The Baby Train

The Baby Train

And Other Lusty Urban Legends

JAN HAROLD BRUNVAND
UNIVERSITY OF UTAH

W · W · NORTON & COMPANY
New York · *London*

Excerpt from "Another Urban Legend," lyrics by Bob Kanefsky
(a parody of "Ferryman," lyrics by Mercedes Lackey
to tune by Leslie Fish), reprinted with permission from
Songworm: Segment Two. Lyrics © 1989
by Firebird Arts and Music, Inc., P.O. Box 14785,
Portland, OR 97214, (800) 752-0494.

"Bedbug letter" reprinted by permission, *Princeton Alumni Weekly*.

First Edition

The text of this book is composed in 11/13 Baskerville,
with the display set in Isbell Medium Italic.
Composition and manufacturing by the Haddon Craftsmen, Inc.

Library of Congress Cataloging-in-Publication Data
Brunvand, Jan Harold.
The baby train and other lusty urban legends / Jan Harold Brunvand.
p.   cm.
Includes index.
1. Urban folklore—United States. 2. Legends—United States.
I. Title. II. Title: Baby train.
GR105.B686 1993
398.2'09173'2—dc20   92–9616

ISBN 0-393-03438-0

W. W. Norton & Company, Inc., 500 Fifth Avenue, New York, N.Y. 10110
W. W. Norton & Company Ltd., 10 Coptic Street, London WCIA 1PU

1 2 3 4 5 6 7 8 9 0

There's a story that Reagan loves to tell about a black welfare woman in Chicago who lives lavishly and supposedly collects something like a hundred and three welfare checks under different names. Now this anecdote has been checked by a number of different people, including Joe Califano, who has written to the president on three different occasions to tell him that the story is mythical and that this woman doesn't exist. The president knows the anecdote isn't true, but he continues to use it.

There are a hundred urban legends just like it, such as the one about the fat lady getting out of a taxi and buying liquor with her food stamps.

—*from* Man of the House: The Life and Political Memoirs of Speaker Tip O'Neill. *With William Novak. (New York: Random House, 1987), 347–48.*

CONTENTS

PREFACE: SOME CAN TELL 'EM, SOME CAN'T

The legend studies in this book—like those in my last one, *Curses! Broiled Again!* (1989)—were first published in my twice-weekly newspaper column "Urban Legends," then revised and expanded, based on further research plus readers' responses. Although folklore, by definition, requires oral tradition to survive, much of the material for my studies in recent years has come to me in the form of letters and clippings and computer bulletin-board entries that echo the word-of-mouth careers of contemporary legends. But I always keep my ears open, and not long ago I had an experience that is unique in my three decades as a folklorist: I witnessed the genesis of a legend first-hand.

The scene was Texas, where I had traveled to attend a scholarly meeting about contemporary legends. Half a dozen of us folklorists were seated around a table at a Chinese restaurant, discussing what to order. We were wavering between two family-style alternatives, which would allow us to sample several dishes.

The attentive Chinese waitress was taking drink orders. Since we were all from different parts of the country, she was having a little difficulty understanding our various regional dialects.

The waitress had just gotten the first four orders down and was waiting for the man on my right to choose when he stated his opinion on the food order. He said, "Let's go back to plan one."

I echoed that, saying "OK, plan one," and then we turned our attention back to ordering our drinks, but the waitress had already left.

A few minutes later she returned with a tray of six drinks: an iced tea, a Coke, two cocktails—and two glasses of plum wine. Plum wine? Who ordered that? The waitress smiled and insisted that we had, and so the two of us without drinks accepted the wine, shrugged, and raised our glasses in a toast.

In time one of the other folklorists figured it out: "Plan one" had sounded like "plum wine" to the waitress.

Since we were all folklorists, we appreciated this apt illustration of how a misunderstood word or phrase may lead to changes in traditional texts.

Later in the evening I heard the first variation of the story. But the teller, a member of our dinner party, messed it up by saying "Plan A," which destroyed the punchline. Some can tell 'em, some can't.

The storyteller's mistake got a big laugh, though, when he had to back up and correct himself, and by the next morning people at the meeting were telling the *new* story about how the guy had garbled the telling of his story about the Chinese waitress. Pretty soon just the phrases "Plan one" or "Plan A" were enough to bring a chuckle, often followed by other anecdotes we knew about misunderstood words leading to comical results.

It started to sound like a set of Chinese boxes at that point, and I won't be surprised if at some subsequent meeting a folklorist gives a paper analyzing this whole thing.

A similar dining-out story—also set in an ethnic restaurant and turning on a misunderstanding of food-related terms—was told to me by a colleague. This man had heard it from his mother who said it had actually happened. But like most urban legends it seemed too good to be true.

My friend's mother had heard about two Texans visiting New York City. Every morning for a week they went into one of the famous delicatessens on Sixth Avenue, wearing cowboy boots and ten-gallon hats, and ordered lox and bagels.

At the end of the week, the owner came over to their table and said that he'd noticed them eating lox and bagels every morning. He said he was happy they were eating at his place, but did they like lox and bagels all that much?

"Sure, we like 'em a lot," one of the Texans answered. "But can you tell us, which is the lox and which is the bagels?"

Reminds me of the time when my daughter held up a cookie she was eating and asked, "Daddy, which is the fig and which is the newton?"

Consider, for a moment, how legends evolve—or, in some cases, *de*volve.

Sometimes we folklorists talk about stories as if they're alive. We say an urban legend like "The Vanishing Hitchhiker" was born in a particular era, spread, changed, and eventually may die out. I find myself speaking of "The Choking Doberman" as "having a life of its own," or of "The Killer in the Backseat" having "mutated to fit a new environment."

I remembered this when I read biologist Richard Dawkins' book about evolution, *The Selfish Gene* (Oxford University Press, 1976). Dawkins alluded to folklore-style changes in explaining how species evolve.

In his view, errors in "copying" are inevitable, and texts always devolve—that is, get worse as they change—while species sometimes evolve (that is, successfully adapt). But I doubt the first axiom, since some urban legends get better and some get worse as they're told. It depends upon the skill of the story-teller.

Dawkins reminds us that "all scribes, however careful, are bound to make a few errors, and some are not above a little willful 'improvement.' " Storytellers, like scribes, also commit human errors when repeating oral tales, and sometimes they too attempt to improve upon what they originally heard. At times, I would insist, they succeed.

For instance, I'd argue that "The Hook" has usually gotten better, not worse, as it has been repeated again and again. "The Hook" is a story—related originally in my first book, *The Vanishing Hitchhiker*—about two kids parked on Lover's Lane with the radio on. Hearing an announcement that a killer with an artificial hand is on the loose, the girl suggests that they leave. The boy pulls out and drives her home. When he walks around the car to open her door, he finds a bloody hook attached to the door handle.

Over the years, tellers drop details that don't fit the plot—say the exact make and model of the car. Or they adapt the legend to fit local conditions, thus making it a bit more plausible. The result may be the tightest, scariest, most compelling and believable version of "The Hook" to come down Lover's Lane since the legend was first told some thirty years ago.

Of course urban legends may also devolve when poor storytellers confuse the plot, pump the story up with extraneous details, mangle the punch line, or give away the ending by saying something like "Let me tell you the one about the hook found dangling on the door handle of the car. . . ." There's no point in telling the story after that! This kind of opening *deserves* to die out.

For example, a reader wrote me about a news item that, he said, "sounds like the old 'Rat in the Hairdo' legend." He was confusing "The Kentucky-Fried Rat" and "The Mouse in the Coke" with "The Spider in the Hairdo"—three quite different legends all dealing with contamination.

Needless to say, I don't expect to encounter any further versions of "The Rat in the Hairdo."

This kind of development was illustrated recently in an experience of my colleague Karen Lawrence. Dr. Lawrence had been named a Guggenheim Fellow and was planning to conduct a study of the ways that travel literature presents female protagonists. An article about her research project in our student newspaper quoted Lawrence as saying that "the female traveler carries different cultural fright from that of her male counterpart." I felt sure she had said "cultural *freight*" to the reporter. When I asked Karen about this, she explained, "Well, actually, I said 'cultural baggage.'" From "baggage" to "freight" to "fright"—that's devolution, for sure, and it happens all the time in urban legends.

For a final example, take the old story about the black man on the elevator who is mistaken for a mugger but turns out to be Reggie Jackson. The man says "Sit!" to his dog, but other passengers on the elevator think he's commanding them, so they sit on the floor.

Later, some people said it was *Jesse* Jackson or even *Michael* Jackson on the elevator, an obvious confusion of first names. Soon other storytellers were inserting different black personalities' names into the story, including Eddie Murphy and Lionel Richie, reflecting these entertainers' growing popularity.

Eventually I heard a highly deviant version of "The Elevator Incident" that named Lionel Hampton, the octogenarian jazzman, hardly likely to seem a threat to anyone! I noted that in most versions of the legend featuring less menacing-looking celebrities, to make better sense of the story, the men are said to be accompanied by burly bodyguards.

All we need now is for someone to mix things up further in this legend and tell the elevator story about someone named "Lionel Jackson." Don't expect that version to survive.

In September 1989 I spent two weeks on the road publicizing my most recent book, *Curses! Broiled Again!* The first leg of the trip took me from New York City to the Rocky Mountains and proved once again that urban legends are popular from the metropolis to the boondocks.

Early Monday morning in the Big Apple someone told a story about some tourists who were visiting South Street Seaport. It seems they picked up a cute little stray doggie and adopted it. It was only later that they learned from a veterinarian that their new pet wasn't a Chihuahua after all. It was a wharf rat. "Here we go again!" I thought. That story is a variation of the legend after which I titled my third book, *The Mexican Pet.*

On Tuesday, taking call-ins on Leonard Lopate's "New York and Company" radio program on WNYC I heard two more local legends. One caller told about a big Bar Mitzvah party during which Cherries Jubilee was served. There were so many guests, he said, that the mass of flaming desserts set off the sprinkler system.

Another caller described a Chinese woman who was carrying a live chicken in her shopping bag when she boarded a city bus. Realizing that the fowl was annoying fellow passengers, the woman calmly reached over and strangled the offensive bird.

After New York, it was on to Minneapolis. On Wednesday morning a caller to the "Boone and Erickson Show" on WCCO talked about two bachelor farmers who had kept the frozen body of their grandfather in their barn during a long and bitterly cold Minnesota winter. The caller said that the bachelors had placed the corpse in a sitting position with its arms outstretched and thumbs sticking up so they could hang their feed sack there until spring when it was warm enough for a funeral. Boone (or was it Erickson?) chuckled at how easily I fell for that tall tale.

Next, in Chicago, I appeared on the program "One Flight Up," on WBEZ.*

One Chicagoan called with a variation of the "Spider in the Hairdo" legend. She said that a woman wanting nice even dreadlocks had been told to put honey on her hair and twist the strands tightly before going to sleep. The next morning her head was infested with cockroaches.

Next stop, Denver. A man called Mike Rosen's KOA talk show to describe a highly successful Chinese restaurant in New

---

*The station is a legend itself. The show's name refers to the fact that the building elevators only reach the thirty-ninth floor, so visitors must walk the last steep flight up to the fortieth where the station is perched.

York that people said was secretly sprinkling opium on customers' food in order to lure them back.

The caller's uncle swore this was true. The proof was that his
uncle once had bought a suit at retail when he was under the
influence of the restaurant's food.

Gimmee a break!

My last date in Denver was with Alan Dumas for his KBX
"Dumas After Dark" show, broadcast from "Muddy's Java
Cafe," a wonderful 1960s-style coffeehouse with a menu and
clientele to match the atmosphere.

After many good phone calls, plus questions from the in-
house patrons, it was time to head for the airport and the last
plane home. But a Muddy's patron handed me a scribbled note
with one more question: "Is it true they cleaned out the water
purification reservoir in Raton, New Mexico, and found a body
at the bottom?"

"I doubt it," I replied as I trotted out to grab a cab. Back at
home the next day, I checked my files and found three similar
stories, which cast some doubt on this one:

A letter from Pocatello, Idaho, repeated a local tradition that
the bodies of two kidnap victims were once found in the city
water supply tanks located in the nearby foothills.

An anonymous photocopied flier taken from a bulletin board
in Eugene, Oregon, claimed that city officials were covering up
the discovery of "various kidnap victims" found in the water
storage tanks in order to avoid "law suites [*sic*]."

A letter from Melville, Saskatchewan, mentioned that the
partly decomposed body of a man had been found in Melville's
water tower. Police had supposedly advised citizens that the
water was still safe to drink.

I was tired from the trip, but suddenly not thirsty at all.

And in January 1991 I received yet another body-in-the-water-
tank story. Luella Snyder of Winnsboro, Louisiana, wrote me
about a local missing-person case that was supposedly solved
when a repulsive odor and taste in the water of the town of

Ferriday, Louisiana, was tracked to the water tank. There, it was rumored, was found the missing man's body. But, reports Snyder:

"This was so widely believed that area newspapers finally published 'not so' articles, pointing out that the water tank was on a high tower with the only access by an open ladder, and that inside the water works building there was no place in the system where a body could be dumped."

Reader mail is always fascinating, but my favorite letters are the ones I file under Nut Mail. Collecting nut mail is a hallowed journalistic tradition. The nuttier the letters, the more columnists enjoy them, although often they demonstrate our failure to communicate effectively in our columns.

Writers of nut mail are not necessarily nuts—although a few certainly are! Most nut mail is just a little bit "off," either because people missed the point of a column or digressed from the topic to their own pet idea.

For example, instead of sending me variations of urban legends, some readers send original stories, poems, songs, or drawings that they expect me to critique or even publish. One man sought a publisher for his book about how to turn lyrics into popular songs. I know zilch about song writing or publishing.

Some people are promoting a product, such as the man selling color photographs of Jesus descending from the clouds. One reader was campaigning to abolish public education, and another quoted messages received from aliens on the dark side of the moon.

Less nutty, but a bit eccentric, was the letter from a man who received two of my books as birthday presents: He included a snapshot of himself in bed, amidst gift wrappings and ribbons, holding up the books.

In one of my treasured pieces of nut mail, the writer sought to correct a spelling error in his previous letter. He wrote a second note, saying, "In my story, please change every instance of 'crouch' to 'crotch'." (The story was actually funnier before the correction.)

A surprising number of readers have sent me accounts of embarrassing events from their pasts—often a prank, an indiscretion, or some dishonest act that they have come to regret. Usually, an urban legend is responsible for jogging their memories of these incidents. One of the worst such confessions I received was signed No Name, but the envelope bore a return sticker showing the writer's (or someone's) full name and address.

The president of an organization called People for Abandoned Pets wrote criticizing me for discussing stories in which animals suffer. Apparently she feared that people might imitate a legend and do something like microwave a poodle.

That seems nutty to me, since "The Microwaved Pet" was a widely told legend long before I ever wrote about it. Besides, I'd never advocate such cruelty, and my business is disproving such tales, not affirming them.

My debunking efforts led a reader to ask, "Are you always so cynical? I'm tired of reading your pessimistical comments regarding legends." The letter continued, "I'm not saying that they are all true, but I'm certain some of your stories have happened. How do you expect to get proof for orally communicated traditions?"

Well, I *don't* expect proof that the stories I study are true, though occasionally I find such evidence. What the widespread variation of urban legends proves is that these stories have a life of their own in modern folklore. It's hard to write about legends without using words like *fictional, untrue,* or *apocryphal,* though I try to find synonyms. Whatever the wording, I suppose I can't help sounding cynical about claims that urban legends are based on actual incidents.

One reader heard a different message in my writing: She wrote, "I've decided that you're a former hippie, since your subculture sympathies show." I may be a bit of a nut about subculture folklore, but I'm not now nor have I ever been a hippie.

Some of my nut mail appears to have been sent to the wrong columnist. I can tell right away when a letter begins "Dear

Abby" or when it contains household hints intended for Heloise. But a mailed slip that held only the notation "R-R6" puzzled me. I tried to figure out what legend that message might refer to.

Just before I relegated the slip to the nut mail folder, I telephoned the feature editor who had forwarded it. She recognized the message at once, realizing that she had mistakenly sent me a piece of mail intended for her newspaper's chess editor, who also happens to have a Scandinavian name. "R-R6" meant simply "Rook to Rook 6"; it was someone's move in a chess game that was being played by mail.

Sometimes nut mail is all in the mind of the receiver.

I'm sometimes asked, "What is your favorite urban legend?" In my opinion, that's like asking a chemist "What is your favorite element?" The legends I collect are data for folkloristic study, and personal preferences shouldn't slant my research.

But, I must confess, I have a special fondness for "The Dead Cat in the Package," the legend about the feline corpse, wrapped for burial, then stolen by a thief who is unaware of what the package contains.

Sometimes the pet's owner watches from a distance as the thief discovers the dead cat in the bag and faints. In a variation, the owner opens her package for another look and discovers that pussy was switched with someone's package of steaks or a ham. In that version, we never learn how the person stuck with the cat corpse reacts.

I first heard "The Dead Cat in the Package" story in 1958; eventually I traced it to about the turn of the century, and yet I hear new versions frequently.

Others share my fondness for the story. My files contain three poems retelling this legend, two of them set to music, and all of them very amusing. Just don't try singing them at your next cat club meeting.

The first is a comical song called "The Body in the Bag" which appears in folksong collections from the 1960s described as an English music hall number.

In the song, a couple's old cat dies; the wife wants her buried, but remembers, "We haven't got a garden 'cause we're living in a flat." So her husband goes off with the body in a bag to dispose of it. On the way, he feels a squirming in the bag and finds that his old cat is still alive and now the mother of kittens. He ends up with the new mother plus "seven little bodies in the bag."

My second dead-cat song is a *filk song,* and that's not a misprint, though the term *filk* did supposedly originate years ago as a typographical error on the program of a science fiction convention. Ever since then, sci-fi enthusiasts have been composing and singing filk songs.

Bob Kanefsky of Palo Alto, California, sent me a tape of the filk song he composed titled "Another Urban Legend." He explained that it's a parody of an earlier filk song called "Ferryman" that was composed by Mercedes Lackey and based on "The Vanishing Hitchhiker."

Both numbers are sung by Leslie Fish on cassette tapes issued by Firebird Arts and Music, Inc., of Portland, Oregon, a major filk song publisher.

Kanefsky's cheery little ballad describes a teenage girl boarding a ferry while carrying a smelly brown paper bag. The girl's poetic plea to the captain is this chorus:

> Ferryman, ferryman, give me a break.
> My parents stuck me with their cat when it died.
> Ferryman, would it be okay with you
> If I toss the thing over the side?

The ferryman says this is definitely *not* OK, but on the return trip her cat bag is accidentally switched with his shopping bag full of Limburger cheese. At home the teenager's parents look into the shopping bag, and they remark:

> But Darling, the thing in this bag isn't Fluffy!
> This has to be one of your jokes!

With that, I thought dead-cat verse had gone about as far as it could go—until I remembered that several years ago Donald

L. Martin of Richmond, Virginia, had sent me the same legend rendered into mock Middle English as a sort of modern Canterbury Tale. I quickly dug out this poem.

Martin followed a version of the legend in which a woman accidentally runs over a cat while driving to a shopping mall. After parking, she gets hold of a plastic shopping bag. Then "the Catte she popped within it."

The woman hopes to dispose of it, but seeing a "cittee Coppe" watching her, she holds onto the bag, I mean the "Bagge." Eventually it is stolen, the thief looks inside and faints; finally, we get "Ye Moral":

All thieves who would their loot enjoy observe the "look first"
    rule:
A Pigge in Pokke or Catte in Bagge is Bait to catch a Foole.

You have a choice of these three versions if you should ever need a legendary dead-cat song or poem. Or you could write your own, perhaps following an obscure metrical pattern called the *catalectic*. This really exists; I looked it up.

Asmut is a new word that I might start to use for urban legends. Writer John McPhee coined the term to refer to tall tales told by sailors, and he defined it as "an apocryphal story much told." I think it has a nice ring to it: "Hey, sailor, how about an asmut?"

In a *New Yorker* article about the merchant marine (March 26, 1990, p. 64), McPhee gave an example of an asmut that dealt with a question that someone supposedly asked a skipper after he had docked his freighter:

"Captain, have you seen any sailboats recently?"

"No."

"Well, you should have. There's a mast and rigging hanging from your anchor."

Reading this in my column, Jess Parker of Bolivia, North Carolina, wrote, "As an old sailor, I have heard this story many times with variations like whales, sharks, dead bodies, and aircraft, or submarine wreckage."

The sailor's yarn seems to be a nautical variation of an apocryphal story much told that I call "The Body on the Car." Supposedly a man who drove home while drunk, checking his car the next morning found the lifeless body of an eight-year-old girl stuck in the grill.

I've never been able to verify that incident, nor a similar story I've heard about a trucker who found a squashed Volkswagen bug stuck to his right front fender.

Those are probably just asmuts, or urban legends.

Actually, folklorists hardly need another term for these stories, since they already have alternate names for the genre such as belief tale, contemporary legend, modern legend, exemplary story, mercantile legend, corporate legend, and others.

The compromise term that most have adopted is *urban legend*, since these stories reflect urban life and attitudes, even if they're not told exclusively about things that supposedly happened in big cities.

One of the first collectors of urban legends was English writer Rodney Dale who in his 1978 book, *The Tumour in the Whale* (London: Gerald Duckworth & Co., Ltd.), called them whale tumor stories, or *WTS*s.

He told a World War II story about whale meat sold in England as a beef substitute. Supposedly, someone saw a chunk of whale quivering in the fridge and upon examining it discovered "a live tumor, gently throbbing."

The term *WTS* never caught on, but Dale doesn't seem to have been serious about it anyway: The dust jacket of his book mentioned "apocryphal anecdotes," while the title page said "modern myths."

Urban myths is a term journalists like to use, though I'd rather reserve *myth* for the kind of metaphorical tribal stories on cosmological themes that the late Joseph Campbell spoke of so eloquently.

A better term proposed by a journalist for apocryphal stories is *dead catter*, referring to the many tales about pussy cats that were supposedly poisoned by nibbling at an entrée, or dead felines boxed for burial that were stolen by unwitting thieves.

"Tumbleweeds" reprinted by permission: North American Syndicate

Never trust a dead cat story, say experienced newspaper writers, since most such stories are legends.

Other journalists call such stories *Mack Sennetts,* after the famed comic silent film producer and actor, because of their slapstick style of humor, or *red wagon stories,* for reasons not entirely clear to me.

Ed Allen, a columnist for *The Sacramento Bee,* sent me a letter from a ninety-year-old woman who reported that when she was a teenager it was said that a girl going out with a "young blade" in his car should have a "little red wagon" of her own to get home in should her date become too amorous.

Supposedly, that led to the term *red wagon stories,* meaning girls' accounts of narrow escapes from ardent suitors. That's as believable as the explanation that the red wagon of a circus or carnival was the ticket office, and sometimes people told out-landish tales hoping to get a free pass.

Herb Karner, retired from the *Tulsa World,* wrote to me concerning legends, "This is the stuff that newspaper people deal with all the time, and we are always looking for these 'brights' to enliven our columns."

Other terms for urban legends surface now and then. I found *nasty legends* in another English book, *monkey sandwiches* from Holland (*broodje Aap* in Dutch), referring to rumors about salami made from monkey meat, and *Klintbergers* from Sweden, refer-ring to the legend collector Bengt af Klintberg.

Some readers have suggested that the best term for urban legends might just be the abbreviation ULs.

But I kind of like *asmut* and shall attempt to convert some fellow folklorists to using it.

From sea stories and journalists' terms, it's not a long leap to lawyers' awareness of folk narratives. At a recent national seminar in trial advocacy held in Washington, D.C., a prominent Texas lawyer told a wonderful story that intrigues me as a possible ancestor of an urban legend that I've been pursuing for several years.

I was not at the seminar, but my urban legend spotter in the audience took notes. Here's the tale the Texan told, saying it happened to him and his brother when they were small boys:

Their mother had baked a Dutch apple pie for a special event. She left it on the kitchen table to cool while she ran an errand, warning the boys not to touch it. But the pie smelled wonderful, and the boys couldn't resist a tiny bite. One bite became several, until a major chunk of the pie had been eaten. Then they heard their mother's car pull into the garage, and they knew they were trapped unless they could quickly cover up their crime.

The future lawyer got a brilliant idea. He grabbed the family cat and shoved its face into the pie, smearing its whiskers with gooey filling and crumbs. His mother walked in, looked at the cat, and saw what she interpreted as guilt written all over its face. She immediately grabbed the cat and threw it out the back door into a stream that ran behind the house.

"And that," the lawyer concluded, "was not the last cat to be sent up the river on crummy circumstantial evidence!"

"Kitty Takes the Rap" is a great story with a perfect punch line that underscores an important principle in the rules of evidence.

It may even be a 100 percent true story, although a few details do bother me, such as, "Do cats eat apple pie?" And how convenient that this was a Dutch apple pie so the cat could be described as "crummy"! What a break that there was a stream nearby so the cat could be sent "up the river" (except, wouldn't the cat have drifted downstream?).

I'm not for a moment suggesting that the Texas lawyer made it all up, but I wonder if he may have enhanced a childhood experience just slightly. If so, he was probably drawing on a folk story that's been told by others.

You see, I heard this circumstantial-evidence ploy as part of the legend I call "Fifi Spills the Paint." So it's hard to believe that the Texas lawyer's version doesn't borrow something from folklore.

My "Fifi" version, which I first wrote about in 1987, is about an interior decorator in Chicago who accidentally spilled a can of paint on a client's priceless Oriental rug. Hearing the client coming into the home, the decorator snatched up their yappy toy poodle, Fifi, dropped her into the puddle of paint, and said, "Oh, Fifi! Bad dog! Look what you've done!"

After I published that story I heard from a man who remembered the same tale told in Portland Heights, Oregon, in 1929 about a painter working on a wooden railing who spilled the paint and blamed the customer's dog. Then I heard from a Boston man who had heard the story from a bartender who said he too had pulled the "Fifi" trick, but with a cat, after he spilled paint on the carpet of a woman for whom he was doing odd jobs. The bartender said he had picked up the trick as a story told by another painter.

Now I had four (or five?) versions of the story about circumstantial evidence used to place the blame on an innocent pet.

I may be misled by circumstantial evidence myself, but I still believe that folklore is involved. The story itself might be a traditional one, and the various sources of the story simply may be repeating it as a joke.

A second possibility is that shoving a hapless pet into the incriminating mess is a traditional way of shifting blame. A person files this idea away in his or her mind and then pulls it out when he or she needs it.

And, I suppose, a third explanation could be that some of these people independently came up with the same clever defense strategy.

Further complicating the matter, Toni Morrison's novel *The Bluest Eye* (Holt, Rinehart, and Winston, 1972) includes a scene involving two children, a cat, and a berry cobbler that sounds suspiciously like yet another variant of the story.

At this point, I sent my column to the Texas lawyer to see if he could cast further light on the matter. The lawyer, Jack B. Zimmermann of Houston, freely confessed; he had heard the story from "one of Colorado's greatest courtroom attorneys, Len Chesler of Denver."

It's time, now, to consider the polite way to debunk urban legends, if you're so inclined. Two readers asked about this in the following letters:

Dear Professor:

Greetings from near Chicago—suburban semirural boredom hell. I really enjoy your books, and I have learned a lot from applying them to real life.

For example, I learned that most people get quite vicious, or at least upset, if you attempt to explain to them that a story like "The Hook" is an urban legend. So it's best to keep your mouth shut.

—Thanks for the enlightenment. Peace & Love.

> *Shellie Smith*
> *New Lenox, Illinois.*

Dear Professor:

If you have any advice on how to gently bring back to earth someone who is telling a story that you know to be an urban legend, I would appreciate it. I am thinking of writing to Miss Manners.

> *Victoria Austin*
> *Castro Valley, California.*

Gentle Readers:

How to respond to someone telling an urban legend as the truth is a serious etiquette dilemma worthy of Miss Manners' attention. But you need not write to America's premiere authority on correct social behavior, since I myself have researched the proper course of action—one that's accepted in all the best spas, country clubs, and hair styling salons.

The mannerly method of dealing with someone who insists on the truth of an urban legend is called "The Polite Persistent Questioning" technique—PPQ for short.

Let us take a typical situation requiring the PPQ approach. Say you are gathered with friends on the patio of a fashionable home one moonless evening, sipping expensive Scotch whisky and daintily nibbling an occasional hors d'oeuvre selected from a tray proffered by an attentive servant.

(Actually, the same advice applies if you're on a camping trip toasting marshmallows by the fire, but my example sounds more like a Miss Manners reply.)

Inspired by the atmosphere, someone begins to tell "The Hook," and you, as an urban legend aficionado recognize immediately that this story is as old as the Scotch you're drinking and as phony as the hostess's smile.

Are you expected by the rules of etiquette to keep your mouth shut and to endure this recital of falsehoods? Must you let it stand as the truth that a couple parking on lovers' lane heard a radio warning of an escaped maniac with a hook replacing his lost hand? Or that they drove off rapidly, and later found a bloody hook dangling from the door handle?

No, indeed. But neither can you simply state outright, "Baloney! That's merely an urban legend that everyone heard at scout camp years ago."

The socially proper reaction to this situation is Polite Persistent Questioning.

At intervals during the recital of such a legend, you may ask some sweetly phrased, but pointed, questions:

—*"Goodness! Why would they give a dangerous maniac a hook? Wouldn't that simply provide him with a powerful weapon?"*

—*"You mean he reached for the door handle with his hook hand? I would think he'd use his other hand for that."*

—*"Isn't that a remarkable coincidence that the hookman was lurking outside the car just at the moment when the announcement came on the radio?"*

—*And the best question of all, "Did the young man really walk politely around the car to open the door for his date, after being angry enough to spin his tires as they left their parking place?"*

The idea of PPQ is not to pit yourself personally against the storyteller and imply that he or she is lying; that would be a worse gaffe than spreading a legend in the first place. Instead you should strive to create an atmosphere of innocently querying the story's details. This might encourage other listeners to raise further questions.

At just the moment when the narrator seems about to retract the tale, you should rescue the poor soul by saying—as if you just happened to remember it—"Oh, I believe that really happened somewhere else! Didn't I read about it in a book by Jan Harold Brunvand called . . . oh dear, what was that title?"

At this point, it is considered socially correct to reach into one's billfold or pocketbook and extract a small card on which is written in black or blue-black ink the full titles and publication dates of Brunvand's books, and to mention that you saw them for sale at some fashionable boutique.

The Baby Train makes five urban legend books that I've written since 1981. My background notes and records for the books now fill eight file drawers, while four more drawers contain the notes and drafts behind each of the five-hundred-plus newspaper columns written since 1987. Altogether, I estimate that I have material relating to the history and distribution of some five hundred urban rumors and legends, and more material arrives steadily. Out of desperation a few years ago, I worked out a rough system of classifying urban legends in order to preserve some order in filing this mass of material. I've refined and expanded the classification as I've worked with it, and I've circulated draft copies to other folklorists for their comments. At the end of this book is the result: A Type-Index of Urban Legends.

At present, the Type-Index includes almost exclusively American urban legends—basically all those discussed or mentioned in my books. Eventually, I hope to expand the Index to encompass American legends published elsewhere, as well as foreign material. For now, the Index will serve as a finding list for readers searching for a particular story and also as a tool for the use of folklorists archiving urban legends and striving to devise a rigorous definition and classification system for this fascinating genre of modern oral narrative.

Besides all of those people who are specifically named in this book, I wish to thank the legions of others—both professional scholars and nonacademics—whose articles, books, letters, and conversations have helped shape my thoughts and writings about urban legends. I owe a special debt of gratitude to my outstanding editors, Chris Hull at United Feature Syndicate and Dan Conaway and Mary Cunnane at W. W. Norton & Company.

My address, for those who wish to send me legends or queries (preferably including an SASE), is as follows:

Professor Jan Harold Brunvand
Department of English
University of Utah
Salt Lake City, UT 84112

The Baby Train

1

Sex and Scandal Legends

"The Baby Train"

Michigan State undergraduates of my era—the early 1950s—firmly believed that one of the married student housing units had the highest birthrate on campus because of the local train schedule.

I heard the story while a student there. It was accepted wisdom that precisely at 5:00 A.M. (or another early hour) each day a freight train roared past an MSU apartment unit situated on the edge of the campus, rudely awakening all the residents.

Since it was too early to get out of bed, and too late to go back to sleep, young love ran its natural course, and the birth rate soared. I've heard of people calling those kids "whistle babies."

I wondered at the time why the train didn't also wake up all the young children in the apartments, and thus ruin the sudden intimacy of the moment. But when I heard the same story told about other universities, I realized that this most likely was only a campus legend.

Thirty-some years later, I learned that the same legend is told in Australia.

Folklorist Bill Scott included it as the final story in his 1985 book, *The Long & the Short & the Tall* (Sydney: Western Plains Publishers). He called it "Not Worth Going Back to Sleep."

Scott heard the story, as he wrote me after I inquired about its origins, "from an anonymous public servant, a casual acquaintance I met at the Leagues Club at Queanbeyan in 1978."

The Aussie version described census officials in Canberra noting that a small town on the coast north of Sydney had a birthrate three times the national average.

They sent an expert out to investigate, and he found "bloody kids everywhere"—so many of them that the local school had built several temporary classrooms and the hospital had added a new maternity wing. After three nights in the town, the census official figured out what was happening:

This town was on the main railway line. The road crossed the line just north of the town and then crossed back about half-a-mile south again.

The Kyogle Mail [a local train] used to reach there and go through about half-past-four every morning. When it hit the road crossing it used to blow its whistle very loud, and wake everybody in the place. Just when they'd be dropping off again it'd blow for the other crossing and wake them all up again.

Well, it was too early to get up but it was hardly worth while going back to sleep again, so they had to fill in time till it was time to get up.

Scott considered this yarn a typical example of Australian humor, and figured that it is probably a relatively new story, since the Kyogle Mail only began running in the 1930s. But his theories fell apart when he found a much earlier example of the story, which may be the ancestor of both our versions.

Scott made his discovery in Fred Archer's 1971 book, *The Secrets of Bredon Hill* (London: Hodder and Stoughton), an account of life in a small Shropshire, England, village during the year 1900.

In this version a parson is visiting members of his flock who live down near the railway yard and who seem to be "breeding like ferrets." The minister asked one young mother why she had produced such a large family in so short a time.

" 'Tis like this, Vicar," she said, "It's that early morning goods train as comes up the incline."

When the vicar failed to understand, the woman explained that the train passed her cottage at half past four and her husband dared not fall asleep again, fearing to be late for work. "It was too early to get up," she said, "so there was nothing else to do but to . . ."

"I know, I know!" the Vicar said, cutting her off abruptly.

Scott is looking for further versions, and he wonders if perhaps much the same story was told about "some Celtic couple awakened by the builders of Stonehenge off to work early!"

And I'm wondering if college students are still telling the campus version.

To my surprise, I found the story again in a setting that's off-campus and quite close to my present home—it turns out to be a legend also told about a small Utah town, and it was originally published by the same local newspaper that carries my "Urban Legends" column today. B. A. Botkin and Alvin F. Harlow reprinted most of the story in their book *A Treasury of Railroad Folklore* (New York: Crown, 1953, p. 376), but here's the full original, as told in Frank Cunningham's book *Big Dan: The Story of a Colorful Railroader* (Salt Lake City: The Deseret News Press, 1946, pp. 257–58). Frank was the nephew of Daniel G. Cunningham, the subject of *Big Dan:*

> Both Frank and Big Dan were amused by a request the Rio
> Grande received from the town council at Nephi, Utah. As
> Dan tells the story, he was requested to forward the message
> on to the head office at Denver. It seems the railroad had a
> branch line on the Marysvale route which ran from Manti to
> Nephi where the Rio Grande connected with the Union
> Pacific. After entering the town limits of Nephi, the D. & R.G.
> tracks crossed a number of streets before reaching the depot.
> According to law, the engineer would blow a crossing signal of
> two longs and two shorts before entering each crossing. This

train was scheduled into Nephi at four o'clock in the morning and the continual whistling of the locomotive awakened everybody in Nephi. As time passed, there were so many babies born in Nephi the infant population created a problem. The town considered the matter and decided to send the railroad a request to set up its schedule an hour so the train wouldn't come in until five o'clock.

According to Dan, the understanding management of the railroad granted the request.

That this Utah connection to the story still exists was proven to me on July 13, 1991, during the annual meeting of the Utah State Historical Society in Park City when Professor William A. Wilson of Brigham Young University told the following version in responding to a paper on railroad folklore given by Karen Krieger of Utah State University:

I've been told that some years ago in Honeyville, Utah, there were three prominent families. Two of these families had numerous children, but the other had very few. Supposedly, the reason for this discrepancy was that at 5:30 every morning a train rolled through town and whistled loudly at the railroad crossing, waking up the partners in two of the marriages. The husband in the third marriage, however, was nearly deaf, and was not awakened by the train whistle, and that's why he and his wife had fewer children.

But even more surprising than these local versions was the response I got to "The Baby Train" from Arthur Goldstuck, author of the first urban legend book from South Africa (*The Rabbit in the Thorn Tree: Modern Myths & Urban Legends of South Africa*, London: Penguin Books, 1990). He wrote in May 1991:

I have some startling news for you. When I read out your letter to my wife Sheryl, she stopped me dead as I reached the line about the baby train.

She told me that she herself (or so she had been led to believe) had been the product of a baby train. Her parents live

on a farm near a small country town called Belfast, in the
Eastern Transvaal province of South Africa. The farm lies
next to a railway line and near the local railway station.

Every morning at 4:00 A.M. a freight train would come
through (and still does), supposedly waking up the household.
And indeed, "It was too early to get up and too late to go back
to sleep." The result, one spring, was a completely unplanned
baby called Sheryl.

In those days it was a very noisy steam train, which has
given way to electric trains that no longer wake the sleeping.

We happened to be visiting the farm a few weekends ago,
and I questioned her parents about the story. Her mother
confirmed that they had always told this tale to Sheryl, and to
their other children, none of whom were blamed on the 4:00
A.M. story. But she could not recall whether Sheryl really had
happened that way.

Sheryl's father, moreover, could not recall ever being
woken by the 4:00 A.M. freight train, but he did not think it
impossible. Nor do I think an urban legend impossible.

Yours in caution, Arthur.

The same theme as in all of these stories, of course, appears
in the rumors of mini–baby booms occurring exactly nine
months after power outrages. A classic version of that story
developed after the famous November 9, 1965, New York City
blackout when numerous couples stranded without television,
radio, or lights supposedly went to bed early but couldn't sleep.
Contrary to folklore, however, there was no upsurge of births in
New York nine months later.

Similarly, a story in the July 13, 1990, San Jose, California,
Mercury News—published just nine months after the 1989 Bay
Area earthquake—declared, "No baby boom spurred by Oct.
17 quake." Who *said* there was a spate of births? *Newsweek*
("People often make the best out of a catastrophe") and *USA
Today* ("Quake registers big on new-baby scale"), that's who.
Sometimes journalists just can't resist the lure of a lively legend.

"Superhero Hijinks"

In 1988 when I was visiting New Zealand, Phil Twyford, a writer for the Aukland *Sunday Star,* gave me a batch of urban legends that his readers submitted in response to an article he had written about modern folktales. One was a real shocker.

It was a weird little sex adventure about a husband in a Superman costume who is injured while approaching his bound and naked wife. The story seemed unsuitable for a family newspaper, so at the time I merely filed it with other such items under Sex, Miscellaneous.

But a similar story later was published in several American papers. Since other columnists had already taken the plunge with this legend, so to speak, I, too, reported what I knew about it, as discreetly as possible.

Twyford's summary was fairly innocuous:

"A couple hear a woman crying out in the apartment next door. They go to investigate, fearing domestic abuse or an intruder.

"In the bedroom they discover their neighbor tied to the bed naked and screaming. Her husband is dressed as Superman and is knocked out cold on the floor. He had been about to jump off the chest of drawers onto her, but had slipped and fallen."

Twyford added that the story had appeared in a local gossip column, and he had heard a Spiderman variation. (Sure enough, a Spiderman version is briefly told by a character in Sue Reidy's story "Alexandra and the Lion" published in *The Penguin Book of Contemporary New Zealand Short Stories* published in 1989.)

After returning from New Zealand, I heard from Mike Lawrence of Chichester, England, who said that Superman, Batman, and Tarzan variations were "doing the rounds at present" over there.

I first read the story as an *American* urban legend in a column by Reese Fant published on August 29, 1988, in the Greenville, South Carolina, *News*. He dubbed it "a semi-new one," described the man wearing a Superman outfit, and said he was knocked out by a ceiling fan. Fant concluded, "I want to see the Superman suit before I'll believe this one."

I heard nothing more of the story until about a year later when St. Louis *Post-Dispatch* columnist Elaine Viets contacted me. She was getting reports of the Batman variation from all over her territory. The popularity of the film *Batman* probably had something to do with it.

The first report came from St. Clair, a town about thirty miles west of St. Louis, but other readers told her they had heard it on the radio about New York and Dallas. "Is some Joker spreading Bat lies?" Viets asked.

Her *Post-Dispatch* column, "Batman with a Twist," incidentally, was released nationwide by Scripps Howard News Service, which may have helped spread the story, as well as inspiring other journalists to report versions they had heard. At any rate, whoever was telling it had been busy in Dallas and Fort Worth during the summer of 1989.

Fort Worth *Star-Telegram* columnist Bud Kennedy reported that local radio personality Betty Ann Stout had told the Batman story in early July, swearing that it happened in Arlington. Then national radio newscaster Paul Harvey repeated Stout's story, except he said it happened in Dallas.

Sure enough, Dallas *Morning News* columnist Larry Powell wrote that he first heard reports of the Batman caper from Dallas, but later he got them from Fort Worth, Mesquite, Coppel, and elsewhere in Texas. But none of these accounts was verified. Powell said he found "no facts, no names, no phone numbers. No pictures. Especially no pictures."

Then he heard that a flashier variation was making the

Reprinted by permission: Bevery Alvarez

rounds in Columbia, South Carolina, as reported by a hairdresser (an impeccable source!) to a legislative reporter.

There the story was that a high-ranking state official had
been caught in the Batman suit while rendezvousing with a lady
who was not his wife in an upscale condo located in an area
called Yacht Cove. But the closest that Bobby Bryant, a writer
for *The State,* a Columbia, South Carolina, newspaper, could
come to "facts" about the alleged incident was that it had earlier been told on a married couple living in a mobile home
whose costume was a Superman suit. Bryant's story published
on August 10, 1989, bore the subheading, "Story of Caped
Seducer Takes on Life of Its Own."

The earliest version of this story I've found in print so far mentions Superman; it's in an English collection by Paul Smith called *The Book of Nastier Legends* (London: Routledge & Kegan Paul, 1986). Smith wrote that "this delightful story only surfaced in the U.K. this year."

Oddly, the cartoon in *Nastier Legends* illustrating the story shows the "hero" costumed as Batman, not Superman, and the couple is depicted hanging upside down, bat-fashion. Evidently the cartoonist knew something that the legend collector didn't about the variations of this story.

And who knows what we'll hear of next—The Phantom of the Opera maybe? Stay tuned.

Letters continued to arrive in my mailbox with reports of the "Superhero Hijinks" legend being told in numerous cities, but with few variations. The typical networks through which urban legends travel were suggested in a version sent from Richmond, Virginia, by a man who wrote:

"I heard it from a good friend and colleague who heard it from his wife, who in turn heard it from her best friend whose husband is a printer. The husband works for a master printer who volunteers some evenings each week for one of the local county rescue squads. He was supposedly on duty one night when the call from Batman's sex partner comes in."

On January 14, 1990, Peter S. Greenberg of the *Asbury Park* (N.J.) *Press* told an unusual version of the Batman story in his "The Savvy Traveler" column. Greenberg said it happened in 1989 to "one very embarrassed couple" in a Boston hotel who were heard calling for help from their guest room by a security guard and rescued by an assistant manager.

In spring 1990 letters began to arrive with queries asking why I didn't rebut Ann Landers and Abigail Van Buren ("Dear Abby") for publishing legends in their columns recently. One letter begged, *"Tell* me that this is folklore; otherwise, I shall have to get a tune-up for my B.S.–detector."

Trust me, readers! I wrote immediately to give the Twin Sisters of Advice some advice of my own. Neither replied. I know that Ann and Abby are busy people, so I composed an open letter to them which should clear things up:

Dear Ann and Abby:

I'm a faithful reader of each of your columns, not just for the advice, but for the urban legends that you occasionally publish.

You both managed to start the 1990s by falling for urban legends once again. I'm sure readers have called your attention to them by now, because dozens of them sent me copies of the two columns involved.

Ann first. On January 30th you published that Batman/bondage story from "A Minnesota Reader," who swore it was true. The Los Angeles Times headlined your column "A Leap of Faith in the Bedroom," because the story told of a husband dressed as Batman who knocked himself out when leaping onto the bed where his naked wife was tied up waiting for him. The neighbors, hearing her cries, dialed 911, and then broke into the bedroom.

Ann, dear, that story has been around for years. Some of the variations mention the husband dressed as Tarzan, Superman, or Spiderman. I found "Superhero Hijinks" published in an English collection in 1986, and I heard it in New Zealand in 1988, and it hit the States in 1989.

A delightful twist on the story has the woman rescue herself, by dialing 911 with her big toe!

I can't fault you for using the letter, but feel free to give me a call next time a reader's story sounds too good to be true.

You were accurate, though, calling it your "laugh of the day." I nearly spilled my cornflakes chuckling over it, and then I turned to my files to find the variations.

On to you, Abby. Speaking of 911, how about your March 6 column? A North Carolina reader wrote you to explain why the emergency telephone number should always be given as "nine-one-one."

The reader claimed, "There are cases pending in courts

across the nation because precious lives have been lost due to the time wasted while children tried to find number 11 on the telephone."

"I should know," the reader concluded, "I work for the Winterville, North Carolina, Rescue Squad."

Well, dear Abby, I first heard that one in 1982, and I believe it goes back to a joke told in the 1940s in which someone looks for 11 on the dial when told to dial "one-one." It wasn't a very funny joke, but it turned into a convincing legend that has been repeated many times, although never, to my knowledge, verified as an actual incident.

I've seen the "Dial 911 for Help" legend retold in periodicals published for paramedics and safety directors, but it is always attributed to word of mouth.

I included the story in my 1984 book The Choking Doberman, and I did a column on it in 1988. Later, I heard from telephone company personnel who said their policy is to advise people to spell out the numbers or use hyphens (9-1-1), even though no one has evidence of a delay caused by searching for 11 on the dial.

I'm not sure hyphens will solve the "problem" however. Won't somebody then start telling a story about a distraught person searching for a hyphen on the telephone dial?

"The Hairdresser's Error"

I heard a scandalous story in Minneapolis in September 1989, while I was in town on a promotion tour for my last urban legend book, *Curses! Broiled Again!* When I got to Ode-gard's Bookstore to sign books, the manager introduced me to a clerk because he thought a story she had told him recently was an urban legend. She was embarrassed telling it, but the manager assured her that I'd be interested.

Despite the story's vague details and her boss's doubts, the clerk believed that it was true. It was up to me to arbitrate this labor-management dispute. Here's the story:

It seems that an older man came into a St. Paul, Minnesota, styling salon near closing time one evening and asked for a haircut. The young female barber, alone in the shop, felt uneasy about this scruffy-looking stranger but agreed to cut his hair.

After pinning a sheet around the man's neck, the stylist turned to get her comb and scissors. Looking back, she noticed a rhythmic motion under the middle of the sheet. Thinking the man in the chair was a sexual deviant and possibly dangerous, she panicked.

The stylist grabbed a large bottle of shampoo and brought it down on the man's head, knocking him cold. Then she called the police. When the police arrived they found the young woman poised over the unconscious man, still wielding the shampoo bottle as a weapon.

The police removed the sheet and discovered that the man had merely been polishing his glasses under it.

I tried to let the bookstore clerk down easy, explaining that I was delighted to have another American version of "The Hairdresser's Error"—only my second. I first got the story in 1986 from Tom Schley of Fairbanks, Alaska, who heard it from a Los Angeles hairdresser.

The California version claimed that the customer was a businessman in a three-piece suit staying in a nearby hotel. He claimed to be in dire need of a haircut because of an early-morning appointment. The female stylist jumped to the wrong conclusion when she saw the sheet moving, and she beaned him with a hair dryer. The man sued her for damages.

The three other versions of "The Hairdresser's Error" that I had at the time are all English, which suggests the story's origin. The earliest comes from Paul Smith's *The Book of Nasty Legends* (London: Routledge & Kegan Paul, 1983).

Smith's version makes no reference to a late hour or an unfamiliar customer, but merely describes a man who absent-mindedly polishes his glasses with the sheet as the stylist starts to blow-dry his hair. The woman screams, "They shouldn't let perverts like you in here!" and hits him with the dryer. There are no police in this version; it's the manageress of the shop who sorts things out.

In the spring of 1989, Penny Long of Manchester, England, sent me the story as she heard it told in a pub. The teller said it happened to a friend of her aunt. Here, again, we meet the anxious businessman staying in a local hotel and needing a haircut after hours so as to look neat for an important meeting. When she sees suspicious movements under the sheet, the stylist stuns the customer with the hair dryer and calls the police.

My last overseas example of "The Hairdresser's Error" shows that the legend has reached New Zealand, via an English traveler. I got it from Hugh Young of Porirua. He wrote, "I hope (probably in vain) that you haven't heard this one yet."

Well, I hadn't heard his particular variation yet, anyway!

As an English woman told it to Young in August 1989, a stranger arrived at a shop on a cold rainy evening and begged the lone female hairdresser to admit him for a trim before his big date that night. A new twist in this version is that after seeing movements under the sheet, the hairdresser grabs a large hairbrush and takes a vicious swipe at the lump in the sheet.

The man screams in pain and shouts, "I was only cleaning

my spectacles, you idiot!" Then, supposedly, he sues her for "grievous bodily harm."

Meanwhile in the United States, two letters received in 1990—one from Bronx, New York, the other from Lincoln, Nebraska—report that "The Hairdresser's Error" is still being told. But the most interesting report came from Laurel L. Cornell of Bloomington, Indiana, who wrote in February 1990:

> I was delighted to see the legend about the hairdresser's error in your column today, because it is the first urban legend I heard and recognized as such. I heard it in Ithaca, New York, in the winter of 1986, from my hairdresser, either when I was holding my own glasses under the cape (I'm a woman), or when I came in for a very late afternoon appointment, and remarked on the lateness.
>
> The elements in the version I heard were the male customer coming in just as the shop was about to close, the woman hairdresser, last one left, being reluctant to serve him, but then thinking she might as well do so, and her beaning him on the head with the blow dryer.
>
> That's where it ended; no lawyers or anything. Actually, when I heard it, I thought of writing you about it, but then thought that being so obviously an urban legend, you must already have heard thousands of versions.

Thanks, Laurel; better late than never. I may be "obviously an urban legend," as you say, but I didn't pick up "The Hairdresser's Error" any sooner than you did, and I'm far from having thousands in my collection of versions of this great story.

"The Butcher's Prank"

I had a 1985 letter in a file marked "The Butcher's Prank" for years, wondering how to answer it or discuss it in a column discreetly. When I received further information and queries about the same story, I decided it was time to face up to the problem of discussing this R-rated legend.

Here's the original letter I received about the story:

Dear Professor:

About forty years ago in Santa Ana, California, there was a butcher who loved practical jokes. One day he stuffed a wiener inside his pants, and when he saw a friend come into the shop, he unbuttoned the bottom two buttons of his fly and stuck about two inches of the wiener out.

When the friend saw this, he delicately called attention to it.

The butcher said, "Is that darn thing sticking out again?"
He went over to the chopping block, took a cleaver, and sliced off the protruding two inches of wiener.

The friend had a heart attack and died. His widow sued the butcher for wrongful death and was awarded a $100,000 judgement.

This was told to me by a friend of a friend of the widow's attorney. Is it an urban legend?

Charles Chenoweth
Santa Maria, California

Dear Charles:

It's either an urban legend or an actual prank once pulled by butchers on their customers. I've recently heard some other versions, including one from Indiana which supposedly happened in the 1930s to the mother of the man who told it to me.

He mentioned a specific meat market, a butcher named Kelly, the use of one of "Benz's famous wieners," and a male customer who fainted.

My Indiana informant said, "My mother insists this really happened, but when pressed, she is not absolutely certain she actually witnessed these events, the story having been retold many times in her presence. "At any rate," he concluded, "the story is now a firm part of our family folklore."

A Maryland family tells an older version of "The Butcher's Prank." George Tobin, of Milford, Delaware, wrote me that his uncle John H. Tobin (Uncle Johnnie), as a small-town Maryland butcher, played the same prank in 1916 using a cut-off cow's udder as the prop.

He pinned a piece of the udder with the teat hanging out onto his pants fly, then donned his work apron before starting his meat delivery route. When a couple of widows who regularly bought from his butcher wagon came out, he lifted his apron and chopped off the teat. Tobin said, "The women screamed and fell to the road in a cold faint."

Tobin concluded, "No legend, buster. That happened!"

I'm inclined to believe that it did *happen*—in other words, that this story is not just an apocryphal anecdote, but an account of a once-popular prank among butchers. I know, also, that the story has been in print one time and probably at least twice.

One reader wrote in 1988 to say he would swear he read "The Butcher's Prank" about twenty years ago in Reader's Digest, with the only difference being that a turkey neck served as the prop. So far this clue has not led me to this particular printed version, but I have got another one.

Hugh W. Thompson of Newark, New Jersey, sent me a photocopy of chapter 23, "The Celebrated Affair of the Butcher and the Cow's Udder," from Lyon Mearson's 1931 book called The French They Are a Funny Race (New York: The Mohawk Press).

This version, which is simply "The Butcher's Prank" story

all over again, claims that "All Paris is following the case."
The only variation is that the trick is played in a restaurant.
The restaurant owner, seeing the protruding appendage,
roars at the butcher, "Regard yourself in front!" The butcher
goes into his chopping routine, and the restaurateur faints,
hitting his head on a table and suffering a fatal concussion.

The widow sues, and . . . but you've heard all this before,
haven't you?

But I still haven't found "The Butcher's Prank" in Reader's
Digest.

"The Bad Bachelorette"

A shocking and rather racist story about a bride's last fling
has appeared occasionally in my mail since I started writing my
"Urban Legends" column in 1987. I assume it's an urban legend, since it crisscrosses the country, is sometimes furnished
with local details, and is inevitably attributed to a friend of a
friend.*

The story deals with the relatively new custom of holding
"bachelorette parties" for future brides, which imitate men's
traditional "bachelor parties," and compete with them in terms
of their raucous behavior. I don't know how popular bachelorette parties actually are nowadays, nor how raucous they
become, but this story deserves the title "The Bad Bachelorette."

I first heard the story from a San Diego reader who said it
was supposed to have happened to a yuppie couple in Los
Angeles in 1985. The bride's female friends had arranged for a
male stripper to perform at her party, and he turned out to be a
tall handsome black body-builder.

The party became pretty wild. At the urging of the guests,
and after having a few too many drinks, the guest of honor led
the stripper into a bedroom for a private show. She ended up
spending the rest of the night with him, and the next day swore
her friends to secrecy.

The story continued by describing the happy marriage that
followed; the bride soon became pregnant, to her and her husband's delight. The yuppie couple enrolled in Lamaze classes,
adopted a healthy lifestyle, decorated a nursery, and eagerly
awaited the arrival of their first child.

---

*A FOAF.

On delivery day, with her tall blond husband holding her hand throughout her labor, while the expectant grandparents waited in the corridor, the fair blond wife gave birth to a beautiful baby—a mixed-race child with a full head of short curly dark hair.

Only the woman and her bridesmaids knew the truth. But it marked the end of the happy yuppie marriage, and the incident put a damper on bachelorette parties among their group.

Later a Milwaukee reader sent me two versions of the same story, as told by his daughter who had heard it from her fiancé who heard it from his sister who said it had really happened to a girlfriend's girlfriend.

This time the young wife had been found to be carrying twins. Her proud husband assisted at the birth, and several other close family members were in attendance. In the first version of the story, the twins were both mixed-race; in the second version, one baby was mixed and the other was white.

In 1989 "The Bad Bachelorette" surfaced again in a letter from Sacramento. This one was told by a woman who heard it from a friend who said it had happened to the friend of one of her suppliers at work. It was the familiar story about the white couple, the black stripper, and the mixed-race baby. My reader asked, "Have you heard that one yet?"

In February 1990 a reader in Brooklyn, New York, sent me the story, saying it was supposed to have happened to a Long Island woman. He also supplied the title I've been using above, commenting, " 'The Bad Bachelorette' has some great urban legend motifs: racist undertones, sexy elements, surprise ending, and a payback for somebody's 'sin.' "

In June 1990, I got word of the story apparently moving from the East Coast back to the Midwest. This version was sent by a New York City woman who heard it told on a flight from Newark, New Jersey, to Chicago. Her seatmate, a woman from Omaha, Nebraska, said it happened to a friend of her brother-in-law who was just completing his ob-gyn residency at a Long Island hospital.

The Omaha woman's story began with the shocking birth of a mixed-race baby to a white couple, then concluded with the husband walking out on his wife. Later the doctor learned about her affair with the black stripper at the bachelorette party and realized what had happened. Confirming the currency of the story in the Midwest, I heard it again in 1991 from a reader in Bloomington, Indiana.

My New York reader commented that she understood that bachelorette parties were becoming very popular, competing with bachelor parties in their debauchery and drunkenness.

Maybe so, but "The Bad Bachelorette" is a legend that had been circulating for at least five years. It may have begun when such parties were just starting to become popular.

Photo Faux Pas and the Infamous Toothbrush Story

A recent article about the problems of identifying suspected purveyors of child pornography began with a vivid account of an incident in which misinterpreted photographic evidence led to the wrongful arrest of an innocent man. According to the story, a grandfather was supposedly arrested "right in the middle of a busy supermarket" after a one-hour photo processing company reported that he had left a roll of film for developing that contained pictures of little children in the nude.

But, as the example concluded, "The story was all a mistake: The camera had been used by the man's grandchildren who had photographed each other without his knowledge, in a playful, and apparently innocent prank."

The article went on to discuss in well-researched detail the "possible weaknesses" in current laws concerning the use of such evidence to identify suspected child pornographers. As for the horror story in the article's lead, the journalist stated, "Prosecutors aren't sure that the incident really happened."

At that, my urban legend alarm went off, as it generally does in such cases. I recognize the illustrative value of a good anecdote, but I also know that reprinting apocryphal stories, even with good intentions, sometimes merely spreads them further. If a story is unverified and sounds too good to be true, then it ought to be assumed to be fictional until proven otherwise.

Although I haven't heard exactly that same overexposure story repeated as an urban legend, I have heard a couple of other similar tales about photographic evidence exposing real crimes. Both first came to me via computer news groups, which nowadays spread legends with, I might say, electrifying speed. These two tales have been hot lately on the computer nets, and the second one has become one of the most common items in my recent mail.

"DOUBLE EXPOSURE"

Some kids broke into a motor vehicles bureau and stole the camera used to make driver's licenses. They used it to make fake IDs for themselves and friends. When they were finished, they dumped the camera where it eventually was found by someone and turned over to the police.

What the kids didn't realize was that the camera automatically took two pictures, keeping one copy inside for the license bureau records and spitting out the other one for the license itself. From the duplicate pictures, police easily identified the thieves and arrested them when they tried to use their homemade ID cards.

Question: Don't state motor vehicle bureaus guard their equipment any better than that, and isn't there more involved in making an ID card or driver's license than just taking a photo? This story sounds too good to be true, and I've never seen a verified news story about such an incident.

However, a January 1991 AP story datelined Peru, Indiana, gives an account of thieves who stole a van and photographed themselves driving it, leaving the owner's camera with the exposed film still intact behind when they abandoned the van. Close, but not quite the same story.

INDECENT EXPOSURES

A day after arriving in the Bahamas, a honeymooning young couple discovered that their hotel room had been ransacked and that everything had been taken except their camera and their toothbrushes, which were left hanging in the bathroom. Hotel insurance covered their losses, and they still had credit cards which they'd carried with them out of the hotel, they decided to complete their vacation and make the best of it.

They reported the crime to the police and filed their insurance claim. Then they bought some new clothes and other needed items, which was literally everything except toothbrushes and a camera. Their honeymoon turned out to be wonderful after all, until they got home and developed the film from their camera. Then they got the shock of their lives.

In one picture, which the thieves had evidently taken, they recognized their own toothbrushes being mishandled and befouled in a most disgusting way: The toothbrushes had been photographed stuck into the rectum of one of the thieves who was mooning the camera.

The many occurrences of this story I've collected since I first heard it in November 1990 differ in saying where the incident occurred, who the victims were, where they came from, and who the thieves were. In no case, however, is the narrator any closer than a FOAF—"friend of a friend"—of these victims, nor has anyone I know about ever actually seen the revealing photos.

Most often the vacation takes place in the Caribbean (Jamaica, Virgin Islands, St. Maarten, etc.), sometimes on a cruise, or in Central America (Mexico, Costa Rica, etc.). Occasionally the vacationers are in New York City, Hawaii, the southern United States, or in Europe (usually Rome, Paris, or on the French Riveria). In a few versions the theft takes place on a camping trip, sometimes while the victims are swimming or hiking. The victims are not necessarily honeymooners, but they are usually said to have come from wherever the storyteller lives (which can be anywhere from coast to coast!).

The thieves may be recognized as belonging to a minority group, and they are sometimes said to be servants in the hotel. Some accounts identify them as Rastafarians. A version told in Pennsylvania says the photo showed "island natives" who were "performing some sort of ritual dance" for the camera. One sent to me from Toronto concluded that the toothbrush photograph was "the 'signature' of this particular gang."

Almost always everything but the toothbrushes and the camera are stolen, but in a few versions nothing is taken, though it's obvious that the room (or campsite) has been disturbed. In a few versions, the victims' home is ransacked while they are on vacation, and the incriminating picture is found in a camera left behind (*or*, the house is ransacked before the vacation, and the roll of film is finished while the owners are away from home). Any way that it's told, you get the picture—right?

The infamous toothbrush story has been told and mailed to me so many times in the past few months that I'm sure it must have come to the attention of numerous journalists. Yet, probably because of its subject matter, the story has seldom been published. The first printed version I found was in the March 1991 issue of the *Ann Arbor* (Michigan) *Observer*. In Jay Forstner's article on urban legends he tells a typical version that he collected locally: honeymooners, Jamaica, Rastafarians, and the photograph showing the toothbrushes "stuck in the one place in Jamaica where the sun doesn't shine."

I still have not seen a purported copy of the actual photograph, which, after all, could conceivably be faked if someone wanted to "prove" the story to be true. However, I do know of two "illustrated" versions of the toothbrush story. One was a comic-strip retelling in the "True Tales of Columbus" series drawn by John Bailey for the Columbus, Ohio, periodical *Hoot* (March 14–27, 1991). Bailey's version shows three young men on vacation in Florida. The thieves take a series of photos as they ransack the room, but the crucial one for this legend is not shown; instead, Bailey drew the three roommates facing forward as they held the picture before them, its back to the reader. He conveyed the nature of the shot with a caption and by the victims' comments, "Urk!" "No!" and "Look how each one sticks out in a different direction."

The second illustrated version of the infamous toothbrush story I have appeared in the August 1991 issue of *Gallery*, which is described by the person who sent it to me as "my favorite smut magazine." This time four campers in upstate New York return from fishing to find their tent ransacked. A color sketch appearing with the story illustrates—rather demurely for a "smut magazine," I think—"an old, toothless, bearded man"

Reprinted by permission: John Bailey

who is photographing himself with the toothbrushes stuck you-know-where. The caption reads "When Brush Comes to Shove."

They say the camera doesn't lie—but where's the film?

Update:

In early April 1992, the day before I returned the final, revised manuscript of *The Baby Train* to my publisher, I received a
letter containing a European version of the tainted toothbrush
story from Peter Burger of Leiden, the Netherlands.* He was
awaiting publication of his own collection of urban legends
titled *De wraak van de kangoeroe* ("The Kangaroo's Revenge"),
and he wrote, "Such a pity this story only came to my notice
after I'd sent my manuscript to the printer!" Here's the story:

A father, mother, and two kids rent a bungalow in one of the
"Centre Parcs" resorts, the best-known and largest purveyor of
holiday homes in Holland. On the appointed day they arrive,
leave their car in the parking lot, and lug their heavy suitcases
to the bungalow. Much to their surprise and dismay, they discover that it is still occupied by four long-haired, leather-clad
bikers. Four Harleys are parked outside, and the owners are
lounging on the terrace drinking beer and smoking.

The bikers are not in the mood to leave on short notice, and
they tell the family to leave their luggage and go for a stroll. For
an hour or so the family walk around, looking at the other
guests and the shops.

On their return they are pleased to find the bikers gone, but
. . . their suitcases are strangely reduced in weight. In fact, they
are quite empty! When one of the children opens a cupboard,
there is all their stuff—the clothes neatly and carefully stored,
everything as if they had put it there themselves. With a sigh of
relief they tell each other that, after all, appearances can be
deceiving. Very nice boys those Hell's Angels turned out to be.

*See below, p. 237, "Tall Tales from the Low Countries" for another story
from Mr. Burger.

They have a good time in the resort, and back home again, they have their holiday pictures printed. The first picture portrays four naked backsides with the family's toothbrushes—well, perhaps you've heard this before?

"The Shocking Videotape"

"Somewhere it may exist," I wrote in November 1990, "this sensational home video of an amateur X-rated performance that I've heard so much about. But I haven't seen it yet, and I don't expect to catch it on television.

"If someone reading today's column," I continued, "owns a copy of America's most legendary home video, don't mail it to me. That would be illegal, and I wouldn't dream of suggesting such a thing.

"But, please, *do* write me if you can verify any details of the story I've heard. I ask this strictly out of professional curiosity, of course."

Here's the rest of that column, beginning with the first version of the story, sent to me in 1987 by an anonymous Indiana reader who explained, "A friend of a friend of mine allegedly heard about this on a radio news broadcast while driving through Iowa":

"A small town couple rented their first X-rated tape, and after watching it said, 'Heck, we could do better than that!' So they set up their camcorder in the bedroom and made their own sex film. Unfortunately, they mistakenly returned their intimate home video in the rental tape's box.

"The next person renting the tape recognized the couple and made copies of the tape. Soon almost everyone in town had a copy of it."

Time passed. Then in 1988 I heard from an Oklahoma man, who wrote:

"I just heard a story about the parents of a high school girl who asked their daughter's basketball coach for a videotape of her performance in a game. The coach was happy to oblige, but sent the wrong tape. It showed the coach having sex with some of the other players."

Soon after that I heard from Philip Hiscock, Folklore Archivist at the Memorial University of Newfoundland in St. John's:

"We've been hearing stories up here for the past year about a homemade pornographic videotape featuring local people and said to have fallen into public hands. Supposedly, some 300 to 400 copies are circulating in this community, though I've never seen one.

"A member of the local police force told me that they investigated the story, found that one of the versions of the legend was indeed true, but dropped it because there is in fact nothing criminal about any of the aspects of it."

In 1989 I received another version of the story, this time from a St. Louis man who wrote:

"A local gossip columnist wrote that a popular female news anchor returned what she thought was a rented videotape. It actually contained racy home videos of the woman herself. Later the columnist retracted the story, saying the tape contained only air-checks of her newscasts."

Then in autumn 1990 the sexy-tape story came up for discussion on a computer bulletin board. This generated variations of versions I'd heard previously, plus some new localities for the supposed event. The first version, coming from Colorado, was written in a telegraphic style:

"Girls' volleyball team from small town takes state championship. Schoolboard requests videos of games from coach. Coach complies, but—oops!—wrong tape, right volleyball team. Coach is fired."

Other comments followed on the bulletin board in rapid succession:

From Massachusetts came the story that it was a small-town Southern sheriff who made the racy tape of himself with his wife, then accidentally returned it in a rental tape box.

From New Jersey came the story that a church youth group was accidentally shown an 8mm amateur sex film by an adult leader; this was supposed to have occurred before VCRs were available.

From Michigan came the story that a high-school teacher showing an educational film accidentally threaded up the wrong movie and left the room without realizing that the class was watching the teacher's amateur sex film.

Next, from several locations, came claims from others who said the class—film blunder had really happened in their hometowns, or at least so they had heard from a friend of a friend.

What a mishmash of videos, films, schools, churches, husbands and wives, sheriffs, teachers, coaches, students, TV anchors, and multiple tape copies of embarrassing moments!

The most suspicious part of the story, I think, is not that someone might make such a film or tape, nor that they might accidentally have released it. But what are the odds of similar things happening many times over in different communities?

Can someone help me to sort the truth (if any) from the legends in all this?

The column was published, and help soon arrived, first in the form of an article I had missed in the October 29, 1990, edition of *Time* magazine headlined "Sex Lives and Videotape." One quoted example in it, though still anonymous, fit some versions of my story very well:

"The sheriff of Morris County, Kansas, filmed his wife and himself with a rented video camera and mistakenly returned the camera to the store—with the tape inside. Copies quickly circulated around the town of Council Grove. Eventually, the sheriff had to resign, and the couple left town."

Now all I needed was some names and dates, and I soon had them in a packet of clippings—but no tape—sent by Professor James Hoy of Emporia (Kansas) State University who wrote "The accidentally distributed X-rated video really does exist, and it was quite a story here a few years ago. The incident has become part of local lore, and I've even seen the tape."

OK, OK Professor Hoy, that's enough; I'm convinced. And I'm also a bit chagrined to find that I missed one of the biggest scandal stories of 1986 at the time when the incident occurred.

For, as *The Kansas City Times* reported in October 1987, one year after the embarrassing incident, "The [couple's] bulletin board and scrapbooks are full of clippings from newspapers, as well as messages from radio and TV reporters all across the country and abroad."

At least I've learned that a real-life incident may underly most versions of "The Sexy Videotape" legend, and if it could happen once, the same kind of mix-up could probably happen repeatedly. Well, I learned one other thing too: Not everyone appreciates this sort of incident. Here's part of a letter from Columbus, Ohio, responding to the original column:

"Jan: Ever hear about the legend of this once strong Godly nation that over a period of time became so preoccupied with illicit sex and corrupt lifestyles that it crumbled to the ground? Your column is usually very enjoyable, but you wasted space and my time with this one."

I guess, for once, I find myself siding with the psychologists, who, according to *Time*, generally approve of do-it-yourself sex videos: "They see homemade erotica as a safe way to spice up a couple's sex life; there's the thrill of the forbidden but none of the danger of, say, an affair."

But I still don't want to view someone else's tape, nor am I ready to make my own. For one thing, I don't own a camcorder, and I sure as heck don't intend to rent one for the purpose.

2

Horrors

"Flights of Fancy"

One summer day a little girl visiting just down the street from my house suffered a concussion when she fell from a piece of furniture she was climbing on. A neighbor told me, "The girl had been watching *Mary Poppins,* and her mother thinks she was just trying to fly like the people in the movie."

Judging from the number of times I've heard this sort of explanation, you'd think that consumers would demand that a warning be aired before this film, not to mention *Peter Pan* and *Superman.* It could read something like, "Kids—Don't try these stunts yourself at home! The actors are trained professionals."

I've heard one account of a child eating lots of spinach, "like Popeye," and then trying to stop a freight train with his body. People also claim that children have gone into sewers in search of the Teenage Mutant Ninja Turtles.

But most of the time the story you hear concerning this theme is the one I call "The Boy Who Played Superman." Supposedly a little boy wearing a towel or a curtain around his neck as a cape jumps from a great height in imitation of the superhero's flying skills, and dies in the attempt.

The story is not entirely fictional; children are impressionable, and sometimes they do try to imitate their heroes. Several readers have written to me describing incidents they witnessed that were similar to the "Flights of Fancy" story. But the hearsay recollections of such accidents happening to other people far outnumber the reliable firsthand accounts of children who try to fly like the fantasy characters they idolize.

Kim Metzger, a comic-book collector and columnist for *The Comics Buyer's Guide,* has attempted to verify "The Boy Who Played Superman" without much luck. "The story is a favorite of the anti-comics crowd," he noted in a column about the legend. For as long as there have been comic strips and comic books, he explained, people opposing them have circulated stories about their pernicious influence on youth.

Films based on comic characters, Metzger added, have further encouraged such claims. After the release of the first *Superman* movie in 1978, for instance, stories about kids' attempts to fly abounded.

But Metzger has located only three news stories describing such incidents.

The first, which appeared in *The New York Times* on February 3, 1979, told about a four-year-old boy in Brooklyn who had fallen from a seventh-floor window. According to the story, the boy's mother told police that after seeing the movie *Superman* a week earlier, her son had, "fantasized about flying like Superman."

Even so, the incident seems unrelated to the legend. For one thing, the *Times* emphasizes right at the top of the story that the boy "fell from a window"—that is, he didn't jump. And the story says nothing about him wearing a towel or curtain around his neck—surely a relevant detail.

It is mentioned in the story that before he fell "the boy was spotted hanging from a window ledge by his fingers." This doesn't sound much like the position one would end up in if trying to "fly" from the window.

The *Times* ran a follow-up story on February 12, under the headline "Boy Who Tried to Fly 'Like Superman' Dies." Again, the story emphasizes that he fell. And the quotation marks in the headline indicate that the newspaper is merely quoting the mother's guess about her son's death.

The second press report about such a death that Metzger found was in an unnamed tabloid. Two boys trying to imitate Superman, the tabloid reported, fell from a window ledge. But in an article published in the same tabloid a week later, the boys' father confessed that he had been abusing them, and that he had invented the Spiderman story as a cover-up.

Metzger and other people have also sent me an apocryphal story, one sometimes mentioned in the press, about actor George Reeves who played Superman in the 1950s television series. Reeves died of a self-inflicted gunshot wound in 1959, two years after the show went off the air. But some people offer a different cause of the actor's death.

After playing the Man of Steel in dozens of *Superman* episodes, according to the story, Reeves began to believe that he himself could actually fly. He supposedly died after jumping off a building in an attempt to do so. Sounds to me like just another "Flights of Fancy" legend.

"Mothers' Double Talk" and
Other Domestic Tragedies

Folklorist Janet Langlois of Wayne State University, Detroit, and I have been comparing notes for several years on legends concerning what she calls "Mothers' Double Talk." These stories of domestic tragedy, Langlois says, "Read like a Don't List for the competent mother."

The crux of the plot is that a mother makes an innappropriate threat to her small son which her young daughter takes literally—with harrowing consequences. (I included a brief discussion of these stories in *The Mexican Pet*, and a variation appears in Hunter Thompson's 1954 novel, *Not as a Stranger*.)

Here's one version sent to me by Edward H. Eulenberg of Chicago, as told by his mother in the 1930s:

"The little boy in the story was usually two or three years old. Despite scoldings, he resisted toilet training until his exasperated mother warned: 'If you don't learn, I'm going to cut it off.'

"She was overheard by the boy's older sister. Then one day, when the children's mother was away, the boy wet again, and the girl took up a pair of shears and cut it off, leaving him bleeding to death."

In some versions of the story, the mother, in her haste to drive the injured child to a hospital, accidentally backs the car over her distraught daughter who has run from the house. Sometimes a third child dies in the mix-up by falling while carrying the knife or scissors.

An English variation of "Mothers' Double Talk" tells of a mother with two small children taking an overnight ferry to Ireland or France. When the baby keeps on crying, Mum snaps, "If you don't shut up, I'll put you out the porthole!"*

Later, when the baby has fallen asleep and the older sister is quiet in her bunk, the mother slips out of the cabin for a cup of tea. When she returns, her daughter proudly announces, "Baby cried again, so I put him out the porthole just like you said."

This version teaches, "Like mother, like daughter." The child learns how to behave as an adult by watching her parent in action.

All of these stories warn mothers not to make idle threats of dire punishment. Behind this practical advice are hints of penis envy and sibling rivalry—it's a Freudian nightmare. Langlois points out that the overburdened mother in the beginning of these tales has become "a free woman" at the end. Thus, the double talk legends pit a mother's desire for freedom against her sense of maternal anxiety, with no resolution in sight—at least not in the legend itself.

Several such stories of maternal failure have prototypes in Europe. For example, a Polish-American woman wrote saying that she remembered this one from her homeland:

"A woman was bathing a child while her two other children were right outside the door. One child announced that he had cut off the other's penis.

"The horrified mother jumped up from bathing the first child, and she threw open the door so hard that she killed the child who had injured the other. When she returned to the bathroom, she found that the first child had drowned."

This variation is found elsewhere in Europe, and since it also applies to the problems of any modern Mom trying to keep

---

*The wording of this threat is similar to that in the Aesop fable "The Nurse and the Wolf" which in one version begins, " 'Be quiet now,' said an old Nurse to a child sitting on her lap. 'If you make that noise again I will throw you to the wolf.' " A wolf, overhearing this, sits outside the window waiting for the child to cry again, but when the nurse sees the wolf, she closes the window and calls the dogs to chase the wolf away.

track of several youngsters, it was adopted into American folk-lore.

Here's another mother/child story I've heard several times, in which one or more children die in a bathtub. Elizabeth Rut-ledge of Ocracoke, North Carolina, wrote in 1988 to say that she remembered this version being "told and retold" in the early years of World War II. A woman whose husband is at the Pacific Front is bathing her two small children upstairs when the doorbell rings. Hurrying down the steps to answer the door, she trips on a toy and falls to the bottom, breaking her neck.

At the door is a military envoy, sent to inform her that her husband was killed in action. When authorities enter the house to check on her, they find the woman dead in the hallway and both children drowned in the bathtub. (A version I heard in New Zealand earlier the same year said the event occurred during the First World War, and the woman did not trip and die, but returned upstairs to find the two youngsters drowned in the tub.)

Rutledge wrote that she later heard the same story in which police officers come to the door to say that the husband had been killed in an auto accident. In some versions the children had begun playing with a radio or a hair dryer in the bathtub and were electrocuted.

A story about multiple accidental deaths of children even appeared in the first edition of *Grimm's Fairy Tales* in 1812—reprinted from a seventeenth-century German book*—but it was dropped from later editions.

In this tale children play at being butchers. Imitating their father's pig-slaughtering, one boy slit his younger brother's throat. Their mother, hearing their cries, runs from the house, and in her distress she seizes the knife and stabs the older child.

---

*See Dieter Richter, "Wie Kinder Schlachtens mit einander gespielt haben (AaTh 2401)," *Fabula*, vol. 27, 1986, pp. 1–11 for the background of the Grimm version. The parenthetical reference is the index number used for this folktale in the international index of tale types.

She then returns to find the baby, whom she was bathing at the time, drowned in the tub.

The Grimm tale (truly!) concludes with the mother hanging herself and the father dying of despondency. No wonder the story was eliminated from the classic fairy-tale collection!

Horrible as the modern versions are, at least in most of them there are some survivors.

Three Sticky Situations

Getting stuck *to* or stuck *in* something may be unlucky in real life, but in urban legends it's downright disastrous. Trust me when I say that the following three sticky horror stories are merely folklore. I hope I don't sound stuck-up saying that, since some people believe these tales. However, I have convincing evidence to back me up.

"THE STUCK DIVER"

A British reader, Sioned Mair Phillips (who helpfully added "Miss" to her signature) wrote to say that the following story is widely known among divers:

A man was diving off Swansea Bay when he spotted a large crab nestling in the rocks. Thinking it would make a nice supper, he put his hand over the crab to pick it up by its back.

The crab, not wanting to end up as anyone's supper, exerted a strong force upwards and trapped the diver's hand between itself and the rock.

When the diver realized that his oxygen supply was getting low, in desperation he pulled out his diving knife and hacked off his own hand.

I heard the variation that validates this as a legend in the early 1970s in California, told about a man hunting abalone along a lonely stretch of the coast. When he reached under a rock ledge for one, it clamped down hard on his fingers and trapped him. No one heard him scream for help, and when the tide came in he drowned.

"THE STUCK BABY"

Rubye Box of San Antonio, Texas, recently wrote me with the following tale:

> *A story I heard twenty years ago upset me very much. I lived in Jackson, Mississippi, when I heard it.*
>
> *A young couple were catching a flight to begin a trip of several days, and they had hired a sitter to care for their baby during their absence.*
>
> *When it was time to leave for the airport, the baby sitter had not arrived, so they telephoned her home and learned that she was on the way. They put the baby in its highchair, left the back door open for the sitter, and rushed to the airport.*
>
> *When the sitter arrived, the wind had blown the door shut, and it had locked. She thought the parents either must have taken the baby with them or left it with someone else, so she returned home.*
>
> *When the couple got back, they found their baby starved to death in its highchair.*

I could sense the shudder behind the last statement in Ms. Box's letter: "I don't know if this story is true or not, but I don't think I shall ever forget it!"

Is it any comfort to know that the same story—never verified—was going around Europe in 1971 and 1972? In one variation the baby-sitter was killed by a car while walking to the couple's home, and she had told no one about her responsibility for the baby.

I've seen "The Stuck Baby" in urban legend books from Norway and Sweden, and in 1984 it was reprinted in England in Rodney Dale's book *It's True, It Happened to a Friend* (London: Gerald Duckworth & Co.) where it was said to be told in England about a Norwegian couple. The title of this version was "Bjorn yesterday."

"THE STUCK SANTA"

This story shows up in my mail annually at Christmas. The following version was sent to me by Tory Brecht of Iowa City:

I'm hoping this truly gruesome story is a legend. It's about a young family who cannot be together for Christmas because the father has to be out of town, leaving mom and children alone for the holiday.

But the dad cancels his business trip and decides to dress up as Santa Claus and surprise his family. On Christmas Eve he climbs on the roof and begins to slide down the chimney.

Unfortunately, he gets stuck in the chimney and dies from asphyxiation. Later that night when the family lights the yule log they smell a strange singed odor. Yup, you guessed it—smoked dead Santa!

And you guessed it too, Tory—urban legend! Variations of this story are widely told, and it was repeated in the 1985 film *Gremlins*, but so far as I'm aware, no one has found an authentic case of a Santa fatally stuck in a chimney.

"The Accidental Cannibals"*

Today's column is truly disgusting—or at least the legend it describes is. But readers keep asking me about stories concerning accidental cannibalism, and I've finally decided to respond, at the risk of getting some negative mail.

Write me to complain if you will, but just don't send me any cremains, or anything that looks like same, OK?

That's the basis of the legend in question—"cremains," or cremated remains, are mistaken for food. Frankly, I dislike the idea as much as the next squeamish soul. But I try to *study* urban legends, not to edit or censor them. So here goes with "The Accidental Cannibals."

I first heard the legend in Romania from a friend with whom I was drinking instant coffee one day. She was reminded of a story she had heard shortly after World War II, when powdered foods first appeared in that country.

A Romanian family was supposed to have received a package from relatives in the United States containing an unlabeled jar of blackish-brown powder, which they assumed was an instant drink of some sort. After the family had used up most of the powder making hot drinks, a letter arrived from the United States explaining that the jar had contained the ashes of their grandmother, who had immigrated to the United States. The American relatives had thought it right to return the woman's ashes to her home country for burial.

In another Romanian version the powder was mistaken for a condiment, which the family sprinkled upon roasts.

The story depicts a drastic mistake that might occur when people jump to conclusions, and underscores the harsh conditions that prevailed in postwar Europe.

---

*column of October 1988.

It also resembles the urban legend about foreigners who think that the baby-food and cat-food containers with babies and cats pictured on their labels contain a food made out of babies or cats.

There's a version of "The Accidental Cannibals" told about a German family who mistook the mailed cremains for flour, and baked bread from the powder. In another German version, the powder is made into soup—and just as they all begin to eat it, an English-speaking member of the family enters and translates the letter that accompanied the package.

A reader in Austria recounted for me a version in which cremains were mistaken for dried coconut: "It was somebody else's food parcel, of course," the Austrian reader wrote, "and nobody knew the coconut-cake maker personally, but nobody ever doubted that the story was true."

I have two versions from England, one of which tells of soup made from powder sent from the States, and the other describing cake baked from the powdered remains of a relative who had died in Australia.

While the legend is generally said to have taken place four decades ago, in the years after the war, it occasionally appears anew in a present-day source. In August 1987, for example, Wilfred R. Woods of *The Wanatchee* (Washington) *World* included it in his "Taking It Over" column. This time Yugoslavs mistook a tin of unlabeled powder for a seasoning.

Folklorist Charles Clay Doyle uncovered what may be the ancestor of the 1940s stories—a very grim anti-Semitic "jest" that originated during the Renaissance. An Italian Jew, in order to smuggle a dead friend's body home to Venice for burial dismembers the corpse and packs it in a large jar with spices and honey. The man brings the jar with him on a ship bound for Venice.

In the course of the journey a fellow passenger, a Gentile from Florence, sneaks some pieces out of the jar and unwittingly snacks on the corpse.

This isn't a story you'd want to tell in an after-dinner speech.

Who knows, even reading about it might kill your appetite.

[The following was deleted from the first column]

I wouldn't have mentioned this last stomach-turning version at all, except that I found an Irish-American folk ballad telling the same story titled "The Pickled Jew" in the book *Folk Songs Out of Wisconsin* edited by Harry B. Peters and published by the State Historical Society of Wisconsin in 1977.

The song was collected in 1941 from a logger who learned it from an Irishman in a lumber camp. The date, plus the European connection, helps to link the repulsive old story to the disgusting recent one.

One stanza of the song, with its refrain quoted right out of the traditional British balladry, goes like this:

"Oh God," said old Isaac, "You're worse than a sinner.
You would eat up my poor brother, Moses, for dinner."
"Oh God," said the captain, "Has me and my crew
Been living three weeks on a barrel of tough Jew?"
　　　Derry down, down, down, Derry down.

MORE ABOUT "THE ACCIDENTAL CANNIBALS"*

Comparing the following two stories from England, you can easily see that they're just variations on a theme:

No. 1: "The parcel of dried fruit for the anniversary cake duly arrived from Australian cousins, with no note or letter. The ingredients, including some greyish powder—to add spice?—were duly mixed and baked, and the cake pronounced by family and friends as 'gorgeous.'

"Then the delayed letter arrived, with the instructions: 'By the way, the grey powder in the packet is Uncle Joe's ashes. Would you please scatter them on his mother's grave?' "

No. 2: ". . . the guilt-ridden Wilkinsons of Sussex . . . having gotten what they thought was a gift package of herbs from

---

*column of February 1991.

Australian relatives, stirred the contents into a traditional Christmas pudding, ate half of it, and put the remainder in the refrigerator.

"Soon thereafter, a member of the family relates, 'we heard from Auntie Sheila that Uncle Eric had died, and had we received his ashes for burial in Britain?' Shocked, the Wilkinsons quickly summoned a vicar to bless, and bury, Uncle Eric's leftovers."

The first story was published in a 1978 collection of British urban legends, along with a variation in which the ashes were packed in a cocoa tin.

The second story was quoted in a December 18, 1990, *Wall Street Journal* article about a British Broadcasting Corporation radio program that features letters in which listeners confess their worst sins.

My conclusion is that a listener to the popular BBC program decided to "confess" to the urban legend called "The Accidental Cannibals." The program's producer, who, according to the *Journal* article, "makes no effort to verify the authenticity of confessions," fell for the fictional story.

"The Accidental Cannibals" has been a popular legend since the end of World War II when powdered foods first became available and were sometimes included in relief packages.

In most versions of the story Americans send their European relatives a family member's cremated remains which are mistaken for dehydrated soup, a powdered drink, or a cake mix. The cremains are cooked and eaten, then later the enclosed letter that identifies the substance is translated.

In England, the usual form of the story is that an aunt's, uncle's, or grandmother's ashes were sent back home from Australia or the United States for burial, but when they arrive they are mistaken for a seasoning. An explanatory letter arrives too late to prevent the family's eating "Aunt Ada's Ashes."

There are too many similar versions of "The Accidental Cannibals" that have circulated too widely and for too many years for me to credit any of them as true. Yet I've always wondered whether cremains might actually be mistaken for a food product.

Here's what a mortician wrote me on the subject:

I have handled many urns of cremains while sprinkling them in various places requested by the deceased. They are so similar to coarse sand or finely ground seashells that I believe no one could mistake them for soup or baking ingredients. Considering that cremation removes all but the mineral content of the body, this isn't surprising.

I believe that fascination with the legend about someone accidentally eating a relative's ashes simply shows most people's total inexperience with the results of cremation.

Coping with people's confusion about cremains seems to be an international problem.

According to a newspaper article I clipped in New Zealand a few years ago, a funeral director in the city of Oamaru, hoping to "dispel some of the myths that have grown up about cremation," arranged an interesting public demonstration.

Citing the "popular misconception" that a person's cremains may include ashes remaining from the coffin, here's what the article says the director did:

"Mr. Perkins has cremated a sheep and will use the remains to show how the casket ash is removed using a sieve, the screws are taken out with a magnet, and the bone fragments are ground into fine ash."

Good show, Perkins! But don't send any unmarked packets of that fine-ground ash to any relatives in England.

"The Exploding Bra"

Most readers who send me stories ask hopefully if they have discovered an urban legend—but not the woman from Secaucus, New Jersey, who wrote to tell about her Aunt Edna's exploding bra. She wanted the story to be true.

"I really hope this is not an urban legend," she wrote, "as it has been a cherished family story for twenty-five years."

Be that as it may, an updated version of the story was referred to in a 1988 television sitcom episode, and I've also received other variations set all the way across the country.

The New Jersey woman, Aunt Edna—I've changed her name—supposedly had an adventure with her bra around 1960. Edna, then a glamorous young lady with a beehive hairdo, gold spike heels, and capri pants wore her brand-new inflatable bra on an airplane trip. When the plane's cabin lost pressure, the bra expanded alarmingly.

One family version of the story claimed that she made it to the rest room in time to remove the bra. But according to another version, the bra exploded while she was wearing it— right in the middle of the aisle. Or so the stories go among Aunt Edna's relatives; the person who sent it to me said, "Unfortunately, I lost track of her years ago."

The writer did recall, however, that the inflatable bra was a popular fashion accessory of the times. She explained that such bras contained hollow soft plastic falsies to be inflated to the desired size by blowing into a small tube.

My correspondent maintained, "This is an article of underclothing I have actually seen!"

Not I, so I took her word for it. But I have some doubts about the story of Aunt Edna's big bang. "The Exploding Bra" story may be part of a larger cycle of legends that embraces exploding bosom stories as well.

In the December 12, 1988, episode of the sitcom "Designing Women" a character wondered whether she ought to spend part of an inheritance to have her bust enlarged with silicone implants. Suzanne (played by Delta Burke) warned her against the procedure, saying, "A Pan Am stewardess I know had hers done, and they exploded on take-off."

Boise State University librarian Dan Lester, who pointed out the sitcom reference, also wrote me, "I first heard of 'The Exploding Bosom' about 1981 or '82 when I lived in Albuquerque. It was told about either a stewardess or a passenger who had silicone breast implants, and these were said to be enclosed in some kind of plastic baggies."

But when Dan mentioned the subject of exploding bosoms to a colleague who had grown up in western Colorado, the colleague remembered a different version of the story. Supposedly a girl wearing an inflatable bra to a prom had it deflate when her date pinned a corsage onto her formal. Yet another colleague, however, said he had heard that story told as true in Chicago.

The line in the sitcom may have been based on a Los Angeles news report that *may* have referred to a stewardess whose inflatable bra *might* actually have exploded. I phrased that last statement with extreme caution because I haven't been able to locate the news story itself, only a claimed reprint without a date.

The following item appears in Jearl Walker's book *The Flying Circus of Physics* (John Wiley & Sons, 1975, p. 46) in the section on atmospheric and water pressure:

Los Angeles (AP)—What happens to a stewardess wearing an inflatable bra when the cabin of her jet plane is depressurized?

Just what you're thinking Herman. Inflation.

As Los Angeles Times *columnist Matt Weinstock told it Friday, this set of potentially explosive circumstances occurred recently on a Los Angeles–bound flight. He gallantly withheld the identity of girl and airline.*

"When she had, ahem, expanded to about size 46,"
Weinstock wrote, "she frantically sought a solution. Somehow
she found a woman passenger who had a small hat pin and
stabbed herself strategically.

"However, another passenger, a man of foreign descent,
misunderstood. He thought she was trying to commit hara-kiri
the hard way. He grappled with her trying to prevent her from
punching the hat pin in her chest.

"Order was quickly restored, but laughter still is echoing
along the airlines."

Weinstock says it really happened.

In this version, the mix-up with the "foreign gentleman," the handy hat pin, the lack of names, and *especially* the columnist's unsupported claim that "it really happened," all make me wonder whether the story is true.

The range of dates and the many variations in the story line as the incident is repeated also cast doubt on the story as a report of actual events.

I'm still not sure we have a legend here, but at least I've been able to verify the existence of inflatable bras. A page from a 1967 Frederick's of Hollywood catalog sent by a helpful reader shows three models of inflatable bras which are called "Float," "Bosom Friend," and "Knit Fit."

And a 1989 mail order catalog from Old Pueblo Traders of Tucson, Arizona, offers a bra that will inflate "to the fullness you desire . . . inflation tube included."

But there's no warning notice in either catalog about the dangers of an explosion during air travel. If it has happened—to Aunt Edna or anyone else—the incident certainly has spun off a wild series of variations.

Exploding Airplanes

In the Ian Fleming thriller *Goldfinger*, James Bond fires his pistol through the window of an airplane in flight. The rapid decompression sucks old Auric Goldfinger through the bullet hole—extruding him, like toothpaste from a tube.

It never occurred to me that this scene might represent, as Mark A. Moritz of Tempe, Arizona, wrote me, "an urban legend that bears exposing." Moritz is a contributing editor for *American Handgunner* magazine. He's also a collector of what he calls *Waffenposselhaft*, a German term that means "gunfoolishness" in English. His letter explained:

Because of Fleming's book, many otherwise intelligent people actually believe that if you fire a bullet through a plane, the plane's insides will be sucked out.

A few years back, when hijacking planes to Cuba became common, the Feds had a Sky Marshal program—armed guards riding on the planes. The marshals carried special low-penetration ammunition, presumably so that they wouldn't have a Goldfinger episode.

Actually, firing a bullet through the skin of a pressurized plane does exactly nothing, since airplanes are already highly porous. Compressors constantly pump air into and out of the plane; otherwise, the passengers would suffocate. (That's the whooshing noise you hear on commercial jets.)

Thus airplanes already have massive "holes" in them, for the air to escape. The size of the hole depends on the size of the plane, but typically, the area is several square feet.

A bullet hole, on the other hand, has an area of less than a tenth of a square inch. (For example, a 9 millimeter bullet has a diameter of .355 inches, so, since area equals πr^2 a bullet hole's area is only about .09 inches.)

*Such a small difference in the total area of a plane's body
would have no measurable effect on cabin pressure.*

*Rapid decompression does occur in cases where the entire
roof tears off a plane, as in the Hawaiian accident, or when
explosives blow a twenty-foot hole in the side of a plane, as in
the TWA incident. But even then both planes landed safely
with few casualties.*

*Decompression from a hole measuring a tenth of a square
inch, though? No way.*

It was a relief to learn from an expert that I won't be ex-
truded through the bullet hole if a terrorist fires a shot inside a
plane I happen to be in.* (Now I wish someone would explain
why after decades of commercial flights I've never seen—nor
met anyone else who has—those little oxygen masks actually
drop out of a plane's ceiling.)

Thanks, too, Mark, for reminding me of one of the few math-
ematical formulas that I can remember from my high school
geometry classes. The formula πr^2 stuck in my head long after
other axioms, like the one about the square of the hypotenuse
(or "squaw of the hippopotamus," as we used to call it), went
thataway.

Back to air-crash myths. An article I saved from the *Los
Angeles Times*, published in 1988, quoted an aviation psycholo-
gist on the subject:

"Most people who fly worry about all the wrong things: tur-
bulence, which often only moves the plane a few inches; light-
ning, which rarely does more than damage the radar domes or
make pinholes in the wings; or catastrophes that really don't
happen any more, such as the wings falling off."

One other cabin pressure story I've heard concerns a mili-

---

*Several readers wrote to remind me that pressurized military fighter
planes have often received bullet holes in combat, and their pilots were not
sucked out through them. Nor (as Gary L. Dikkers, Lt. Col, USAF, wrote)
does the pilot usually endure much more than a lot of wind and noise when a
plane loses its canopy, which is certainly an instance of rapid decompression.

tary pilot flying out of an air base somewhere in the southwest. While cruising at 25,000 or 30,000 feet, he looks down and sees a large rattlesnake coiled on the cabin floor.

Since he's flying solo, a bite would surely be fatal since he probably would not be able to land.

The pilot saves his life, as well as the taxpayers' money, by staying aboard and not ejecting. He kills the rattler by decompressing the cabin until the snake dies from lack of oxygen.

The pilot, of course, is protected by his oxygen mask.

"The Failed Suicide"

Many teachers use jokes and anecdotes to enliven their lectures and underscore main points. Here's an example that involves a rather ironic urban legend. At least I think it's an urban legend; I'm still seeking more proof.

Sir Sidney Smith, a British expert on forensic medicine, gives this account of teaching via storytelling in his book *Mostly Murder* (London, 1959):

> *When I lectured to my students on multiple methods of suicide, I generally finished up by relating the most outstanding case of all, a classic of its kind, which, unfortunately, is not susceptible to confirmation. . . . The story is that a highly pessimistic individual had determined to take his life, and wanted to make sure there would be none of the slip-ups he had read about. He decided that hanging would be an efficient method of self-destruction, and selected a tree with a stout branch overhanging a cliff, the sea being fifty feet below. . . . In order to prevent any pain in the hanging process he procured himself a large dose of opium. Although these arrangements seemed fairly complete, he decided that in order to make certain of a successful result it would be a good idea to shoot himself as well. The noose adjusted, the poison taken, and the revolver cocked, he stepped over the cliff, and as he did so, fired. The jerk of the rope altered his aim, and the bullet missed his head but cut partly through the rope. This broke with the jerk of the body, and he fell fifty feet into the sea below. There he swallowed a quantity of salt water, vomited the poison, and swam ashore a better and a wiser man.*

The only other published version of "The Failed Suicide" that I have found, so far, came from a reader who copied it from a 1944 London *Daily Express* column called "50 Years Ago." It sounds like a concise summary of Sir Sidney Smith's anecdote:

"A British suicide took poison and tried to hang himself from a cliff above the sea, shooting himself in the head as, noose around his neck, he jumped out of this world. But he missed and shot through the rope, falling into the sea below; the brine he swallowed neutralized the poison, and the sea washed him ashore."

Smith cites no parallels for "The Failed Suicide," but since he called the story "a classic of its kind," and emphasized that it "is not susceptible to confirmation," I suspect that other accounts of the story exist.

I've been racking my brain to remember where I read (or heard?) a similar story that supposedly happened, not in England, but on either the San Francisco Bay Bridge or the Brooklyn Bridge. Maybe I'm hallucinating about this after having read too many wacky stories, but I swear I somewhere ran into an American version of the failed-suicide story.

At any rate, I've heard two variants of a different failed-suicide story.

One involves a man who had an argument with his wife. The wife stormed out of the apartment, and the husband decided to hurl himself from the window into the street below.

By the time the man had scrawled a suicide note and opened the window, his wife was just leaving the building at the main entrance directly below their window. The man jumped and landed on his wife. She was killed by the force of the collision, but he survived.

In the second version, the man had been fired from his job. He leaped from the office window and landed on his boss, who after the unpleasant duty of firing an employee was on his way to an early lunch.

Life's rarely so neat and ironic, so I'm assuming there's a strong dose of urban legend to all these stories.

"Psychic Videotapes"

Can someone invent a legend that sounds genuine and then later hear the story being repeated in variations? In other words, can you invent a piece of folklore?

Folklorists' stock answer is "No," because legends, like other folktales, usually develop from collective efforts. Countless people retell a story, each unconsciously adding or changing details until it acquires a life of its own in oral tradition. Everybody telling legends is part of this composing process that scholars call *communal re-creation*.

Still, John W. Cork of Los Angeles thought he'd try to start an urban legend. He sent me his creation, a story he called "The Psychic Videotape":

> *A young married couple who had just moved to [insert city name] rents the movie* Always *at a local video store [insert name]. At the end of the film after the credits roll and the screen turns to snow, they are startled to see the ghostly image of Richard Dreyfuss, star of the film.*
>
> *He says "Call your mom!" and disappears.*
>
> *Neither of the viewers call their mothers, but the next morning the wife gets a call from her brother. He tells her that Mom died in her sleep last night.*
>
> *All the tapes of* Always *at the video store were checked for the image, but none had it.* Always *has become the hottest rental at that store since the story got out, but so far Richard Dreyfuss' ghostly image has yet to warn another viewer.*

Reading Cork's story I thought, "Hmm, not bad." He cleverly grafted the traditional motif of a spiritual death warning onto a technological theme. "The Psychic Videotape" legend could fit any big city or video rental store. The story could also be interpreted—in typical urban-legend fashion—as a ploy to promote tape rentals.

Incidentally, Cork concluded his letter saying, "I am *not* in the video rental business."

As far as I know, this invented legend has not caught on. But a similar story about a ghostly image on a videotape was running rampant by autumn 1990.

It turns out that in the 1987 film (released on videotape in 1990) *Three Men and a Baby*, you can make out the shadowy figure of what appears to be a young boy standing near a window in the rear of a scene involving Ted Danson and Celeste Holm, who plays his mother. Apparently, nobody noticed the image when the film ran in theaters, but thousands spotted it in the videotapes.

The boy seems to be wearing jeans and a T-shirt and staring stiffly ahead, partly obscured by sheer curtains. Some people claim to see a rifle leaning against the wall next to the boy. The other characters in the scene ignore the boy, and he never appears elsewhere in the film.

This oddity is explained, according to the story people began telling, by the notion that a New York apartment used for the filming was leased by the filmakers from a couple who moved out after their son committed suicide there. Some say the boy shot himself, others believe that he fell out of the window near where his ghost appears.

When the couple saw the film, they supposedly recognized their son wearing the same clothes he had died in. To account for the delay in spotting the ghost, some people claim that the New York couple never managed to catch the film in a theater, and only spotted the ghost image when they rented the video.

Several further variations, none of them true, help validate this story as a genuine legend: Some people say the son was murdered, or that the couple has appeared on a national TV program discussing the case; others claim that those who filmed the scene never saw the boy, or that the boy visible on the tapes does not show up at conventional screenings of the film.

People not inclined to tell ghost stories have suggested that the boy may have been the son of a member of the film's cast or crew who accidently found himself in camera range and "froze." Others speculate that he may be a young relative of Leonard Nimoy, the film's director who had promised the boy a chance to appear in the movie.

Then there are the inevitable claims in stories about big business that the film production company must have inserted the "ghost" scenes in order to build interest in the video rentals and in the film's sequel. Though the story did boost rentals of *Three Men and a Baby*, there's no evidence that it was deliberately planted.

Chris Hicks, film critic for the Salt Lake City *Deseret News* dubbed the strange story "Three Men and a Spectral Vision." "Every film commentator in the region," he told me in mid-August, 1990, "has been inundated with calls about it."

Shortly after I spoke to Hicks, a television newscaster in Las Vegas called saying that the same story was circulating both locally and on computer nets. Before long I was receiving calls and letters about the ghostly videotape story from all over the country, and several national publications had mentioned it.

The story is easily debunked. As journalists who queried Touchstone Pictures division of the Walt Disney studios learned, the apartment scenes in the movie were filmed not in a Manhattan apartment but on a soundstage in Toronto. There was no actual New York apartment, no dead son, and no bereft parents.

But there definitely *is* an unexplained human figure visible in the background of the scene in question. It turns out to be a slightly smaller than life-sized cardboard cutout of actor Ted Danson who appears in the film in the character of an actor. The cardboard figure, explained the studio, represents part of an advertising display that his character used to decorate the apartment.

That's the reality of the *Three Men and a Baby* ghost, but

there's also a folkloristic side to the story. Spectral images in photographs are nothing new, but have long been a part of folk tradition. One popular cycle of stories tells of a face showing up in the window of an abandoned house when it is photographed. The face is recognized as that of someone who died in the house long ago, often as a murder victim.

Other old legends claim that in a group photo of some mining, logging, or other work group the face of an extra person appears. It is recognized as someone who had been killed in an accident on the job, and the eyes of the figure in the photo are blank.

So it seems that when a "ghost" image actually appeared in a contemporary film, people telling and retelling the incident collectively revived and adapted the old "spiritual photograph" tradition in order to make it fit the theme of a ghostly videotape.

Note: Charles Greg Kelley included several verbatim texts of this legend and a short discussion in his article "Three Men, a Baby, and a Boy Behind the Curtain: A Tradition in the Making," *Midwestern Folklore*, vol. 17, 1991, pp. 5–13.

"No News but Bad News"

Robert Rodriguez, a New York City storyteller and teacher, wrote to ask if I know a story he likes to tell called "No News." He summarized it like this:

A man returning home after a few months away is met by his servant who tells him his dog died from eating burnt horseflesh after the barn burned down from a spark blown from the fire that consumed his house.

The house fire started from candles placed around the coffin of his mother-in-law who died after learning that her daughter ran off with the hired man.

"Other than that," the servant said, "there's no news."

I'm impressed that an urban raconteur is still telling this old chestnut, a story known to folklorists as "The Climax of Horrors" and assigned number 2040 in our standard index *The Types of the Folktale.* Three years ago I replied personally to a query about this story. But since it's neither urban nor a legend, I never mentioned it in a column until Rodriguez wrote me.

That original question came from a woman in her seventies in Raleigh, North Carolina, whose great-grandmother told it as a Civil War story. In her version, the young heir of a southern family had been hospitalized for some time after the war. A servant sent to bring him home was cautioned not to upset the heir in any way which might endanger his precarious health.

When the young man asked "Moses, why did you come for me driving this team of old nags?" the servant answered, "These are all we have since the other horses died." The servant went on to explain that the horses died in the barn fire caused by sparks from the house fire set by candles burning at the foot of the heir's father's casket.

These summaries can't do the story justice, since its humor

depends as much on the style in which it's told as on the absurd placement of the worst news last.

When good storytellers perform "No News" they dramatize the series of questions and answers. That's exactly how the story appeared in *McGuffey's Fifth Eclectic Reader,* a schoolbook first published in 1879. McGuffey's titled it "How to Tell Bad News" and phrased it as a dialogue between "Mr. H." and his steward that began:

"Mr. H.: Ha! Steward, how are you my old boy? How do things go on at home?

"Steward: Bad enough, your honor; the magpie's dead."

It turns out that the bird ate itself to death by consuming the flesh of the horses that died from overwork hauling water to put out the house fire set from torches lit during the funeral of Mr. H.'s mother.

I wonder how schoolchildren a century ago reacted to that gruesome little tale!

There are many other versions of "The Climax of Horrors" that only a folklorist enamored of Type 2040 would care to read. Probably our American versions stem from a British original.

I found a rather funny one in a 1958 book by Vance Randolph called *Sticks in the Knapsack and Other Ozark Folktales* (New York: Columbia University Press). Randolph collected his version, called "The Loss of Old Bugler," in Fayetteville, Arkansas, in 1921 but said it had been a common story in the 1880s.

A farmer returning after two weeks in Little Rock asks his cousin if anything important had happened while he was gone. The cousin replies, "Well, I hate to tell you, but old Bugler is dead." Bugler was the farmer's best hound, and he died from eating too much horse meat. The cousin then explains about the burned barn and house and the wife's funeral.

The Ozark version has a unique ending. When the bereaved man groans, "No wife, no house, no barn, no horses, and three little children on my hands!" the cousin brightens up and reports: "It ain't quite that bad. You ain't got no motherless children to worry about, since all three of 'em died in the fire too."

Maybe this is the original "Good News/Bad News" joke, if you can call this sort of story a joke.

Note: After my column on "The Climax of Horrors" appeared, I received the following letter from Ithaca, New York:

Dear Sir:

When I was ten or so we used to play a record on the (wind up) Victrola that had your horror story on one side. It was titled "No News, or What Killed the Dog." The reverse side was "The Three Trees." I am now 71 years old, but I remember it well.

The Jersey Devil

New Jersey, as far as I know, is the only state in the Union with an "official state demon." The Jersey Devil, which is supposed to haunt the sparsely populated pine barrens that cover the south central part of the Garden State, was adopted as the state's mascot in 1939.

Eat your heart out Wolverine State, Badger State, Beehive State, Peach State, Sunshine State, and others! Only New Jersey has a devil all its own.

The term *Jersey Devil* refers to a conglomerate of themes from presumed historical writings, folklore, poplore, and most recently urban legends. So, because of the legend's many variations, not everyone agrees how the Devil of New Jersey looks or behaves.

Most accounts state that the Jersey Devil was born to a witch living at Leeds Point in Atlantic County in 1735. Some versions claim that she cursed the child—her thirteenth—and it was born a monster.

Other sources say that the newborn was a normal child that sprouted batlike wings and other monstrous features such as a long tail; a dog's or a horse's face; cloven hoofs, pig's feet, or claws; and sometimes a body shaped like a kangaroo's.

Depending on the account, the Devil's size in the legends varies from a meager eighteen inches tall to an impressive twenty feet in length. Most accounts agree that the creature can shoot flames from its mouth and that it utters bloodcurdling screams as it flies through the woods.

And what does a Jersey Devil eat? Just about anything it wants, including wild animals, domestic stock, stolen supplies, and even humans.

One account of its origin states that the Devil devoured its twelve siblings, its parents, and the midwife before flying out the window and starting its career of terrorizing the residents of south Jersey.

The Jersey Devil was a mere footnote in South Jersey history, representing the credulity of eighteenth-century folk, until 1909 when a series of supposed Devil-sightings inspired a Philadelphia entrepreneur to stage a hoax. He painted a kangaroo green, attached false wings to the poor creature, and exhibited it in a cage strewn with bones.

The recent history of the Jersey Devil belongs more to poplore than to folklore as people ceased fearing Devil visitations and started putting its image on T-shirts, postcards, buttons, menus, and the like. There are even Jersey Devil cocktails sold in some South Jersey bars.

In 1989 I heard from Charlie Simpson of Bensalem, Pennsylvania, who sent me two modern legends pinned on the old Jersey Devil legend. One is a horror tale, similar to "The Boyfriend's Death" legend, that he calls "Thump, Thump, Drag." In it, two young women are baby-sitting in a house "way out in the boonies." One decides to walk home; once outside, the Jersey Devil catches her and chops off most of her arms and legs, leaving her to "thump" and "drag" her way back to the house where she finally bleeds to death.

Simpson's second story is the more standard "Boyfriend's Death" legend in which a parking couple are menaced by a maniac. The madman hangs the murdered boyfriend's body upside down from a tree limb overhanging his car. The girl inside the car, not knowing what has happened, hears the scratching of the corpse's fingernails on the roof. In Simpson's version, of course, it's the Jersey Devil lurking outside their car.

I received additional Jersey Devil stories from Janice E. Brooks of Sharon Hill, Pennsylvania, who collected them while studying folklore at the University of Pennsylvania. Brooks found teenagers telling a Devil version of the classic "Hookman" legend, as well as talking about a photograph snapped at the edge of a pine barrens swamp that revealed a monster standing in the shadows behind a person.

But Brooks's best example of the Devil infiltrating an urban legend is a story about a girl staying in her house during a fierce storm. She is alone except for her dog.

Several times during the night she wakes, and her dog licks her hand. At dawn she finds that her dog has been slashed to death, and written on the wall in its blood are the words, "Jersey Devils lick hands too."

I'll remind you that the usual punch line of the licked-hand story is "People can lick too" which is written in the dog's blood on the bathroom wall.

Note: Angus K. Gillespie's useful article "The Jersey Devil" appeared in a double issue of *Journal of Regional Cultures,* vol. 4, no. 2, Fall/Winter 1984, and vol. 5, no. 1, Spring/Summer 1985, pp. 59–73.

Mothman—Big Bird or Big Fantasy?

What human-shaped creature has huge red eyes, a ten-foot wingspan, stands seven feet tall, is gray, and scratches car roofs? Give up? It's Mothman, a West Virginia flying monster.

Normally I bypass supernatural lore, but scratching on a car roof sounds like it belongs in an urban legend. Besides, recently a caller to a radio talk show where I was a guest wondered what I knew about Mothman.

According to the caller, the monster was supposed to have been created by an accident in a chemical plant, and he thought that the Mothman scares had occurred about twenty years ago. Supposedly, numerous West Virginia teenagers saw Mothman when they were out parking. The creature was usually perched near highways, flying overhead, or sitting on car roofs, and was even said to have killed somebody.

I found no death claims in my notes on this legend, only reports of Mothman scares occurring in 1966 and 1967 near Point Pleasant, West Virginia. Accounts of Mothman usually state that at least one hundred people saw the monster, and perhaps twice as many others were afraid to report their sightings.

Unfortunately, the only written sources are books for children, or sensationalized and undocumented accounts of "mysteries in the mountains" that fail to quote identifiable persons. Something real may have triggered the Mothman scares, but the stories—whatever their sources—also incorporated existing folklore.

Scratching on car roofs, as we have seen, is a familiar detail from the urban legend "The Boyfriend's Death."

In *Living Monsters,* a children's paperback book, we read about how characters named Lou and Carla spotted Mothman as they drove home late past an old power plant. They also heard a "scratch . . . scratch . . . scratch" on their car roof. They reported the incident to "Officer Mac" of the Point Pleasant Police Department, who—despite the actual scratches in their car's paint—pooh-poohed their account.

Later, the book continues, many others in town saw Mothman, and eventually Mac's police car was found near the power plant, with its top torn open. The book concludes, "No one ever saw Mac again."

Similar children's books with titles like *Weird and Mysterious* repeat this tale as well as one about "a girl named Connie" who supposedly saw the creature unfold its wings and raise itself "straight up, like a helicopter."

A California schoolteacher sent me a copy of the response her class got when they wrote to the Point Pleasant Chamber of Commerce asking for further details about Mothman.

The Chamber's secretary replied that she knew nothing about Officer Mac, but enclosed photocopies of other Mothman articles from the popular press. One claimed the Mothman sightings were connected with UFOs; another said a nearby military storage site was Mothman's home. The letter also mentioned books that I've been unable to locate titled *The Mothman Prophecies,* and *They Knew Too Much About Flying Saucers.*

Sightings of huge birdlike figures have occurred repeatedly in many locations, leading some investigators to believe there must be *something* out there that was actually seen by people.

Other local monster figures—like "The Green Man" of central Pennsylvania, and "Hyrum the Ax Murderer" of Utah's Uintah Mountains—are also said to have been created by accidents involving chemicals, explosives, or electricity. For variety, you sometimes hear about a wandering swamp creature, like the "Lizard Man" that supposedly was sighted several times during the summer of 1988 near Browntown, South Carolina.

There's not *much* variety, though: "Lizard Man," according to press reports of the rumors, was seven-feet tall, had red eyes, and was said to have "chewed up" some car roofs.

I wonder: Why should creatures from space, or monsters spawned by industrial accidents, be so attracted to the tops of our cars?

"Homey the Clown"

Omigosh, here's that story again about clowns abducting children!

In the spring of 1981, there were widespread rumors that vans full of phantom clowns were preying on young children. But not a single kidnapping clown was arrested, and authorities debunked the stories.

Killer clown rumors surfaced briefly again in 1985, then faded until June 1991—exactly ten years after the first cycle of similar stories. This time the setting was New Jersey. My first report of the return of the phantom clowns came in a letter from Orrin C. Judd of West Orange, New Jersey, postmarked June 12, 1991, who wrote:

"My mom teaches school in South Orange, New Jersey, and the kids at school are all terrified by the rumor that there is someone dressed as a clown driving around kidnapping children. The story has grown to the point where the clown has a name, Homey, and now they are saying that there are a whole bunch of clowns riding around in a van."

The next day I got a note from Joseph Zarra of Belleville, New Jersey, enclosing a clipping from the *Newark Star-Ledger* of an article published on June 7th, headlined, "Child-Abducting 'Clown' Rumor Persists in Plaguing Essex Towns." It's the same old story.

First-, second-, and third-grade children in several communities were claiming that a van containing a clown, or several clowns, was cruising the streets looking for young victims to kill or abduct. The name Homey came from a character who frequently appears on the television series "In Living Color."

An East Orange police officer commented, "It just spread, from one kid to another, and continued until there was a kind of a hysteria."

One child, who later retracted his story, told police that a clown holding a machete in one hand and an Uzi machine gun in the other fired five shots at him before he drove him off with his book bag.

New Jersey police questioned seven hundred schoolchildren, many of them "petrified" by the rumors, and concluded, "We couldn't substantiate the existence of a clown. We have no sightings, no assaults, no homicides."

Lori A. Windolf of Montclair, New Jersey, sent me the front-page report on the phantom-clown scare that appeared in *The Montclair Times* on June 6th. In a well-researched article, reporter Lucinda Smith debunked the "nasty rumors" and "gruesome stories" that were spreading in the area among schoolchildren.

Parents and grandparents expressed their concern to Smith; psychologists sought reasons for the rumors, and Montclair Deputy Police Chief John Corcoran summed up the situation: "If any parent wants to know what's true, they should call us. We'll check it out and give them a straight answer. On this Homey the Clown thing: nothing to it at all."

The Homey story faded in New Jersey, but resurfaced four months later in the Midwest. On October 11th the *Chicago Tribune* headlined a story "Police Taking Clown Sightings Seriously," and reported that "sightings have come from Oak Park and various parts of Chicago of an African-American male who is dressing up as the sock-wielding, child-taunting, militant character made famous by comedian Damon Wayans on Fox-TV's 'In Living Color' comedy-variety program."

The Windy City police took the stories seriously enough, at least, to issue to the press dry statements couched in drab officialese, such as "I can tell you with reasonable certainty that that [*sic*] does not have merit," and "If you're a clown going to work, you're gonna get stopped!"

Despite numerous reports of clown-sightings by young children, all sounding very much like the earlier Homey stories, no actual clown-clad attackers of children were ever seen by an adult or apprehended. On October 22nd, another Chicago newspaper, the *News-Star,* asked in a headline, "Homey Sightings: Menace or Mirage?" and in an article pretty much put the rumors to rest, at least for the present.

The clown rumors were not confined to the United States. In the January 1992 issue of *FLS News,* the newsletter of the [British] Folklore Society, appears this notice: "In September and October 1991, stories began circulating amongst schoolchildren in the Glasgow area, concerning approaches by ill-intentioned adults dressed as clowns. These stories caused a fair degree of panic amongst children, parents and teachers."

Mysterious America, a 1983 book by Loren Coleman, gives a good account of the 1981 phantom clown scares (Boston: Faber and Faber). In May that year, reports of clowns riding in vans and threatening children surfaced in Boston and some of the surrounding communities. Shortly afterwards the same story showed up in Providence, Rhode Island; Kansas City, Missouri; Kansas City, Kansas; Omaha, Nebraska; Denver, Colorado; and Pittsburgh, Pennsylvania.

Many of the children's stories included specific details: They said that the vans were black, green, blue, or yellow, and the clowns were armed with swords, knives, or guns.

The only other clown scare I'm aware of in the United States occurred in late March 1985, when the Phoenix, Arizona, area suffered a brief period of similar stories spreading among schoolchildren.

Although no police authorities anywhere have verified the existence of phantom clowns, some people take the threat seriously. A warning circulated in a 1986 newsletter claimed that clowns were responsible for children being "spirited away to join the throngs of missing children whose pathetic faces peer at us from milk cartons, shopping bags, and telephone bills."

If child-abductors disguised as clowns exist, then why do they cease their nefarious activities for such long periods of time? Who is sending in these clowns, and why don't the police ever catch them?

Probably the source of the stories lies more in folklore than in actual crimes. Loren Coleman suggests a connection to the Pied Piper of Hamelin who, according to legend, lured away all the children of the German town, never to be seen again. Another possible background tradition for the modern phantom clowns are the age-old stories about Gypsies stealing children.

But exactly how such ancient legends can keep recurring in the form of scare stories told by American youngsters is hard to explain. Perhaps one underlying fact is that many little children are frightened by clowns in their grotesque costumes and heavy makeup, despite parents' belief that all kids love clowns.

The Well to Hell

In January 1991, my Swedish counterpart, the urban legend collector and researcher Bengt af Klintberg, sent me this note from Stockholm:

Dear Jan:
The other day I heard a fantastic story about a deep drill hole in the Kola Peninsula in Siberia from which was heard cries and laments that obviously came from Hell itself! My informant told me that this story had spread to Fundamentalists in the United States. Have you heard it?

—Bengt.

Dear Bengt:
Yes, indeed; I've been hearing about the "Well to Hell" for more than a year now, mostly told on Christian television and radio broadcasts and repeated in letters to newspaper editors. Evidently the story stemmed from a misunderstanding of a scientific project, though there's a hoax involved too. Here's the background:
The California-based Trinity Broadcasting Network aired this bizarre story repeatedly more than a year ago, then in the February 1990 issue of its magazine Praise the Lord *published a translation of it credited to a Finnish newspaper. This account stated that "Scientists are afraid that they have opened the gates to hell."*
The article went on to explain that geologists working somewhere "in remote Siberia" had drilled a hole some 14.4 kilometers deep (about 9 miles) when "the drill bit suddenly began to rotate wildly." A "Mr. Azzacov," identified as the project's manager, was quoted as saying they decided that the center of the earth is hollow.

Supposedly, the geologists measured temperatures of over 2,000 degrees in the deep hole. They lowered "super sensitive microphones" to the bottom of the well, and to their astonishment they heard the sounds of "thousands, perhaps millions of suffering souls screaming."

The story concludes, "After this ghastly discovery, about half of the scientists quit because of fear," and Azzacov is supposed to have said, "Hopefully, that which is down there will stay there."

After hearing the "Well to Hell" story from a caller to his Los Angeles–based radio talk show, host Rich Buhler set out to track it down. He revealed his findings in an article published in the July 16, 1990, issue of *Christianity Today* (vol. 34, no. 10, pp. 28–29).

The Finnish periodical turned out to be not "a respected scientific journal," as some had claimed, but a newsletter published by a group of Finnish missionaries. From there, Buhler traced the story from person to person back to a vague claim that it had appeared in "a Christian newsletter from California."

So far the history of the story simply went around in circles.

But further clarification came from a Norwegian article that had been sent to the Trinity Broadcasting Network, along with a supposed "translation," by a man from near Oslo who had visited California. But this Norwegian, named Age Rendelin, was both a schoolteacher and a prankster.

When Buhler called for more information, Mr. Rendelin confessed that after hearing the story about screams coming from the deep well while he was visiting California, he simply clipped a Norwegian newspaper article on another topic—a Norwegian building inspector—and made up a translation to see if he could fool anyone.

Buhler's article was summarized in the *Secular Humanist Bulletin* of October 1990, with the closing quip that "when it comes to rumors, it's not where they start, it's where they Finnish." Another periodical to comment skeptically on the "Well to Hell" story was *Biblical Archaeology Review* in its issue of November/December 1990 (vol. 16, no. 6, p. 6). The report began, "First it was Noah's Ark, then it was the Ark of the Covenant. Now hell itself has been discovered."

Where did the original teller of this story got inspiration for such a bizarre yarn? A letter to me from Liam Wescott, a geologist in Fairbanks, Alaska, provided a likely answer. Wescott cited an article in the December 1984 issue of *Scientific American* titled "The World's Deepest Well."

The article's author, Soviet geologist Y. A. Kozlovsky, describes an experimental well that had, at that time, reached 12,000 meters—by far the deepest drill hole that had been bored up to that time. The scientists encountered rare rock formations, flows of gas and water, and temperatures up to 180 degrees, but no hollow center and certainly no screams of the damned.

Wescott guessed that the "hole truth," as he put it, concerning the story of drilling down to the Gates of Hell might simply be explained by the possibility that someone who heard about the Soviet geological project had combined it with traditional accounts of hellfire and damnation.

I think he's probably right, because the actual Siberian well, according to the article, was drilled on the Kola Peninsula, exactly the place where the version of the fictional "Well to Hell" story that Bengt heard was supposed to have taken place.

The story got a re-run in the April 7, 1992, issue of the tabloid *Weekly World News* which bore the lurid headline on page 1, "Satan Escapes from Hell" and the subhead, "13 Alaskan oil rig workers killed when the Devil roars out of well." A photograph showed a huge cloud in the shape of Satan's head pouring out of a flaming oil derrick.

Who ya gonna call when a cursed well goes wild? Dr. Azzacov, of course. As a sidebar to the story, the *News* summarized the "Well to Hell" story from two years earlier, this time giving Dr. Azzacov a first name (Dmitri) and explaining that he was lecturing "at a university in Yugoslavia." I was tempted to laugh this off as a perpetuation of the hoax, but the *News* also published an actual photograph of Dr. Azzacov's face!

Drug Horror Stories

The ongoing "war on drugs" will probably generate a new round of the kind of horrible stories that constitute much of the lore on drugs.

Perhaps you remember the favorite LSD scare legend told during the 1960s. Supposedly, a group of college students, high on acid, sat on a hillside and stared straight into the sun until they went blind. The incident never occurred, however, or at least it was never verified. Still, the story is frequently repeated.

Or you may have heard about heartless fiends who smuggled cocaine into the United States inside the body of a dead baby. The *Washington Post* included the story in a 1985 article on crime in Miami, but retracted it later, admitting that although the story was well known among drug agents, none could confirm it. (See *The Mexican Pet*, pages 145–46.)

An authority on drugs who analyzes this kind of "drug horror story" is Dr. John P. Morgan, Program Director of Pharmacology at the City University of New York Medical School. He made me aware of what he calls "the mythic nature of many drug tales." It turns out, for example, that the most common theme in horror stories about PCP (or Angel Dust) is that people under its influence have supposedly plucked their own eyes out in a drug-induced frenzy.

Morgan sent me an article he and his colleague Doreen Kagan published in the *Journal of Psychedelic Drugs* in 1980 (vol 12, nos. 3–4, pp. 195–204). It's titled "The Dusting of America: The Image of Phencyclidine (PCP) in the Popular Media."

The two investigators studied hundreds of newspaper articles about PCP between 1958 and 1979. They concluded that "mythic" stories about "dangerous, criminal, or self-destructive behavior by the drug-crazed" were typical of these media reports. They wrote that the stories "resemble the myths, ballads, and folktales previously generated and transformed by oral transmission."

My own guess is that in addition to distorting the facts of actual cases, journalists sometimes incorporate oral traditions into their reports—as when repeating the dead-baby anecdote. Morgan and Kagan mentioned media stories describing PCP users trying to cook a baby, attempting to fly off a roof, pulling out their own teeth, and gaining the strength to pop off handcuffs. Such stories probably echo apocryphal oral tales about drug abuse.

Even drug horror stories with a grain of truth are sometimes distorted in the media. For example, one repeated incident tells of a Baltimore student who actually did blind himself in jail in 1971. He may have acted under the influence of PCP, but this was never proven, and the student denied it.

Later references to the incident in the press, however, claimed incorrectly that he "tore his eyes out of their sockets," and stated that the cause was known to be an overdose of Angel Dust.

In March 1991 an amateur videotape of the beating of Rodney G. King by police officers in Los Angeles drew national attention and again raised the question of whether horror stories about Angel Dust were true. Police claimed that they believed King to be high on PCP, and, according to a Los Angeles *Times* article, a sergeant involved in the beating told investigators that "he feared King could, in a moment, turn into the 'Hulk,' grabbing away police weapons and putting officers in a 'death grip.'"

The *Times* story, written by Claire Spiegel, was headlined "Effects of PCP: Myth vs. Reality" (June 17, 1991). It cited medical researchers—including Dr. John Morgan—who blame the media "for creating a bogyman out of PCP based on a few recycled horror stories."

In their 1980 article Morgan and Kagan identified prototypes of PCP horror stories in accounts of "drug-crazed cocaine fiends" published in the early 1900s, in vivid descriptions of effects of "the killer drug marijuana" in the 1930s, and in the LSD scare stories of the 1960s.

Such stories were intended to deter potential users from trying drugs, but Morgan and Kagan saw a possible danger in them. Some people, they suggest, may respond to drug horror stories by considering them a challenge to be tried rather than a risk to be avoided.

This is exactly what has happened with the latest drug horror story that Morgan has investigated—"the recent spate of stories about toad licking." He explained in a letter to me that the stories describe "Young people who supposedly have been licking Colorado river toads to get high." Since the skin secretions of certain toads contain what Morgan identified as "psychoactive chemicals," he admits there's a possible logic to the bizarre stories.

The toad species involved here, *Bufo marinus,* is known as the cane toad and, according to a *Scientific American* article by John Horgan [*sic;* not Morgan, this time] "Bofo Abuse," (August 1990, pp. 26–27) cane toad–licking lore has inspired "drug-war hysteria in the U.S." Native to warm climates in the Americas, *B. marinus* was introduced to Australia in the 1930s in hopes of controlling beetles in the cane fields. From their skin glands, these toads secret a substance called bufotenine which was reportedly licked off as an intoxicant by some native peoples.

American researchers, beginning in the 1950s, conducted experiments synthesizing and testing the effects of bufotenine. Negative side effects suffered by some subjects of experiments led the U.S. Drug Enforcement Administration to ban the substance in the late 1960s, and this action, apparently (and ironically) led some people to try licking live toads. But, writes Horgan, "these adventurers became sick rather than high, and toad licking never caught on."

Enter the media in the mid-1980s. Newspapers began publishing largely-unverified stories about alleged cane-toad abuse in the United States and Australia. The articles became more and more sensational with tongue-in-cheek headlines like

"Toads Take a Licking From Desperate Druggies" and "How Low Will People Stoop to Get High?" And, to complete the circle, "reality imitated fiction," as Horgan wrote, when some teenagers began to try toad licking simply because they had read about it in the paper.

In case you're tempted to try toad licking, be warned that cane toads, according to *Scientific American,* are "plump, greenish-yellow and pebbly in texture [and] some attain the girth of Frisbees."

UPDATE:

In June 1992, Dale Kostiew of Winnipeg, Manitoba, wrote me about a horrendous drug horror story that a coworker assued him was true, although nothing like it had appeared in the local news media. It was the dead baby story agian, this time told about a Canadian couple cross-border shopping in Fargo, North Dakota. The couple's baby is stolen from the car seat in their supermarket shopping cart, a watermelon substituted in its place. A week goes by and police still have no clues—until (as the story concludes):

A different couple is stopped at the Emerson border crossing into Canada. They tell the guard to go ahead and search their car, but not to wake the baby. While the guard is checking out the vehicle, he notices a red mark on the baby's neck. Closer inspection reveals that the baby's neck has been slit, and when the baby is examined further, they find that the body has been slit down the front, the infant's organs removed, and the body has been stuffed with drugs. It was, of course, the first couple's missing baby.

3

Crime and Punishment

Foiled Again! Lessons from Folklore

People today sometimes tell legends for the same reason the ancients told fables—to recommend a course of action. Aesop's fables, for instance, ended with a stated moral, such as "Don't count your chickens before they're hatched." Our contemporary fables, sometimes called "exemplary stories" by folklorists, usually just imply their message.

An example of this kind of story was sent to me by Stephen G. Bates, an attorney in Cambridge, Massachusetts. Bates writes:

In a family history written in the 1940s, my grandfather, Robert W. Bates, told a story that, on reflection, seems like a legend.

His great-aunt Jessie Holland told him the story around 1900. Once when she was alone in the house, she came downstairs in the dark late at night. Near the bottom of the stairs she reached for the bannister and instead felt a human head.

Being alone in the house, and wanting to avoid a confrontation, she thought quickly and then said, 'My! That careless maid has left the mop out again.'

Then she walked quickly to the front door, rushed outside,

*and cried for help, thus saving herself from the rather
dimwitted burglar.*

The implication for those hearing the story is that if you
think and act quickly and cleverly enough, and remain cool-
headed, you may be able to save yourself from danger. It's a
good lesson, even though you're not likely to find yourself with
exactly that opportunity to foil a gullible housebreaker by
means of the same trick.

I have not heard this "mop-head" motif in other family stories, but by coincidence the very same week I got a letter from
another reader in Massachusetts describing a different way of
dealing with a possible attack. Mark Lutton of Malden, Massachusetts, wrote that he heard or read somewhere that joggers
claim the best way to deal with a mean dog approaching you on
the street is simply to say to it, "Go for a walk?" Since that's
likely to be the one expression that every dog knows, it is supposed to be effective in calming them down.

Lutton had an occasion to try the trick. "In the early 1970s
when I was in college," he recalls, "I was walking through an
unfamiliar part of Boston. I walked past a house with a big
German Shepherd on the porch, and just as I passed, the dog
suddenly jumped up, ran at me, and started barking furiously.

"I was afraid it might attack me, when suddenly the jogger's
advice came to mind. As soon as it stopped barking for a moment, I said to the dog, 'Want to go for a walk?'

"The dog cocked her head and looked at me with that puzzled expression dogs have, and I repeated it, 'Want to go for a
walk?'

"The dog tipped her head the other way, and then as I
turned to go she began to trot quietly along beside me. We
didn't get far together, though, since her owner came out and
called her back home."

I suspect that Lutton has told his personal-experience story
to other people who, like me, may have filed it in their memory
banks for possible future use in an emergency. I recently tried

the technique on a neighbor's two large and noisy dogs who bark at everyone who passes. But saying "Want to go for a walk?" to them merely intensified their eagerness to escape the yard and take a walk.

If I ever have to use the trick on a loose barking dog, I hope it works better. And I hope that I never have to try the folkloric defense I have heard recommended to drive off a would-be mugger—just start picking your nose.

Annual Campus Crime-Rumor Scares

During the autumn 1988 semester at four universities in the South and Midwest, rumors began to fly that a psychic had predicted on a TV talk show that a mass murderer was going to terrorize the campus on Halloween night.

The most common programs named were "The Oprah Winfrey Show," "Geraldo!" and "Donahue," and the universities were Florida State, Purdue, Slippery Rock (Pennsylvania), and Ohio Northern. Together the incidents show that students should be wary of urban legends as well as of mass murderers.

Student newspapers tried to calm students' fears by publicizing denials that such a prediction had occurred on any of the mentioned TV shows. Still, local police and college administrators promised that extra precautions would be taken.

At Florida State, the student paper *The Flambeau* reported that students were saying that a psychic, a guest on "The Oprah Winfrey" show had predicted the following: "A knife-wielding maniac, perhaps dressed as Little Bo Peep, would slash his way through a sorority house or a dormitory." A publicist for the Winfrey show called this rumor "absolutely untrue," pointing out that they had not had a psychic on the program for two years.

ONU, too, had the Bo Peep detail in its version of the story, as well as the notion that the name of the fated campus would begin with an "O" and that the landscape surrounding the campus would be "very very flat."

At Purdue University in West Lafayette, Indiana, as the student paper *The Exponent* reported, the version of the rumor going around was that a guest on Phil Donahue's show had said that the murders would occur in Meredith Hall, a women's dormitory. Others claimed that a Purdue student's parents had read about the prediction in a Minnesota newspaper. Neither the national TV interview nor the hometown news report existed.

The various rumors sliding around Slippery Rock mentioned virtually every television talk show that exists and included details of the alleged prophecy such as that the killings would occur at a college named after a local town with a body of water running through it. But, as university authorities pointed out, a great many colleges and universities fit that description, and similar rumors had sprung up around Halloween for more than twenty years.

All of these rumor scares contained further specific details, although not all students had heard all versions of the story. At Florida State, for example, some students believed that the psychic had predicted that the killer would stalk the halls of a U-shaped building on the campus of "a large university having a graveyard nearby"—an accurate description of FSU.

Others were saying that the psychic had mentioned that the killer was coming to a university bordering the state of Georgia. Supposedly, too, the prophecy had specified that the killings would occur on the dorm's fourth floor.

Meanwhile up at Purdue, as well as ONU, some students were saying that the psychic had predicted the deaths of twelve students living in an X-shaped dormitory. Another persistent detail was that the murders would occur at either the highest or lowest spot on campus.

Joining the original rumor in Florida and Indiana was the report that the university administration had ordered the evacuation of all campus residences, a course of action that was never considered, although Little Bo Peep costumes *were* banned at some Halloween parties.

Still, on all four campuses—and doubtless on others where such rumors have circulated—some dorm residents moved out for Halloween night. Other students grouped up in their rooms and barricaded the doors. Even some who pooh-poohed the rumors, took extra precautions on the theory that a madman might hear the stories and try to act them out.

Rumors about predictions of campus murders recur frequently, generally around Halloween. Usually the stories specify that the killings will occur at a college whose name begins with a certain letter, or one situated near a certain configuration of hills or rivers. Generally the target building is said to be a campus residence of a particular shape, size, or name. In recent years the rumors may include claims that a satanic cult is planning the murders.

Shortly before Halloween in 1991, suddenly the campus rumor scares were back. The first report I found was in *The Daily Free Press*, student newspaper of Boston University, on Friday October 11th. Again students were claiming that a psychic appearing on "The Oprah Winfrey Show" had predicted a massacre, this time in an L-shaped campus building. Allegedly, the attacks were supposed to happen on the weekend of October 25th.

The BU story was soon joined by numerous variations attributed to several northeastern colleges. On October 28th, for example, *The Boston Globe* reported that University of Massachusetts students were saying that mass murders would occur around Halloween "at a campus with a pond and a building named for President John F. Kennedy." At other colleges the details mentioned included a domed stadium or a dorm situated near a cemetery. Some students, the *Globe* said, were citing CNN or "A Current Affair" as the source of the story, though most still stuck with Oprah Winfrey's program, which by this time had spokespersons busy denying that a psychic had recently been on the program or that any guest had ever made such a prediction.

In the next two days the Associated Press circulated widely printed articles now mentioning that at "no fewer than six colleges from New Hampshire to Connecticut" the latest campus rumor was spreading. A new theory was reported here—that the writings of Nostradamus had prophesied the killings. When *USA Today* picked up the story for its October 30th edition, they added Syracuse University to the list of institutions suffering the

rumor scare, and cited another variation in the basic prediction—that the massacre would occur in a year (like 1991) with a
"reversible number."

No mass murders happened on any campus on Halloween
1991, but the next day—Friday November 1st—a student at
the University of Iowa did shoot four people, wound two others, and kill himself. Early news reports of the incident briefly
mentioned the recent campus scare rumors, although none had
circulated about Iowa, or at least in 1991 they hadn't. But
folklorist Bill Ellis reminded me that earlier editions of the rumors had sometimes mentioned that the crimes were supposed
to occur in a state that began and ended with a vowel.

The legend goes back at least as far as 1968 when a similar
rumor raged through eastern and midwestern universities. The
story at that time was that Jean Dixon had predicted campus
murders on a radio program not long before.

Those rumors often noted the precise murder weapon (a
hatchet or a fire ax) and stated the expected number of victims
(9, 10, 12, or 20). It was supposedly predicted that the killer
would strike at a school whose name began with a *D* or a *B*, or
one that was situated near a mental institution.

The details about the particular weapon, the maniac who is
supposed to wield it, and the murder threat aimed at a women's
dorm are also features of "The Roommate's Death," a classic
campus horror legend.

This legend typically tells of two female students who are
staying alone in a college dormitory over a holiday break. One
of the young women is slain in the hallway by an ax blow to her
head, while the other one cowers behind the locked door of her
room and summons help the next morning through a window.

That story, too, like the one that goes around campuses in
autumn, is nothing but a grisly rumor.

Crime Victims Speak, and Folklorists Listen

Part of a folklorist's job is listening to people tell the most incredible stories.

Balancing the fascination of fieldwork, however, is routine filing and library research. And then there's the comparing of notes with other folklorists. Which is how I came to know the work of folklorist Eleanor Wachs, who studies violent crime the way I do choking Dobermans and Mexican pets.

For over a decade, while I've been collecting urban fictions told as fact, Wachs has gathered the sometimes embellished but presumably true stories told by and about crime victims in New York City.

I group my urban legends in broad categories like "Automobiles," "Animals," and "Crime," and give them titles like "The Hook," "Alligators in the Sewers," and "The Attempted Abduction." Wachs's filing system is simpler: She arranges the stories she hears as *M*'s, *R*'s, or *MR*'s—Muggings, Rapes, or Murders. The stories, told to her over the years by New York residents, usually take the form of: "Did I tell you about the time my neighbor was mugged?" or the like.

Reading her book, *Crime Victim Stories: New York's Urban Folklore* (Bloomington: Indiana University Press, 1988), I noted that some of the individual story categories, such as "The Fated Victimization," "The Trickster Offended," and "The Clever Victim," sounded much like legends. All the accounts Wachs presents were first told as literally true, she writes. But Wachs discovered that "threads of legend plots . . . form the kernel of some of these crime-victim stories."

When New Yorkers tell about muggings, for example, they sometimes include details borrowed from the urban legend I call "The Middle-Class Mugger." In this legend, a man beats up and takes a wallet from a stranger who had bumped him on the street, believing that the stranger picked his pocket. When he returns home, though, he discovers that he had left his wallet on the dresser that morning.

Another of Wachs's New York crime-victim narratives tells about a man on a bus. Out of the sleeve of his trenchcoat drops a woman's hand with valuable rings still intact on the bloodied fingers. The tellers of this horror story are never first-person witnesses of the event, and they seem to be retelling a version of the legend I call "The Cut-Off Finger" (about which more below) as if it happened to a FOAF.*

One of the most dramatic stories Wachs collected described an elderly blind woman, alone at home, whose door was forced open as far as the door-chain would allow by a would-be robber. According to the story, the intruder grasped the woman's hand and scratched her arm with sandpaper, attempting to force her to undo the chain.

But the woman, taking strength from her fear and outrage, clenched her fist and broke all the man's fingers—"like spaghetti." He ran away, and later was captured at an emergency room where he sought treatment.

Wachs points out incongruities in the story, aside from its lack of a first-person source. Sandpaper seems an unlikely assault weapon; a chained door must be closed before it can be unlatched, and an elderly woman would probably lack the muscle to break anyone's fingers by force alone.

These details showed Wachs that her informant was probably borrowing from a version of the well-known urban legend "The Robber Who Was Hurt." This legend usually describes an attempted entry by a man who sticks his hands or fingers into a half-opened door, window, or mail slot. A woman inside injures the intruder with a knife, a hot poker, or an electric iron.

The hurt robber is recognized when he shows up back home or at a hospital seeking treatment for the injury to his hands or

---

*Friend of a friend.

fingers. In Wachs's version of this story—as in many legends—a supposed true account is enhanced with a detail lifted from a piece of folklore.

MORE ABOUT "THE CUT-OFF FINGER"

A reader named Juan Carlos Aguilera wrote me from Madrid to ask if I'd heard this urban legend that's popular in Spain:

"The police stopped somebody on a bus who was carrying a cut-off finger with a diamond ring. Just then a lady on the bus screamed and fainted, because she discovered that she was missing both her ring and her finger."

Si, Juan, I replied, I know that story. "The Cut-Off Finger" legend circulates internationally, probably going back to an old folktale called "The Robber Bridegroom" or "Mr. Fox."

Another good example of the modern European version of that folktale appeared in a 1986 book of Swedish urban legends. It was told to a Swedish TV correspondent stationed in Paris. (See Bengt af Klintberg, *Råttan i Pizzan: Folksägner i vår tid,* Stockholm: Norstedts Förlag, pp. 178–79.)

According to the version the correspondent heard, a young man boarded a metro car with blood dripping from his jacket pocket. When other passengers offered help, he ignored them. Then police entered the car, and when they spotted the blood, they detained the man for questioning. In his pocket they found a woman's cut-off finger with a diamond ring on it.

The folklorist who collected the legend said that when a similar story is told in Sweden, it is given as a warning to people traveling to North Africa, where finger-chopping is supposedly a standard practice of ring thieves.

While I was translating the Swedish text, I paused to open the day's mail, and what did I find but another version of "The Cut-Off Finger," this one from South America. The story was sent to me by Christopher Chennell of McMinnville, Oregon, who heard it in 1978 when he lived in Medellin, Colombia. His version went like this:

> *Someone entered a bus and sat down next to another passenger. Soon the newcomer noticed blood spots on his seatmate's shirt, and he asked if he could be of any assistance.*
>
> *This offer was brusquely declined. Other passengers began to notice the blood, and they questioned the apparently injured passenger, who became increasingly agitated and still refused aid.*
>
> *At the next stop, the newcomer bolted from the bus; in his haste something dropped from his pocket. It turned out to be a severed bloody hand (only one finger, according to my wife) with an expensive ring still on one of the fingers.*

Among urban crime legends, many more stories describe criminals who get their fingers bitten or torn off than the victims of finger-choppers. The latter theme appears as either of the two stories that Eleanor Wachs calls "The Rider with the Extra Hand" or "The Mutilated Shopper."*

In the first group are stories such as outlined here, in which the finger-chopper has already done his dirty work and is carrying the finger around in his pocket dripping blood on fellow passengers who are riding public transportation. In the second category of these tales, a woman has her finger cut off while she is trying on new clothes in a department store's dressing room. Her attacker steals her diamond ring.

Both versions, I believe, echo the old folktale about "Mr. Fox," who was described as a seducer of women, a murderer, and . . . you guessed it, a cutter of hands. Here's part of an English version of the story published in 1890:

---

*See Eleanor Wachs, "The Mutilated Shopper at the Mall: A Legend of Urban Violence," in Gillian Bennett and Paul Smith, eds., *A Nest of Vipers: Perspectives on Contemporary Legend V* (Sheffield, England: Sheffield Academic Press, 1990), pp. 143–60.

"Mr. Fox saw a diamond ring glittering on the finger of the young lady he was dragging, and he tried to pull it off. But it was tight . . . and so Mr. Fox drew his sword, raised it, and brought it down upon the hand of the poor lady.

"The sword cut off the hand, which jumped up into the air, and fell of all places in the world, into Lady Mary's lap."

Lady Mary in the story was the intended bride of the dreadful Mr. Fox, and had been secretly watching his crime. According to the folktale, she stayed hidden, kept the hand, and used it as evidence to expose Mr. Fox as the young woman's killer.

In the edition I have of Joseph Jacobs's *English Fairy Tales*, quoted above, there's a great illustration of Lady Mary rising from the dinner table and holding the severed hand right in Mr. Fox's face while her horrified brothers and friends look on. Following this revelation, the men drew their swords and cut Mr. Fox into a thousand pieces, and everyone lived happily ever after.

But that was not the end of the story, since "The Cut-Off Finger" lives on as an urban legend that's told around the world.

City Life

The stories that I call "urban" legends, while being characteristic of modern life, are not necessarily always about living in cities. But here are five tales I've heard that definitely reflect urban lifestyles and problems:

"ALL THAT GLITTERS"

(Told to me by an Associated Press writer based in New York City)—A woman riding a Manhattan subway feels her gold neck chain being snapped loose just as the train slows down at a station. Reacting automatically, she reaches over and snaps off the chain that's around her attacker's neck, and he runs out the door and up the stairs.

Later, a jeweler tells her that the chain she grabbed was pure gold. Her own chain was an inexpensive fake.

"THE MISGUIDED GOOD DEED"

(From the *New York Times* "Metropolitan Diary" column, January 21, 1990)—A woman on a subway sees an expensive-looking leather glove lying on the floor just as a well-dressed man is leaving the train. She snatches it up and throws it onto the platform before the train doors close.

The other passengers all stare at her, and then one of them, a mild-looking man, asks plaintively, "Why did you toss my glove out the door?"

"THE D. C. SCHOOLCHILD'S QUESTION"

(Sent by Ray Milefsky of Washington, D.C., who has heard it told at many parties)—A white liberal D.C. couple decide to enroll their son or daughter in a racially-mixed public school. Well into the school year, the puzzled child asks, "Daddy, we've been studying about inventors and famous people in school. Why haven't white people invented anything or become famous?"

The parents immediately withdraw the child from the school and enroll him or her in a private school, or else move to the suburbs.

Mr. Milefsky commented, "The repeated recitation of this story makes it seem like some kind of tribal folk wisdom passed down to confirm common values and beliefs."

I would add that the story also gives a reverse twist to the question that may have been asked by countless black children who have studied American history in predominantly white schools.

"THE STOLEN SOD"

(Told by horticulture instructor Steve Pietrolungo of Simi Valley, California)—Sod is very popular in Southern California, providing an instant lawn that rolls out like a carpet. Supposedly a church group that had just installed 1,000 square feet of sod around their building arrived the next morning to find nothing but bare soil. During the night someone had rolled up the sod and carted it away.

When Pietrolungo identified this story as an urban legend in one of his classes, a student claimed that over 10,000 square feet of sod had mysteriously disappeared the day after it was rolled out as part of the preparation for the 1984 Summer Olympics.

Pietrolungo explains, "Sod is so heavy that it takes a fork lift just to lift a pallet with only 500 square feet." Rolling, loading, and moving such large amounts undetected overnight seems unlikely at best.

"THE VEGGIE MISSILE"

(Appeared in an article on urban legends in the Christmas 1989 Literary Supplement of *The Weekly Mail,* a Republic of South Africa newspaper)—"During the 1976 Soweto uprising, a bunch of township youths paint a potato green. As an armoured car rolls past them, with a soldier sitting in the turret, they lob the 'grenade' into the car. All the soldiers inside scramble out, sans weapons, and the youths leap in and commandeer the vehicle. The story is, naturally, hushed up by the authorities."

Arthur Goldstuck, who wrote the article, commented, "This story is uniquely 1970s South African. Or 1960s Saigon. Or 1940s France."

I'm not so sure of the truth or falsity of any of these five city stories, but they are all urban legends that are for once, about the city.

From the Annals of Modern Crime

Here are four crime stories I've heard lately that seem just bizarre enough to be legends. So far, I haven't spotted anything quite like them in documented news reports.

"THE NEW IDENTITY"

This is a crime narrative with academic legend overtones. I heard it told at a folklore conference:

The FBI furnished a former Mafia member who had served as a government informer or witness with an entirely new identity. They gave him a detailed but fabricated background biography, extensive plastic surgery, a new wardrobe, and a new career. Then they moved the man to a state where he had never lived, and set him up in an apartment to start his life anew, hidden from the crime syndicates.

All seemed to be going along fine until he checked his mail for the first time. There in the box was a fund-raising letter from the alumni organization at his alma mater. It was addressed to the name that his new identity was supposed to be covering up!

Moral: You can outrun the mob, but forget about ditching the alma mater.

"WATCH THE BORDERS"

I heard this tale from someone whose college roommate said he had heard Watergate conspirator G. Gordon Liddy tell it in a lecture given in 1982 or 1983:

J. Edgar Hoover, former director of the FBI, had a rule stating that all FBI memoranda were required to be shorter than two and one-half typed pages and with wide margins all around. Hoover himelf once received a memo that violated this prescribed length and format.

The writer had managed to cram more words into his memo by reducing the size of the margins. Hoover responded by writing on the memo, "Watch the borders!" When Hoover's subordinates saw the note, they assigned hundreds of special agents to guard our national borders with Mexico and Canada.

"CRIME PAYS, IF YOU'RE NOT GREEDY"

This was sent by Jackie McDade, a Nevada native, who now lives in San Pedro, California:

There was a blackjack dealer in a Nevada casino who customarily wore cowboy boots and tucked the legs of his pants into the boot tops.

One day, while raking in the gamblers' silver dollars, he got the bright idea of dropping a dollar down his leg into the top of his boot. The dollar slipped into the boot without anyone noticing, and he kept repeating the trick. At the end of his shift he had about $20 in his boot, and he walked off the floor with the money undetected.

The dealer continued this little income augmentation scheme, and no one was the wiser. But after several weeks of stealing small amounts, he was ready for a larger heist.

The next day he dropped dollars into the boots more frequently, and he managed to collect about $200 during his shift. The dealer thought he was getting away with the theft, until he tried to walk away from the table. He hadn't counted on the weight of that much money in silver. At his first step, the dealer fell to the floor, and silver dollars spilled out in all directions revealing his theft.

(McDade reminded me that nowadays most casinos use chips rather than silver dollars. To me it also seemed incredible that the dealer could hit the boot tops with every single dropped coin.)

"TAINTED MONEY"

This is another Nevada casino story that I heard recently:

A cashier in Las Vegas was arrested for cocaine use after failing a drug test. But she convinced the authorities that the cocaine must have come from all the bills she counted, some of which must have been handled by drug dealers or users.

Since her problem was ruled to be job-related, the cashier was able to collect disability.

"The Body in the Bed"

The first time I heard about the smelly hotel room in Las Vegas I thought the story sounded highly suspicious. After I collected many varying versions from several states, I'm sure it's a legend. Here's the story as I heard it from Trisha Topham, a teaching assistant in English at the University of Utah:

"Last week at my book club meeting I was half listening while two women talked about a new story they'd heard. They were saying something about a decaying corpse in a Las Vegas hotel room, when suddenly another woman shrieked and said, 'My sister-in-law told me that same story, and she said it happened to her best friend.'

"The three compared stories and agreed on most of the details.

"Seems that a couple checked into a hotel room in Las Vegas and immediately noticed a terrible smell in their room. They asked housekeeping to come up and check out the problem.

"A maid came, looked around, found nothing, and sprayed the room with air freshener. But the smell continued, and they had the maid come back a couple more times, but with no improvement.

"Finally the couple looked in the bed, because the smell seemed to be coming from it. They found the body of a prostitute; in one version, the body was inside the mattress, and in the other inside the wooden platform on which the mattress was supported.

"The woman who said she knew the source of the story rushed to the phone and called her sister-in-law, demanding to know if the story was true. Of course it was true, she learned, except that it had really happened to a friend of the sister-in-law's best friend."

Topham had taken a folklore course, and she knew a FOAF story when she heard one.

Another Utah student told me much the same story, except he had heard that it was the body of a Mafia hit victim that was found in the mattress.

I had first received the story in April 1991 from Professor James Hoy of Emporia State University in Kansas. He had heard it from one of his students, with the only variations being that the tourists were two local women, and that the decomposing body was found stuffed between the mattress and box spring.

Another midwestern version came shortly afterwards from Thelma Moore Johnson of Sioux City, Iowa. She had heard from a high school librarian that a couple from their own city were the discoverers of the smelly room in Vegas. Both Johnson and Hoy, incidentally, mentioned that it was supposed to be an expensive hotel where the incident happened.

The Iowans, in Johnson's version, spent one night in their room, despite the terrible odor. They complained to the desk clerk when they went to breakfast, and coming back to their room after a day on the town, they found the police investigating a body that the maid had discovered under the bed.

Before long I got a letter from Linda Crosser of Walnut, California, who had heard "The Body in the Bed" story from someone in her sewing class. It supposedly had happened to some close friends of the narrator.

The basic details of this version are familiar by now: fancy hotel, bad smell, attempts to remove the smell, and discovery of the body. But a new twist is that the body of a teenage girl was found under the mattress and inside a hollow section that had been cut out of the box spring.

Subsequently, I received "The Body in the Bed" from readers in Chicago and Minneapolis; both had heard that it was the Mirage Hotel, although one was also told it happened at the Excalibur. In the first version the body had been there "for weeks," and in the second the hotel awarded the couple free lodging in first-class rooms for a lifetime.

The expensive item (a posh hotel room) with the rotten smell in this legend reminds me of the old "Death Car" story. It describes an expensive automobile, such as a Corvette, that is on sale for $500 because its upholstery still reeks with the smell of death from a person who committed suicide in it.

"The Death Car" has been around since the 1940s, with only the make, model, and price of the car changing from year to year. Whatever the details, the smelly car is always a bargain, though nobody has yet been able to locate such a car.

Maybe the next step in the development of "The Body in the Bed" legend should be saying that the high-priced Las Vegas hotel room can now be rented at a bargain rate.

If that twist actually enters the legend, remember that you heard it here first.

"The Slasher under the Car"

Has there been a rash of injuries and attacks caused by ankle-slashers lurking under women's cars in America's shopping malls? For years I've been hearing stories about such crimes, without ever finding evidence that any such thing has happened.

A Columbus, Ohio, woman wrote me in 1987 saying that many women coming to a rape crisis center have told her different versions of the story, but she had never seen a news report of such crimes. She wondered how the slasher would know that a lone woman had driven a car to the mall, or that she would return alone. Why wouldn't the women shout for help? Why does the man hide *under* the car rather than waiting inside, and why does he slash at the ankles?

Another woman, who also doubts the story's authenticity, wrote that she heard it in 1985 in Birmingham, Alabama. Men were said to have waited until the woman had her right foot inside the car and then grabbed at the left foot.

Back in 1984 I received an earlier midwestern report of "The Slasher under the Car" from a woman in Fort Wayne, Indiana. She heard that the event happened at a shopping mall near Chicago. When the slashed woman reached down toward her injury, the man grabbed her hands and pulled her under the car.

Another version from 1984 pinpointed the crime site as a mall in Crown Point, Indiana. This attacker would roll out from under a woman's car, cut her ankles, and then steal both the packages and the car.

None of those who wrote me about "The Slasher under the Car" had come any closer than a FOAF to finding proof that such crimes had ever occurred. Women appeared to be the chief narrators of this legend, using it to warn others against patronizing certain malls, or against parking a long distance from other cars, especially at night.

A variation minus the slashing was told by a police officer in Phoenix, Arizona, as part of his safety course. A Phoenix doctor wrote me that he heard this version just before Christmas 1984, from his office manager who had attended such a course. The officer said the assailant used a tire iron to break women's ankles with a single blow.

Another detail that the Phoenix police officer included was that the attacked women suffered such intense pain from the blow that they were unable to cry out, so the man easily overpowered them. When a student in the class asked why there had been no press coverage of the crime, the officer said, "Plenty of things like that never get into the papers."

A reference to "The Slasher under the Car" circulating even earlier came from a woman who heard it in 1978 in Fargo, North Dakota. This version has two specific details not found in all others: The slasher specifically aimed for the victims' Achilles tendons, and he had supposedly attacked twenty-eight women.

So far, the earliest report of this legend that I've encountered associates the event with the 1950s and the Northland shopping mall on the outskirts of Detroit. My source, former Michigan resident Cheryl Kirtley-Hodess of Ellicott City, Maryland, wrote to me about it because during the 1989 Christmas season she heard the same story told on a mall near Baltimore.

But as the Baltimore *Evening Sun* reported, on December 8, 1989, "The unsubstantiated story has grown to such heights that Baltimore County police and White Marsh Mall security are having difficulty keeping a lid on it."

The Maryland authorities were receiving ten to twenty calls a day from people inquiring about the alleged slashings, with some callers claiming that the man under the car was a rapist "who forces his victims under the cars, assaults them, and then wraps them in Christmas paper."

Also during the 1989 Christmas season "The Slasher under

the Car" legend hit the Tacoma (Washington) Mall, prompting local police to issue a statement that no such attacks were known to have actually happened. Nevertheless, authorities opened a security office in a prominent mall location for the duration of the Christmas season.

An article in the Tacoma *News Tribune* referred to the stories about "mythical ankle-slashers" as being examples of "urban American folklore, like the one about the woman who put her wet poodle in the microwave oven." Tacoma shoppers feared that gang members armed with knives and razors were preying on them by waiting under cars to slash ankles. This was said to be part of an initiation rite.

Slasher stories continue to surface at widespread locations. On December 1, 1990, the *Los Angeles Times* reported that a notice sent out on a computer bulletin board in El Segundo, California, was warning people about a slasher alleged to be "stalking women shoppers in the Galleria at South Bay." Police said there had been no such incidents.

In March 1991, the *Asbury Park* (New Jersey) *Press* quoted police statements denying rampant rumors about crimes at Freehold Raceway Mall. These stories said that a rapist lurking under women's cars at the mall "slashes his victims' Achilles tendons so they cannot run."

Then in October 1991, at about the time campus crime-rumor scares were emerging again (see above, pp. 116–19.) mall-slasher stories began to circulate in the Chicago and Little Rock areas. On October 11th, a story by Peter Kendall in the *Chicago Tribune* reported, "In recent weeks, countless people around Joliet and Aurora have heard and retold the same horrible tale." The tale Kendall described was pretty standard: Men were lurking under cars in mall parking lots, waiting to slash women's ankles. The attacks were thought to be the work of local gangs, and one Joliet minister who said he believed the stories, was quoted saying that he would not allow his name to be given in the newspaper for fear of retaliation by gang members.

On October 17th John Hoogesteger's byline appeared on an article in the *Arkansas Gazette* that reported rampant rumors of ankle slashers attacking women at two Little Rock suburban shopping malls. The newspaper assured readers that police authorities had investigated the claims and found them baseless. The article also mentioned that during the recent Arkansas State Fair a false rumor claimed that young men with knives stuck in their shoes had been slashing at women's ankles.

"Wild Rumors in Wichita" trumpeted a headline on December 29, 1991, in the *Wichita Eagle*. The story, written by Laurie Kalmanson, mentioned unverified local stories about teenage gangs throwing people over the second-level railing at a shopping mall, about a psychopath carrying a hatchet who supposedly had hidden in people's cars, and, naturally, about a "mini-skirted woman who had her ankles slashed by a knife-wielding hoodlum hiding beneath her parked car."

Danny McKenzie, a columnist for the Jackson, Mississippi, *Clarion-Ledger* debunked the local version of the ankle-slasher story on March 9, 1992. In this instance, members of black gangs were said to hide under a woman's car, slash at her ankles, and then when the victim reached down towards her injury, grab her hand and cut off a finger. These assaults were thought to be part of a gang initiation rite. But, wrote McKenzie, "no one—*absolutely no one*—has come forward with any solid proof that this dastardly deed has been done."

It's possible that this bizarre crime has actually happened. The following appeared in a 1989 car-safety booklet prepared by the Michigan State Police together with Chrysler's Jeep Division: "Thieves have been known to hide under a vehicle and grab a woman's ankles."

On the other hand, the same booklet retells as fact a version of "The Assailant in the Back Seat" legend, attributing it only to "a woman in a suburban Pittsburgh shopping mall."

Finally, a story on March 27, 1990, in the *Ball State Daily News*, Muncie, Indiana, quotes a director of a national crime-fighting organization who described "The Slasher under the

Car" as a real threat. According to the article, the man said:

"Look under your vehicle as you approach it. . . . Criminals are now hiding under cars, from where they can grab your ankles and pull you under."

The director added this example, "A criminal hiding under a car once slit the tendons on the backs of a guy's ankles, so men are vulnerable too."

Now *that's* a new twist on the story! It may be that some police authorities and safety directors have believed a widespread urban legend about shopping mall crime and are now even themselves adding to the variations of the story.

UPDATE:

In her column of April 23, 1992, Abigail Van Buren began with this letter, prompting dozens of urban legend fans to forward copies to me:

"Dear Abby: I am 16 and am terrified to go to the mall. At our local shopping mall, crimes have been going on that are never reported in the newspaper because there are so many of them.

"A friend of mine had been shopping and was just about to get into her car, when a man who had been hiding under her car grabbed her ankles. Another man, working in cahoots with the man under the car, was hiding behind another car nearby, and he jumped out and grabbed my friend's purse, and the two of them got away and were never caught.

"The security guards never seem to be around when you need them. Please warn people, Abby.—"

And Abby *did* warn people—to avoid malls with high crime rates or lax security, never to shop alone, and always to check under the car before getting in. There was no warning, however, about falling for urban legends.

"The Colander Copier Caper"

Rodney K. Gregson, a fifteen-year veteran of the Los Angeles Police Department, wrote in June 1990 to tell me a funny story about a faked lie detector used to fool suspects in criminal cases.

He commented, "This story deals with two items found in all police stations—a photocopy machine and a not-very-bright arrestee—and with one item I've never seen in any station, a metal colander."

Already this was beginning to sound familiar! Gregson's story turned out to be one I had read previously in a book claiming it as an actual news item from a Pennsylvania town.

First, Officer Gregson's version goes like this:

The suspect is put in a metal-framed chair with the colander inverted on his head and wires running from it to the photocopy machine. The officers have prepared a sheet of paper with the word "lie" (or, in some versions, "false") neatly inscribed on it.

The suspect is told that he's hooked up to a lie detector, and officers start to ask him questions like "Where is the gun?" or "Did you do this alone?"

When he answers with what the officers can tell is a lie (Trust me—we can tell when someone is lying!), one officer pushes the print button on the machine and out comes a sheet saying "lie."

Believing that he can't fool the machine, the suspect starts confessing his crimes, at which point an officer surreptitiously switches the "lie" paper with one saying "true".

Officer Gregson concluded, "Knowing the slightly skewed (some would say warped) sense of humor that cops have, I would not doubt that this event might really have happened."

Why did the LAPD officer send me the story, then? Because, as he put it, "I've heard it in several parts of the city, but the officers telling it never played the trick themselves and were never even there when it was used." In other words, this is a FOAF story, and it's likely an urban legend.

The claimed news report from Pennsylvania that I had read appeared in the 1989 book *News of the Weird* by Chuck Shepherd, John J. Kohut, and Roland Sweet (New York: New American Library, Plume Books). It reads like this:

"Police in Radnor, Pennsylvania, interrogated a suspect by placing a metal colander on his head and connecting it with metal wires to a photocopy machine. The message, 'he's lying' was placed in the copier and police pressed the copy button each time they believed the suspect wasn't telling the truth. Believing that the 'lie detector' was working, the suspect confessed." (pp. 110–11)

To check on this version of the story, for which *News of the Weird* cites no source, I wrote to the police chief in Radnor, a town west of Philadelphia. I received this reply, dated October 10, 1990:

The fake lie detector incident referred to in your letter did not happen in Radnor.

We do not know how the story originated; however, over the years, we have received numerous letters inquiring about this incident.

Articles have been sent to us which appeared in the Wall Street Journal, Playboy *and other publications.*

Our guess is that some reporter had the story and used Radnor as the place of occurrence.

                    Sincerely,
                    Maurice L. Hennessy
                    Chief of Police, Radnor Township

I certainly hope nobody gave Chief Hennessy a copy of the "National Lampoon True Facts Calendar" for 1991 with a different story for each date, because on the page for Friday,

January 18, we find this version of the story:

"A judge admonished the Radnor, Pennsylvania, police for pretending that a Xerox copy machine was a lie detector. Officers had placed a metal colander on the head of a suspect and attached the colander to the copier with metal wires. In the copy machine was a typewritten message which read 'He's lying.'

"According to UPI, 'Each time investigators received answers they did not fancy, they pushed the copy button. Out came the message, 'He's lying.'

"Apparently convinced the machine was accurate, the suspect confessed."

(Probably the phrase "metal wires," among other similarities betrays a common source for these two Radnor, Pennsylvania, versions.)*

Next, a lawyer sent me the same fake lie detector story as he remembered it being told in 1983 by an instructor at the U.S. Naval Justice School in Newport, Rhode Island. Supposedly, officers of the Naval Investigative Service had used the same colander-on-the-head trick to interrogate an enlisted man who was suspected of a series of petty thefts.

Besides NIS agents, however, the lawyer also wrote that he had heard that the same phony lie detector had been used by FBI agents or by detectives in some big-city police department. Let me guess—could it have been Los Angeles or Philadelphia, by any chance?

The lawyer offered another hint of how the story had traveled. He said, "I've heard it or read it a couple more times in different contexts, always in speeches or publications directed at criminal defense lawyers."

---

*The same text, minus the reference to Radnor, appeared in the "Country Life" column of the British humor magazine *Punch* for the week of February 19–25, 1992, where it was credited to a Reno, Nevada, newspaper. Along with a version published in the April 1992 issue of *Life*, however, was the statement, "The police in Radnor, Pa., claim the story is apocryphal."

Before I could ponder the significance of this hint and figure out a way to query more law-enforcement personnel about the caper, I came across yet another version of the story attributed to a different part of Pennsylvania. An article by William Ecenbarger titled "Copier Communiqué" appearing in the October 1990 issue of *USAir Magazine* retold the story this way:

> *Perhaps the most unusual government use of a photocopier occurred in 1977 and was later revealed before Judge Isaac Garb in Bucks County, Pennsylvania. Police took a suspect into custody and asked if he would submit to a lie-detector test. He agreed, whereupon he was led to a Xerox machine in which police had already inserted a typewritten card that said "He's lying." The suspect was seated next to the machine, a metal kitchen colander was placed on his head, the photocopier and the colander were "connected" by a piece of wire, and police began their interrogation. Whenever the suspect gave an answer the police didn't believe, they pushed the button, and out came a photocopy of "He's lying." The suspect, apparently convinced there was no way to beat the machine, confessed. Judge Garb, however, was unconvinced, and threw out the confession.*

(Incidentally, I got the *USAir Magazine* story from Robert Hicks, a criminal justice analyst for the Commonwealth of Virginia who got it from a professional colleague, Police Lieutenant John H. Lawrence of Melvindale, Michigan. Both remembered hearing the story previously, but could not remember where or when. I know the feeling.)

Next I wrote to William Ecenbarger, who lives in Lebanon, Pennsylvania, hoping he'd have firsthand knowledge of "The Colander Copier Caper." No such luck, for he had merely clipped the item from a column by Clark DeLeon published in the Philadelphia *Inquirer* on July 22, 1977, a copy of which he included. I found that Ecenbarger had summarized the story accurately, and the only further information included in the column was that the incident had happened in a "small police department in the county."

DeLeon had handled the story with humor, headlining his column "Whatever Happened to Rubber Hoses?" and nominating the incident for his "dumb crook series." But, adding a sense of verisimilitude, there was even this quotation, supposedly from Judge Garb: "It's the sort of comic relief you need around here once in awhile."

Still straining to get at the truth, I called Clark DeLeon in August 1991, hoping against hope that he could identify a source for his 1977 column some fourteen years later. But DeLeon's best recollection was that he must have heard the story from someone in law enforcement; not surprisingly for a daily columnist, he had no backup data on file for this story, but he did tell me that a newspaper reporter from Harrisburg had assured him that an actual Pennsylvania Superior Court ruling had in fact overturned a conviction based on a colander copier confession.

Time to consult the pros: I asked Susan Miner, Reference Librarian at the University of Utah College of Law if she could track down anything—*anything at all*—relating the Pennsylvania Superior Court system, or anywhere else, to a case involving colanders, copiers, or lie detectors. Believe me, I felt more than a little foolish raising this question among the serious pinstripe types I saw in the library; they all seemed to be busy researching torts, wills, contracts, and whatever, so I armed myself with a legal-sized yellow lined pad and kept my voice down.

Ms. Miner linked her desktop terminal to the mighty Lexis database, typed in the key words, and found one solitary reference to "The Colander Copier Caper." Alas: the reference was not to a court case.

The computer produced a reference to a book review published August 3, 1987, in *The National Law Journal* (p. 39) of a collection of legal anecdotes, *Disorderly Conduct: Verbatim Excerpts from Actual Court Cases,* compiled by Gerald F. Uelmen, Charles

M. Sevilla, and Rodney Jones and published by (of all companies!) my own publisher, W. W. Norton & Company. The review mentions that the stories were "drawn from letters received from lawyers around the world describing actual
events," and quotes Uelmen's own favorite story. I quote it
below from the 1989 paperback edition of the book itself:

"Two police officers extracted a confession from a suspect by
advising him the Xerox machine was a lie detector. First they
put a colander—a salad strainer—over the suspect's head and
wired it to the duplicating machine. Then, under the Xerox lid
they placed a slip of paper reading 'He Is Lying!' Every time the
suspect answered a question, an officer would press the duplicating button and out would pop a Xeroxed 'He Is Lying!'
Finally shaken, the suspect told all. His confession was thrown
out by a judge who was not amused." (pp. 47–48)

The brief foreword to *Disorderly Conduct* restates the claim that
all the stories are about things that "actually took place in a
courtroom," but, unfortunately, no individual sources are
cited. (Nor is it clear why the word "colander" needs a gloss for
lawyers to understand it.)

How shall we evaluate all the evidence about "The Colander
Copier Caper" and the various claims that it really happened?

Possibly some police unit acted out a legend they'd heard,
and played the trick on a prisoner, although that seems unlikely, considering the strict rules of individual rights and use of
evidence that modern law-enforcement personnel adhere to.
Does Judge Garb exist, and did the caper really occur in Bucks
County? So far I cannot find the proof.

More likely, I think, various police officers with their
"slightly skewed" sense of humor have told the apocryphal colander story to newspaper reporters as a joke, and it was accepted by some of them as truth. During a slow night on the
police beat, the legend could have found its way into print.

Judging from my collected references, at least, I'd guess that
there are probably several further published versions that es-

caped the dragnet. Those that I did find, taken together, have probably reached a large number of people, both via reading them and hearing the story retold.

Now if I could only get one of those policemen or police reporters who claim the story is true to sit down next to my copy machine with a colander on his head, I'll bet I could get to the truth behind this case at last.

Crime and the Quake

I live in Utah about six hundred miles from San Francisco, but even at this distance I felt some shock waves from the Bay Area quake that occurred on October 17, 1989. However, these were folkloric effects, not literal aftershocks.

Of the many stories told about the quake, the ones most likely to be urban legends concern cars, always a favorite topic of modern folklore.

For example, Peggy Sue Davis of distant Pasadena wrote that she has heard several versions of a story about someone calling home on a car phone just after the quake began. The person reports that he or she is driving on I-880, the Nimitz Freeway, and will get back home as soon as possible.

Suddenly the phone line goes dead, because the freeway had just collapsed. The caller is never seen alive again.

Davis also sent me a story I'm calling "The Smashed Car Thief." It's a tale that I've collected from other sources as well. Davis heard it from a friend whose business partner got it on the telephone from a friend in San Francisco. He said it had happened to yet another friend's friend from Fresno.

"At least I think that's the connection," Davis wrote, "but at that point it got pretty convoluted."

Her source was clearer about the make of car involved: "A brand-new 700S BMW—gorgeous—a $65,000 car."

This is what supposedly happened: The Fresno friend of a friend had driven to Candlestick Park that day to watch the third game of the World Series. After the earthquake hit, he made his way back to the parking lot to recover his expensive new car, but it was no longer in the spot where he had parked it. Evidently the car had been stolen. So after managing to get back home, he filed a police report.

About a week later the police called the Fresno man to tell

him that his car had been found by workers excavating the collapsed I-880 freeway, with the crushed body of the car thief inside.

The same story circulated in Fresno itself, as I learned from Professor Joel Best of the California State University at Fresno's Department of Sociology. Best sent me an account from a paper written by one of his students whose father told it on Thanksgiving Day. This version claimed that a couple from Clovis, a small town outside Fresno, had driven their Porsche to Candlestick Park for the baseball game on that fateful day.

One of the details in this version is that the car thief who is found crushed in their car on the Nimitz Freeway was a black man. This, of course, introduces a racist element into the little drama of crime and punishment.

Glenn Scott of the Modesto *Bee* heard another localized version of the story, as reported in his column of December 29, 1989: This time it was a Modesto couple who drove their new BMW to the ball game and found their car stolen after the quake. "Weeks later they received a call. Workers clearing the debris from the collapsed portion of the Nimitz Freeway had hoisted up one of the last sections of concrete to be removed. Beneath it was the BMW, squashed flat as a pancake. Trapped inside was the car thief."

Still other versions of the story mention a white Mercedes with gold trim or say the car was crushed not on the freeway but in the Cypress Parking Structure. But among them all, I prefer the variation sent to me by Barbara Bernstein of San Francisco. She heard that the stolen car was a new Porsche "and the owners found out what had happened when a policeman showed up at their front door holding their [crumpled] license plate."

I found an equally doubtful story in a November 26th article about quake narratives. San Francisco *Examiner* columnist Rob Morse introduced the tale by commenting, "Some stories sound suspiciously like urban legends."

According to Morse's report, four Japanese seismologists

landed at the San Francisco airport shortly after the quake and told a cabby, "Take us to the epicenter." A couple of hours later, geologists at the quake's epicenter in the Santa Cruz mountains looked up to see a cab bouncing down the road.

Yes, I agreed; that story does sound too good to be true.

However, Morse accepted without question another story he heard about a man having his "1972 Mercedes 250C" stolen during the height of the post-quake confusion. I suspect that this car thief too was said to have been found later, crushed inside the vehicle on the damaged Nimitz Freeway.

I'm also slightly skeptical about a "wake of the shake" story included in Herb Caen's San Francisco *Chronicle* column of November 28th. Caen wrote that "Two newly arrived Norwegians drove up to Stanford Court on Nob Hill last wkend[*sic*] in a four-wheel drive truck they'd rented at the airport. Having read those 'San Francisco in ruins' fables in the Oslo press, they confessed sheepishly to mgr. Creighton Casper that they thought they'd need the truck to get through the rubble."

This sounds to me like another California car-in-the-quake legend; either that, or a particularly unfunny dumb-Norwegian joke.

"The Kidney Heist"

There's a real shocker of a story going around about thefts of organs (and I mean human kidneys not Wurlitzers), so brace yourself. I first noted "The Kidney Heist" legend in the late winter of 1991, and it has remained a hot story thereafter, both on the grapevine and in the media.

A typical version of the story tells of a group of young men who went to New York City for a weekend of fun. One of them was attracted to a woman he met in a bar, and told his buddies he was going to spend the night at her place and would get in touch with them later.

They didn't hear from him until late the next day when he phoned to say "I think I'm in such-and-such a hotel in room number so-and-so, but something's wrong with me and you'd better come and get me."

When the friends arrived at the hotel room they found their friend in bed and the sheets splattered with blood. He was very weak. When they tried to help him out of bed, they discovered a fresh surgical closure on his back and still more blood, so they rushed him to a hospital.

There it was discovered that the man had had one of his kidneys removed, and they concluded that he had been drugged so his kidney could be taken for sale on the black market for human organs.

That's the version of the story I got in a letter dated March 8, 1991, from Felicia Strobhert of Stone Mountain, Georgia. She had heard it the night before from an Ohio friend who got it from a relative in Virginia. A few days later, on March 11th, I received "The Kidney Heist" story again, this time from Dan Verner of Manassas, Virginia, who had heard it that day.

As Verner was told the story, four Washington, D.C., business partners—three women and a man—went into New York

City as part of their work nearly every Thursday and Friday. Sometimes they would stay over to see a show and not return home until Sunday morning.

One such weekend the man remained at a bar Friday night while the women went off on their own. They worried when they did not hear from him, but Sunday morning he called their hotel.

"Please," he begged, "You've got to come and help me," and he gave them an address. They raced there in a cab and found the man lying against a building wearing the same clothes he had on Friday when they last saw him.

The man was soaked with sweat and seemed dazed, so they took him to a hospital where it was discovered that he was doped up on morphine, had 110 stitches across his abdomen, and was missing a kidney. The surgery, according to a doctor, had been "done by an expert."

Two weeks later, on March 27th, Joe Baldanza of Weymouth, Massachusetts, telephoned. He had just heard "The Kidney Heist" story from a business associate and couldn't wait to learn if I'd heard it. Then the phone rang again, bringing me a report of the same legend circulating in the Midwest.

George Hesselberg, columnist with the *Wisconsin State Journal* in Madison, first heard that the organ theft had happened—in New York City again—to a man from Romance Foods company in Kenosha, Wisconsin. As summarized in Hesselberg's column on Sunday, March 31st, the president of Romance Foods had heard the story too, but from an employee of Hewlett-Packard in Chicago. She'd heard it from "a friend in New York who heard it from a friend of the family of the man who had his kidney stolen."

Determined journalist that he is, Hesselberg called the friend in New York who told him she had heard it at a dinner party from yet another friend "who swears it happened to another friend." Then Hesselberg called me, and we had a nice chat about urban legends. As Hesselberg reported it, "before I could tell him my story . . . Brunvand told the same story to me, in more detail."

By then "The Kidney Heist" story was breaking wide open. Sunday's *New York Times* (We're still on March 31st here!) included an article by Joe Morgenstern, scriptwriter for the episode of NBC's series "Law and Order" to be broadcast on Tuesday, April 2nd. He had made "The Kidney Heist" legend the basis of that episode, having been told by a friend that it was an actual crime reported in a newspaper article, although, Morgenstern admitted, "I never found anyone who had actually seen it." (Although promotional advertising for that episode implied that the plot stemmed from news stories, a disclaimer at the end of the actual broadcast said, "This story is fictional. No actual person or event is depicted.)

The morning of the day of the "Law and Order" broadcast, Lloyd Grove in a *Washington Post* article tied the upcoming TV episode to urban legends in an article that quoted yours truly as well as Nebraska folklorist Roger Welsch. Grove also reported that a *Post* editor who had heard the story at a Bethesda, Maryland, dinner party had "promptly assigned a reporter to check it out." But the reporter merely uncovered a series of variations on the theme, none of them verifiable.

By the time the New York *Daily News* got around to covering the story on April 29th ("Tale full of kidney beans . . .") there was speculation to report that the legends might be based on the "Law and Order" episode. But I continued to receive the story from people who had not seen the broadcast and had heard such details as that the illicit operation was performed in a dentist's office, that the wound was sewn shut with dental floss, that the incident had actually happened in New Jersey or in California, and that recent medical school graduates do illegal kidney transplants in order to earn enough money to pay back their student loans.

Meanwhile, "The Kidney Heist" was also being told in Europe, as attested in a letter to me from Peter Burger of

Leiden, The Netherlands, who had collected a version in which a Dutch tourist in Tunisia loses a kidney. I also received an article by Bengt af Klintberg published in the Swedish newspaper *Expressen* for May 26, 1991, titled "Den vandrande njuren" (The Wandering Kidney). Later Bengt wrote to say that the tentative title of his next book of urban legends would be the same phrase.

Mark Moravec, a folklore researcher in Ballarat, Australia, has been collecting "The Kidney Heist" in his country, except that usually the incident is said to have occurred not in Australia but in the United States, often Los Angeles, to an Aussie on holiday there.

French folklorist Véronique Campion-Vincent has supplied the likely background for "The Kidney Heist" legend in her article "The Baby-Parts Story: A New Latin American Legend" (*Western Folklore*, vol. no. 49, 1, January, 1990, pp. 9–25). She documents thoroughly how similar organ theft rumors had been rampant internationally for the past four years.

Claims that babies were being kidnapped and murdered for their vital organs first arose in Honduras and Guatemala in 1987, then spread to South America in 1988, and eventually centered on Mexico where some newspaper articles insisted that the stories are true. In all accounts, it was suggested that wealthy people in the United States were paying huge amounts for organs taken from murdered Third World children. These incredible stories ignored the complexity of organ transplant operations, which would preclude any such quick removal and long-distance shipment of body parts.

"I have closely tracked this groundless rumor, which has appeared hundreds of times in the world press since January 1987," wrote Todd Leventhal, a Policy Officer for the United States Information Agency in a letter published on February 26, 1992, in the *New York Times*. Leventhal complained that a *Times* article published on February 5th had treated the baby parts story as factual. He listed several international agencies that had investigated the rumor and found it baseless, but admitted that still "it persists and is widely believed in many parts of the world."

David Schrieberg, Mexico bureau chief for *The Sacramento Bee*, had debunked the baby-parts story in the December 24, 1990, issue of *The New Republic*. He quoted from descriptions of the supposed crimes in Mexican newspapers, and reported hearing accounts of a traveler caught with a leaky suitcase "full of children's eyes and kidneys, wrapped in plastic and chilled with melting ice." Another investigative article debunking the story was Debbie Nathan's piece "Body Snatchers: The Logic of Myth in the Third World" published in the December 21, 1990, issue of *The Texas Observer*.

Mexico City's English-language newspaper, *The News*, on February 28, 1990, published an account of a kidney theft that sounds like a version that may lie behind the recent American legend. This article described how an eight-year-old child was found "wandering around the streets in a daze and with a healing surgical scar on her body . . . a kidney had been surgically removed."

But it never happened in Mexico, and I'm confident that the adult kidney-heist stories being told in this country and in Europe are false as well.

Bulletin: Just as I finished writing the above, Michelle Hudson of Jackson, Mississippi, sent me Orley Hood's July 21, 1991, column from the Jackson *Clarion-Ledger* on "Stories I've heard lately, which may or may not be true." Story No. 1 is "The Kidney Heist."

In early August I got the story from Randall S. Hoopes of Wilmington, Delaware, from Sarah P. Beiting of Kalamazoo, Michigan, and from Julie Hoffman of Oconomowoc, Wisconsin. Then Jim Kline of Lakewood, California, wrote on August 12th to report that the night before at a dinner party he heard "The Kidney Heist" told as something that had happened recently to Linda Ronstadt's brother while he was on a trip to Mexico.

By mid-winter the story had spread north of the border. On

January 31, 1992, *The Buffalo News* reported a recent tongue-in-cheek column published in the *Toronto Star* that told of a Canadian visitor who came to Buffalo shopping and ended up being mugged for his left kidney. Despite the column's disbelieving tone, the *News* article mentioned that "several worried organ owners" had called the Buffalo paper to ask about black-market body parts, and that the *Star* had received more than 100 calls since its column had appeared.

4

On-the-Job Legends

Career Decisions

There are many legends about notable careers that began by accident. Here's a classic example, as told to me by Robert L. Brust of Walnut Creek, California:

"My grandfather used to tell about a country lad who went to the big city to seek his fortune, but had no luck finding a job. One day, wandering through the red light district, he spotted a Help Wanted sign in a window.

"They were looking for a bookkeeper, but after the madam quizzed the boy about his education and discovered that he could neither read or write, she turned him away.

"Feeling sorry for him, she gave him two big red apples as he left. A few blocks down the street, he placed the apples on top of a garbage can while tying his shoe, and a stranger came along and offered to buy them.

"The boy took the money to a produce market and bought a dozen more apples, which he sold quickly. Eventually he parlayed his fruit sales into a grocery store, then a string of supermarkets. Eventually he became the wealthiest man in the state.

"Finally, he was named Man of the Year, and during an interview a journalist discovered that his subject could neither read or write.

" 'Good Lord, Sir,' he said. 'What do you suppose you would

have become if you had ever learned to read and write?'

" 'Well,' he answered, 'I guess I would have been a book-keeper in a whorehouse.' "

Brust believed his grandfather's story until he heard another version about a piano player who was turned down for the bordello job and went on to become a famed concert pianist. The punch line was similar.

Another version of this legend was the inspiration for William Somerset Maugham's 1929 short story "The Verger," the title of which is a British term for a church caretaker. In the story, Maugham's hero is fired by the vicar when it is discovered that he is illiterate. Quite by accident, he becomes a tobacconist and eventually owns a string of shops in London.

One day, when taking his day's receipts to a bank he is asked to sign some papers, and the banker discovers that he can neither read nor write. Astonished, the banker asks "Good God, Man, what would you be now if you had been able to?"

The successful man replies, "I'd be verger of St. Peter's, Neville Square."

This story was adapted for the 1950 film *Trio* based on Maugham's works. Accused of plagiarizing the plot from another work, Maugham explained that he had heard the story from a friend and that it was "a well known bit of Jewish folklore." (See Ted Morgan, *Maugham*, New York: Simon and Schuster, 1980, p. 545.)

I was reminded of another accidental career-decision story when I read in January 1990 about the death of football great Bronko Nagurski. The Associated Press report said:

"According to football lore, he was discovered in 1925 when Minnesota coach Doc Spears drove past a farm and saw a muscular boy plowing a field—without a horse. Spears supposedly asked Nagurski directions, and Bronko picked up the plow and pointed [with it]."

The part about plowing without a horse appears in a nineteenth-century story called "The Young Giant," one of the

Grimm fairy tales. This tall tale has equivalents in the folklore of many other countries.

The feat of pointing with a plow has been told on nearly every strongman of local legend both in European and American folklore. For example, in the Upper Peninsula of Michigan they tell it on the French Canadian Max Duhaim (see Richard M. Dorson, *Bloodstoppers and Bearwalkers,* Cambridge: Harvard University Press, 1952, p. 89); in Indiana it's told on "The Strongman of Salem" (see Ron L. Baker, *Hoosier Folk Legends,* Bloomington: Indiana University Press, 1982, p. 145); and in New York State the subject is "Joe Call, the Lewis Giant" (see article by C. Eleanor Hall in *New York Folklore Quarterly,* 9 [1953], p. 183).

Another football coach, among many, on whom the plow-pointing story is told was Bennie Bierman of the University of Minnesota, as reported in Richard M. Dorson's book *American Folklore* (University of Chicago Press, 1959, pp. 257–58).

In overseas versions, the strongman's discoverer was usually a military recruiter scouting rural regions for soldiers to enlist in the czar's, king's, or emperor's army. Whenever a country lad pointed to the city with his plow, the recruiter signed him up.

"The Bedbug Letter"

A reader in Staten Island, New York, who neatly printed his letter but scrawled an illegible signature, wrote "I'm sending you a story that might bear checking out." He recounted a job-related legend I'd never heard before, which I called "The Bedbug Letter."

The story goes that an elderly woman found a bedbug in her sleeping berth on a train. She wrote a letter of complaint to the president of the company, and—surprisingly—received a prompt answer.

In a carefully worded letter the president expressed his horror at the incident and apologized profusely to the passenger, promising that nothing like this had happened before nor would ever happen again. But accidentally attached to the letter was a routing memo addressed to the president's secretary. This note read, "Send this SOB a copy of the bedbug letter!"

That story seemed too good to be true, which meant (I wrote in a column) it was probably a legend. Confirming my guess, a card arrived from another reader saying simply, "My father told me that tale in the late 1940s." Then, before too long I heard the same story from another reader, who wrote:

Dear Professor:

I heard this story from a college friend whose mother worked for the railroad in Cheyenne, Wyo. It probably dates from the early '50s.

It seems that a woman arose from her Pullman sleeper and was outraged to discover that she had been bitten by bedbugs during the night. She wrote a letter to the railroad company and in due course received a beautiful apology from the company.

The letter assured her that the railroad's standards of hygiene had always been of the highest, their care of linens and compartments were impeccable, etc. The writer added that although they had never before received the slightest complaint about bedbugs they would thoroughly clean and fumigate the Pullman cars and were sending her some kind of compensation.

I don't remember whether it was a free pass, a basket of flowers, or something else, but the letter concluded by saying that the woman would never again have any reason to regret her continued patronage. The letter was signed by the company president.

But clipped to the letter was a handwritten memo to the president's secretary; it read, "Send this dame the bedbug letter."

—Carol Kimball, Denver, Colorado

(*Memo to myself:* Send this person the bedbug letter letter. And I did.)

Recently I heard "The Bedbug Letter" again; this time the story of corporate double-talk was read on the air from a listener's letter to a CBC (Canadian Broadcasting Corporation) radio program that I happened to be listening to while driving.

My wife and I were creeping along in our camper-van on the New York Thruway near Buffalo in early November 1991, during the first major snowstorm of the season. We had our radio tuned to a Toronto station, which was airing part of a series devoted to consumer problems. The announcer read the letter telling "The Bedbug Letter" absolutely straight, right up to the line "Send this guy the bedbug letter." Neither he nor the letter-writer gave the slightest hint that this might not be a 100 percent true incident.

Then, would you believe, the tale popped up again in the *Princeton Alumni Weekly* for October 9, 1991, as spotted by my friend David Stanley of Salt Lake City and passed on to me when we got home. In an article by Forrest D. Colburn, assistant professor of politics, titled "The Wit and Wisdom of the Faculty," we find this:

> *Sometime back, I told Henry Bienen, a Woodrow Wilson School professor who directs the Center of International Studies, that I had written to a politician. He said I would probably get a response similar to the famous "bug letter" from the Pennsylvania Railroad. Did I know about that letter? No, I admitted.*
>
> *According to Bienen, a passenger once wrote a letter to the railroad to complain about all the roaches she had encountered on a train. Shortly thereafter, she received a letter apologizing profusely for the presence of bugs. The author of the letter promised that the authorities would take immediate remedial action. Attached inadvertently to this reply was the passenger's own letter. At the top of it was stamped: "Send her the bug letter."*

The variations here help to identify "The Bedbug Letter" as a traditional story. This time it's the Pennsylvania Railroad, a plague of roaches instead of bedbugs, and a rubber stamp in place of the written memo. But the point of the story remains intact: Big company executives may write you one thing but be thinking another.

Could the story of "The Bedbug Letter" possibly be true? Here's what another Princeton alum wrote in the *Weekly* for February 5, 1992:

> *As corresponding secretary of the George Mortimer Pullman Encomium Society, Appalachian Chapter, it is my grievous duty to call to your attention some most regrettable errors in the article "The Wit and Wisdom of the Faculty," by Forrest D. Colburn (PAW, October 9th).*
>
> *A minimal amount of research by the author or by his mistaken informant, Professor Henry Bienen, would have revealed that the passenger was male, not female, and that the*

"bugs" complained of were not roaches but bedbugs. Moreover, the matter of complaint was addressed not to the railroad but to the Pullman Palace Car Company. Here are the verified particulars: A certain Phineas P. Jenkins, a salesman of pig-iron products for the Monongahela Ironworks Company of Pittsburgh, was traveling from Chicago to Cleveland on the night of March 4, 1889. After Jenkins wrote George M. Pullman, the president of the car firm, about the sleepless night he'd endured being "viciously attacked in the dark by a horde of ravenous bedbugs," he received the following reply:

"We are in receipt of your letter of the 5th instant, and I cannot begin to express to you, sir, how embarrassed and chagrined I am to learn of this most unfortunate incident involving a unit of our property. You have called it an 'outrage'; I agree totally. You have asked what we intend doing about it. Allow me to tell you.

"Because you were admirably foresighted and enclosed your ticket stub and receipts, we were able quickly to identify the sleeping car in question. The car was located on March 8th, immediately removed from passenger service and sidetracked in a remote area until it could be transported by a specially dispatched locomotive to our maintenance facility at Alton, Illinois.

"There it has been stripped of all furnishings. The bedding, upholstery, curtains, carpet and all other combustible materials have been burned. The toilets and their fixtures have been scrubbed down and sterilized with carbolic acid. By the time you receive this letter, the car will have been fumigated and steam cleaned from end to end . . ."

Pullman went on to report that the responsible personnel had been reprimanded, docked two weeks' wages, and assigned to refresher training in maintenance and sanitation. He concluded by stating that the Interstate Commerce Commission prohibited him from refunding Jenkins's fare or reimbursing him for medical or other expenses.

   When Jenkins received the reply, he found his original letter mistakenly enclosed with it. Across that letter, Pullman had hand-written (not stamped, as your article erroneously stated) this note to his secretary: "Sarah—Send this S! O! B! the 'bedbug letter'."

M. William Adler '48
Weston, W. Va.

Roughneck Fishermen Throw 'em Back

"I am positive," writes David R. MacDonald, a geologist in Saskatoon, Saskatchewan, "that this story about a roughneck's revenge is told in every oil patch between Texas and the Beaufort Sea." That sounds like quite a claim, and—for a folklorist—one well worth checking out.

First I looked up "roughneck" (an oil drilling crew member), "oil patch" (a district that contains oil wells) and the Beaufort Sea (the part of the Arctic ocean that's northeast of Alaska and northwest of Canada). Then I read the story, greatly enjoying MacDonald's tale of a worker's sweet revenge:

"Near the completion of drilling an oil well, a roughneck dropped a hammer, a wrench, or some other tool down the hole. A crew was brought in at great expense and loss of time to fish for it.

"When it was finally brought to the surface, the toolpush [drill foreman] handed the tool back to the roughneck and said 'You're fired!' The roughneck said 'Fine,' and he dropped the tool right back into the hole again."

Not to brag, but it took me only about fifteen minutes of leafing through reference sources to find a parallel for the story as it was told by offshore oil workers in the Louisiana Gulf Coast. After checking a bibliography of occupational folklore, I located an article by Mary C. Fields, "The View from the Water Table: Folklore of the Offshore Oilfield Workers," published in the Winter 1974 issue of the journal *Mid-South Folklore*. (vol. 2, no. 3, pp. 63–76). Bingo!

Here's Fields's version, quoted in an oil driller's actual words:

There was an old boy that fooled around and kicked a twelve-pound sledge hammer. They were sitting around the

*hole with the top off of it, and he stumbled or fell or
something and kicked it off in the hole.*

*They couldn't drill it up or sidetrack it or fish for it, and
they messed with it for days, and they finally caught the thing
and got it back to surface.*

*And this had cost them maybe two weeks fishing time, a lot
of work when they should have had the well completed and
been gone.*

*As quick as they got it out of the hole, the toolpusher told
him, 'Well, we just don't need your kind around here
anymore.'*

*The guy said, "Well, then I guess I don't need this
anymore," and kicked the sledge hammer back in the hole.*

To my surprise, I did not find the "Fishing for Revenge"
story in the standard study of this general topic, Mody C. Boatright's 1963 book *Folklore of the Oil Industry* (Dallas: Southern
Methodist University Press). But he did include another anecdote about fishing in an oil patch that he had collected in
Texas.

Seems that one toolpush (or toolpusher, take your choice)
needed a special device for pulling lost objects out of the drill
hole. It's called a "bulldog spear," or "bulldog" for short, and it
consists of a grabber gadget which has an automatic latch that
clamps onto the lost item and cannot be released until brought
to the surface.

According to the story, an American oil driller working in
Mexico asked a man going back to the States for a visit to bring
him back a sixteen-inch bulldog. You guessed it; the man returned leading a nice little brindle bulldog on a leash.

I am positive, to echo Mr. MacDonald's words, that similar
stories based on technical jobs, jargon exist in most other occu-
pations.

But my favorite story from Boatright's collection is on a different theme. It's about a Texas oil millionaire who tells guests
at his mansion that he has three swimming pools. One is filled

with cold water for people who like a refreshing swim. The second contains warm water for those who wish to be more comfortable as they paddle around. And the third pool contains no water at all, "for those who do not wish to swim."

"The Wife on the Flight"

The business world, like any area of modern life, has its share of legends, and I don't just mean Lee Iacocca. As a matter of fact, though, I have heard an apocryphal story about the chairman of Chrysler Motors.

It's rumored that Iacocca's parents spent their honeymoon at Lido Beach near Venice and really named their son "Lido"— · not Lee—in remembrance of that time. Not true, says Lee; and not much of a legend either, say I.

A typical business story with a much better plot line is "The Wife on the Flight."

This legend was sent to me by the man who discovered and named it, John Robert Colombo, a Toronto radio commentator and columnist. He told "The Wife on the Flight" this way in his *Toronto Star* column for December 3, 1989:

"An airline company's promotion department suggested in its advertising that executives should take their wives on business trips, and it kept records of which ones did. Subsequently the department asked the market-research department to carry out a survey with three hundred of the wives to get their impressions of this scheme.

"In due course the research department sent a letter to those wives asking how they enjoyed the trip. From ninety percent of them came back a baffled reply, 'What airplane trip?' "

Colombo first encountered this story when he was copy-editing the manuscript of a book called *The Darlings: The Mystique of the Supermarket*" published by McClelland & Steward in Toronto in 1970. The book's author, according to Colombo, was "the late Robert F. Chisholm, Toronto socialite and supermarket executive."

Colombo asked Chisholm, whom he describes as "a canny fellow with a dry wit," when and where the incident about

Reprinted by permission: Robert Noyce/Deseret News

wives *not* on flights occurred. Chisholm told him the story was merely hearsay, something he had heard on a business trip to the United States in either late 1969 or early 1970.

The editor/columnist included the story in his book *Colombo's Canadian Quotations* in 1974, and he saw it reported as news from America in *The Observer*, an English weekly paper. But Colombo wrote that he has also heard the story told "half a dozen times," including twice recently on Canadian radio programs, and sometimes mentioning United Airlines.

First he heard it told in autumn 1989 by the host of a CBC Radio talk show with the added details that the carrier involved was American Airlines, and the incident had happened just "a year ago." Then, after mentioning the story on the air himself in mid-September 1989, Colombo heard from a listener who called to tell him a much older version.

The caller, an American woman married to a Canadian, said that when she worked as an air cargo manager at La Guardia

Airport in New York City from 1942 until the end of World War II she heard the same story told as true.

She said that a sales manager for American Airlines launched a promotion aimed at getting returned servicemen's wives to try commercial flights. The woman claimed that about two hundred free tickets were issued to servicemen-turned-businessmen, all earmarked for their wives to use when accompanying them on business flights.

A follow-up survey, she said, showed that most of the wives who had been listed as ticket users had never actually taken a business flight with their husbands.

Colombo wrote, in a letter to me, " 'The Wife on the Flight' sounds like an urban legend to me, but it may well be based on an actual airline promotion."

I agree that it's probably a legend, considering the stories' variations, their time span, and Chisholm's mention of hearing it told in the business world.

Still, although I've heard other business-scam anecdotes, I have not collected other versions of this particular story.

Mistaken Identities

At one time or another, everyone has mistaken someone's identity. It's an embarrassing situation, but at least it makes a good story.

For example, many people whose jobs involve scheduling strangers for some kind of service or treatment have probably occasionally made minor errors in identifying patrons, and they're usually happy to tell you about these slips.

Here's an actual case of one such goof as described in a letter I received from June Marie Schasre of Buffalo, New York, who said she had dozens of funny experiences while working as a medical technician:

One day the receptionist phoned to say that a patient was on his way down to the lab for a Basal Metabolism Rate test.

Shortly a man appeared at my door and asked, "Is this the lab?"

I was busy with some tests, so I just nodded and led him to an examining room. I told him to remove his coat, jacket and shoes, to loosen his tie, and to lie down on the couch and wait for me to return in a half hour.

A short time later another man appeared and said he was there for a BMR, and when I asked the first guy, I discovered he had just come to check some filters on the lab equipment.

He said he had gone along with my request because, "You're a cute chick, and I wondered what would happen when you came back."

I'm sure that this personal experience contains the stuff of legend. After all, Schasre couldn't resist retelling it to me and undoubtedly to others as well.

I became convinced of the story's legend potential shortly afterwards when I received a letter from Les Murray of Bunyah, New South Wales, Australia. Murray wrote to tell me the story about "The Caned Telegram Boy," which, he said, "is a myth gleefully recounted by all high school teachers in this country."

To me it sounds like a legend that was probably carried to Australia from Britain, since it refers to schoolboys being "caned," that is punished by being struck with a cane or stick. That's the sort of thing that happens in a lot of English novels that I've read.

Murray told the caning story in his letter like this:

A notoriously irascible headmaster comes out of his office to deal with a line of shivering boy miscreants, and he awards two, four, or six cuts of the cane to each, including the tall kid at the end of the line.

"Hold out your hand!" he barks, and the boy does so with no more than a strangled "Bbbbut . . . !"

Only when the boy is wringing his hand with pain does the headmaster notice the Postmaster General patch on the boy's grey shirt and the telegram held in his other hand.

Murray added, "I know that this tale goes back to at least the 1930s, and yet my wife taught school under two headmasters about whom the story was told, and one of them even pretended that he had been the headmaster in question.

"Just yesterday," Murray wrote, "I was talking to an inspector of schools exactly my age who swore that *he* saw it happen at Forbes High School in New South Wales in 1955."

If actual cases of mistaken identity sometimes evolve into legends, then Les Murray's information shows how the story may develop one step further. What he indicates here is that a legend about a possible real-life situation—punishing the wrong schoolboy with a cane—apparently was retold as if it were a firsthand personal experience.

Either some Australian headmasters have cast themselves in the leading role of "The Caned Telegram Boy" legend, or else several hapless telegram boys have been victims of similar mistaken identities.

Another mistaken identity story cropped up in the city where I lived in the winter of 1990.

Everybody in Salt Lake City knows about Karl Malone, the star forward for NBA's Utah Jazz. Nicknamed "The Mailman," Malone can be counted on to deliver plenty of points per game, usually with a flamboyant style of play that fans love to talk about.

But in December 1990, a different kind of Karl Malone story was buzzing around town. While it inspired a local sportswriter to suggest jokingly that we rename him "The Skycap," the story made others in this predominantly white community realize how prevalent racist stereotypes still are.

Malone, a 6-foot-9, 256-pound black athlete, was at the Salt Lake International Airport waiting in the baggage claim area for his brother to arrive. A white woman approached him, and, as Malone was quoted by the sportswriter, "She said she needed a porter-boy. You know, someone to help her with her bags."

On the spur of the moment Malone decided to play along and not inform the woman of her mistake. He picked up the woman's bags, and in chatting with her learned that they both originally came from Louisiana. When asked about how he made his living, Malone said he told her that "I drove a truck during the day and did this at night, for a few extra bucks."

When they reached the woman's car—said in the article to be a blue Mercedes—the woman offered him a tip, but Malone refused it saying, "It's OK, I really play pro basketball." Observing her shocked reaction, Malone told the sportswriter, "It was really funny. . . . I was having a good time."

As the story of the Mailman working as a skycap circulated orally and in the media for the next few days I heard varying details about where Malone was waiting, what the woman said to him, where she came from, the kind of car she had, and whether her husband was at the wheel and had recognized her helper.

After telling the story, some people commented that similar mistaken identities must be fairly common and that they must be particularly galling for blacks—that "having a good time" while making light of such incidents must be soured by the obvious taint of racism that's implicit in such situations.

You can't miss this message when you reread the news story and choke on the term "porter-boy."

One Salt Lake citizen wrote a letter to the editor of a local newspaper, branding the story "a dramatic, sad commentary on the state of European-American images of African-Americans."

An article by Douglas C. Lyons, "Racism and Blacks Who've 'Made It,' " in the October 1989 issue of *Ebony* magazine recounted experiences of prominent blacks similar to Karl Malone's and made the point that "You're never too famous, too rich, or too accomplished to escape racial prejudice."

Lyons told a story about how the Reverend Jesse Jackson was waiting in front of a New York City hotel for his ride to several important engagements when an elderly white woman approached, thinking he was the bellhop who had assisted her.

She thanked Jackson for helping her with her baggage on the elevator, and tipped him a dollar. According to the article, Jackson reacted much as Karl Malone did; he "took the dollar, thanked the woman, and climbed into his waiting stretch limousine, which was driven by a white chauffeur."

There's no reason to doubt the truth of this story, but as a folklorist I wonder if it was "improved" slightly in multiple retellings so as to emphasize the age of the woman, the small size of her tip, and the perfect on-cue arrival of the limo with its white driver.

Another mistaken identity story in Lyons's article illustrates a different strategy that some blacks may adopt in dealing with mistaken identities. This time the subject was David Wilmot, the Dean of Admissions of Georgetown Law School in Washington, D.C. Here's the story:

"Wilmot was standing in front of a posh Washington hotel, waiting for the parking attendant to bring him his car. Suddenly a white man rushed out of the hotel and asked Wilmot to fetch his car.

"Did Wilmot get mad? No, he got even. 'The little boy came out in me,' he says.

"I took his claim ticket and told him that I would be right with him. When my car arrived, I drove off with his claim ticket. I must have smiled all the way back to campus.' "

"The Technology Contest"

John Grover of Bountiful, Utah, sent me a fine version of an urban legend I call "The Technology Contest." He remembered hearing it told in Youngstown, Ohio, in 1939 or 1940, but never again since World War II. Here's an abbreviated version of his story, which he prefers to call "The Legend of the Wispy Wire."

Just before the war a German manufacturer sent a request to an American steel company asking it to make a sample of a special steel wire—four feet long and as thin as possible.

The most experienced metallurgists and wire-drawers in the company's Youngstown plant were assigned to the job. After a truly Herculean effort, the perfect piece of wire was ready.

So fine and delicate was this wire that a breath would blow it away. It could barely be seen with the naked eye. Company employees curled it up in a black-velvet-lined jewel box. A special courier carried the box to Germany to get the response of the manufacturer who had ordered the sample.

The courier was welcomed at the plant and given a glass of schnapps while the box was taken to another room for experts to inspect its contents. Before the man had finished his drink, the box was returned—now sealed with wax—and the courier given the instructions, "Your answer is in the box. Please do not open it until you return to your plant."

Back in Youngstown, with all the top employees of the steel plant looking on, the company president opened the box, expecting an order for large quantities of this high-quality wire.

But the box contained only the original piece of wire, coiled just the way it had been packed. Experts inspected the sample closely, wondering what "answer" they were expected to find in the box. Finally, one of the metallurgists started to inspect the wire with a jeweler's eyepiece, and he suddenly gasped and stood bolt upright.

He asked the courier, "How long did you say they had the wire?"

The courier answered, "Not more than two minutes, or three at the outside."

"Good heavens, man, look!" the metallurgist said, handing over the eyepiece.

First the courier and then all the top engineers in the steel plant looked again, using the magnifier. They all gasped at what they saw. The Germans had taken their piece of fragile, almost microscopically thin wire, and in less that three minutes had drilled a hole down its center!

Grover thought this story was "past ripe" when he heard it the first time, and he recalls that it was debunked by the time the United States entered the war and it would have seemed unpatriotic to tell it thereafter. He wondered if I had ever encountered the story.

Yes I have, but (sad to say) I cannot remember exactly where or when. In 1940 I was seven years old and living in Michigan, so it's possible that I heard it at about the same time Grover did. The drilling of the wispy wire was also the climax of the version I recall, although I remember nothing about a velvet-lined box, a courier, or a glass of schnapps. To the best of my recollection, the foreign manufacturer who ordered the sample was in Japan rather than Germany.

Thinking about the story now, I wonder if its ancestor isn't the one about Robin Hood shooting an arrow into the shaft of his rival's arrow sticking in the bull's-eye of the target, a feat allegedly repeated with a rifle or six-shooter by various American frontier heroes who fired one bullet through the hole left by another.

After I wrote a column about the "Wispy Wire" version of "The Technology Contest" legend, asking readers to send me variations. I received five responses, all different.

Bob Spack of Hendersonville, North Carolina, wrote saying that in 1943 he heard the wire story told about a "peacock proud" Swedish steel company. They shipped their finest wire sample to a Swiss watch company on request. The wire was returned—from one neutral country to another, in this case— with several holes drilled through it.

The version sent to me by Stanley G. Thomas of Burlingame, California, also mentions a Swiss company. This time an American tool manufacturer sent a sample of a drill with a remarkably small diameter to a well-known Swiss watch manufacturer. The Swiss shipped the bit back with a hole drilled through its shank.

Clifton E. Davis of Worthington, Ohio, wrote that he remembered the story from his junior high school days and believed it had circulated before World War II. As he heard it, the Americans sent a sample of their best extremely thin wire to Germany where technicians drilled a hole through it lengthwise. Then the same piece of wire was sent to the Japanese who demonstrated their skill by reaming out the hole even further.

The way Charles A. Mencio, an industrial design consultant in San Antonio, Texas, heard it, a German company requested a sample of American industry's precision engineering. The U.S. company responded with "a mated machine screw and nut so fine that it could only be distinguished as such through powerful magnification." The Germans topped this, "by drilling the screw, castellating the nut, and inserting a tiny cotter pin."

Not only does this version contain the three-part punch line of a typical folktale, but it introduces the technical term "castellate" (having a notched profile, like a castle's battlements). I checked with a hardware store, and found that "castle nuts" do have little battlements all around one edge, through which a cotter pin might be inserted if the screw's shaft were drilled.

My fifth version of the story came from James R. Hopkins of Mt. Vernon, Ohio, and features Queen Victoria. Supposedly Her Majesty sent gifts to a new emperor of China; among them were a very delicate English vase and the finest (thinnest) sewing needle ever manufactured in Britain. The new ruler sent back to her a group of gifts manufactured in China, including an even more delicate vase. Inside was the English needle, now completely hollowed out.

I've located another possible prototype for "The Technology Contest"—a legend about a contest in lifelike painting. One artist challenges another to show his skill in depicting reality. The second artist paints a highly lifelike portrait of a saint, adding a picture of a fly to the saint's nose. As the first artist views the work, he reaches out and tries to brush the fly from the canvas—and thus loses the contest. In other versions, an artist paints a mare so lifelike that it deceives a stallion, or paints grapes so realistic that they attract birds.

But the second artist wins the challenge by painting a curtain on the canvas on his easel that is so realistic that the first artist reaches out and tries to remove it, intending to inspect the painting underneath.

"Give Me a High Three"

Eugene L. Davis, an engineer in Houston, Texas, has the instincts of a folklorist, and some pretty good stories to tell too. He sent me five examples of his favorite yarns, with details of their variations, plus the times and places in which he heard them.

My favorite of the legends in his letter was "The Sawed-off Fingers," or "Give Me a High Three," as I've dubbed it, a grisly little fable about industrial safety.

Davis remembers that he first heard the story in 1945. It was told by a fellow Navy man about his family's business, a mirror factory in Louisiana. The story went like this:

A man operated a band saw in our woodworking mill, and one time he accidentally severed two fingers on one hand. After recovering, since the loss of fingers did not affect his performance, he returned to work on the same machine and was there for many years without another accident.

One day the manager brought some family friends on a tour of the mill, and one of the visitors was an attractive woman. She ooohed and aaahed at everything she saw.

When the visitors came to the band saw station, the blonde moved in for a closer look, and she noticed the man's missing fingers.

She asked the man how his accident had happened. "Like this," he replied, and he promptly cut off two more fingers.

Mr. Davis speculates whether the safety lesson—keep your mind on your work when operating dangerous machinery—is the reason for the story's survival. I think that's likely, but the story may also reflect an old taboo against women entering men's work places. In the old days, women often weren't allowed to go on merchant ships or down in mines. Conditions were thought to be too much for them, and besides, they might distract the workers.

At any rate, Davis heard the story told three more times in varying circumstances over the next forty-four years.

The second time was in 1959 when he was a graduate student at Georgia Tech in Atlanta. The sawed-off finger incident was told by a fellow student, who said it had occurred at a furniture factory in south Georgia.

Then in 1975, when Davis was employed at the Johnson Space Center in Houston, a colleague told him that the sawed-off finger incident had happened at a local factory. The wife of the man who told the story worked as a secretary there.

In January 1989, Davis heard the story again, this time from his son-in-law, who said it was "just a joke that was making the rounds" at *his* factory. Now the victim was a refrigeration mechanic who reacted to a female trainee's question by losing another finger in a compressor.

I'm glad that this Texan wrote me such a long and engaging letter, since by doing so he gives me the opportunity to relate my own version of "The Sawed-off Fingers."

The way I heard the story many years ago, it was a Swedish-dialect story. It was probably recited to me by one of my Norwegian relatives with a lot of side comments about "dumb Swedes."

It seems that this Swedish worker in a lumber mill pushed a piece of wood too far forward while sawing one day, and he sliced one of his fingers clean off.

"How in the world did you manage to do that, Ole?" asked a coworker.

"Oh, it vus easy," Ole said. "I yust pushed it in, like dis, and—voops! der goes anudder vun!"

Swedes, I am sure, will know the same story as a Norwegian-dialect joke, and it probably has other variations as well.

As a folklorist, I expect such alterations in detail as such stories circulate. But before I heard from Eugene Davis I didn't know that "The Sawed-off Fingers" is also told to underscore a safety message in factories.

After the above column was published, I received this additional version from Mary Powell of New Braunfels, Texas:

"I first heard a variation of that story from my grandfather. The incident, told as true, took place on a farm in Indiana sometime before 1920. It seems a simple farmhand had been careless with a posthole digger and had cut off two toes. When asked about his accident, he did it again. There didn't seem to be any safety message that I recall, only gales of laughter about just how dumb human beings can get."

A Dirt-Cheap Way of Selling Real Estate

If you're trying to sell your house and it's been on the market or months, sometimes it seems that only a miracle can help. And that's exactly what many home sellers have been hoping to induce lately, by burying a statue of St. Joseph in the yard.

Believe it or not, many happy people around the country claim that this odd little ritual has actually helped them to sell a long-listed piece of property.

I first read about the practice in an article that appeared September 29, 1990, in the *Dallas Morning News* headlined "If you need a miracle . . . St. Joseph gives home sellers a prayer in locating a buyer."

The writer, Bill Marvel, alluded to "a recent *Wall Street Journal* article" on the topic, which I haven't been able to locate. He also quoted a local merchant who said, "This came out of Chicago."

Evidently, the practice of burying a statue of St. Joseph to ensure the marketability of a piece of property is fairly well known. But I'm not aware of anything like it in standard folklore references.

However, I've received two further newspaper articles about similar practices in Iowa and Pennsylvania, and I've located two reprints of news articles reporting the practice from Washington, D.C., and Atlanta.

The Dallas report summarizes local variants. Some people say the statue must be buried upside down in the front yard. Others claim it should be right side up. Still others say it should be lying on its back and pointing toward the house "like an arrow," or that it should be facing toward the house, or even that it should be buried in the backyard, usually in a flower bed.

It's typical of folk tradition that almost every possible variation on the basic theme exists somewhere.

No matter how the statue of St. Joseph is interred, folks in Dallas agree on what should be done after the property sells: "The grateful seller must dig up the statue and display it on the mantle or some other place of honor."

A local manager of a religious supplies store is quoted saying that she stocks two kinds of St. Joseph statues, a regular $41 devotional model, and a cheaper model, "the burying kind"— three inches tall, plastic, imported, 75 cents.

A Catholic church spokesperson commented, "The practice verges on superstition."

The second news story I received about the miracle-inducing statue appeared in the *Cedar Rapids* (Iowa) *Gazette* on October 14th. This report, by Rick Smith, advises "burying the statue head down, feet pointing toward heaven."

Here, too, after the property sells, the statue is supposed to be dug up and displayed in the seller's new home. The article contains testimonials from local people about the ritual's success, using the $2.25 plastic statues available from religious suppliers there.

One Cedar Rapids person claimed that when a St. Joseph statue was buried facing the street, a house across from it soon sold, and it wasn't even listed for sale at the time!

Iowa folk quoted in the article also mention St. Louis and Philadelphia as places where saint-burying is supposedly practiced by hopeful home sellers. A local Catholic church official commented, cautiously, "It's almost like a superstition-type thing . . . but that's probably a prejudicial judgment on my part."

My third report of the ritual comes from Harrisburg, Pennsylvania. It appeared in the October 28th edition of the *Sunday Patriot-News*. The article, by Jennifer Danner, was headlined "Home Sellers Bury St. Joseph for Luck."

Similar variations on the theme are reported: statue buried head down, head up, front yard, backyard, facing in, facing out, and so forth. Like the other two articles, the story quotes both

Catholics and non-Catholics who have tried the procedure and have sold or not sold houses, as well as Catholic officials who affirm that burying a statue of St. Joseph carries no official sanction.

"It seems to me to be an act of superstition," said Father T. Ronald Haney, secretary of communications for the Catholic Diocese of Harrisburg.

In Harrisburg, the burying kind of statue costs "about a dollar at The Catholic Shop on Second Street, where business has been brisk."

On November 15th, as reported in *Skeptical Inquirer* (vol. 15, no. 3, Spring 1991, p. 237) the *Washington Post* carried a report about burying a saint Joseph statue: "Be sure the saint's head is pointing toward the street, and don't dig up the figurine until after you've closed the deal."

One local agent was quoted in the article as saying that she kept a box of St. Joseph statuettes under her desk. But the National Board of Realtors "failed to return a telephone call inquiring about its opinion concerning the efficacy of the statue ploy."

Finally, *The American Folklore Society Newsletter* (vol. 20, no. 3, June 1991, p. 1) noted that on December 23rd an article on saint-burying appeared in the Atlanta *Journal and Constitution*. The article specified that the statue should be buried upside down and next to the For Sale sign. As in Washington, the report from Atlanta claimed that some agents "have begun laying in private stocks to distribute among selected clients."

By the end of the year, the practice had made it into a reference book. In chapter 11, "Garden Ornaments," of Steve Ettlinger's *The Complete Illustrated Guide to Everything Sold in Garden Centers (Except the Plants)*, published in 1990 (New York: Macmillan, p. 319), under the heading "St. Joseph," we find, "Patron saint of workers and families. Also, sometimes buried in the front lawn of a house that is proving difficult to sell in order to find a buyer."

Personally, if I had a house on the market, I'd try a different surefire method of moving it. Just put a Sold sign on your lawn, and soon potential buyers will start calling to see if the sale really went through.

Tales from the Greenroom
_____

Most people outside the entertainment industry have probably only heard of "the greenroom" through guests' remarks on television talk shows. For example, Tony Randall may say to Jay Leno—or, until recently, Johnny Carson—"As I was listening to your monologue back in the greenroom it reminded me of . . ." or "We were talking back in the greenroom about . . . ," and so forth. I don't remember Johnny ever asking Tony, or anyone else, to explain "greenroom," because the word belongs to a professional lingo that the regulars understand. From such offhand comments, viewers at home may get a vague idea of a waiting room decorated in shades of green. Occasionally, during a studio tour, or when David Letterman goes backstage, followed by a cameraman, we may get a glimpse of the greenroom itself.

But have you noticed that the greenroom is almost never green? I've been in dozens of greenrooms. Every TV studio has one, and many have a sign saying Greenroom on the door. But these rooms are never, as I recall, painted green. For that reason I always ask a technician, a producer, or a guide, "Why do you call this room the greenroom?"

"Oh," I've been told repeatedly, "that's because green is a very restful color," or "green is restful to the eyes after being exposed to the bright lights on the set."

When I point out that the room isn't green, they may say, "Well, it used to be green" or "The waiting room in our old studio was painted green, so we still call it that."

If green is such a restful hue, I wonder why more greenrooms aren't repainted. Maybe institutional beige, the usual waiting-room color, is also a very restful color.

Veteran television pros may tell a different story, such as,

"Calling this the greenroom is an old theatrical tradition." Some TV folk say that a famous London theater originally had a green waiting room, but they're never sure exactly which theater it was or why it was painted green.

Hearing these greenroom tales, I did what any English professor would—looked up the word in the standard historical dictionary for the English language called *The Oxford English Dictionary* (or the OED). I found ten quotations, the earliest being from the year 1701:

"I do know London pretty well, and the Side-box, Sir, and behind the Scenes; ay, and the Green-Room, and all the Girls and Women-Actresses there."

Another quotation from England, dated 1736, described "most of the players drinking tea in the Green-room." Nowadays, the waiting-room scene in television studios is similar, but with coffee and soft drinks added to the menu.

In 1823 the American author Washington Irving described one of his characters as "a green-room veteran [who has] written for the London theatre." The OED also quotes an 1887 reference to "actors' gossip and green-room whispers."

When I showed these "greenroom" references to my wife, she said, "Why isn't Jane Austen's use of the word listed?" She got out her well-read copy of Austen's 1814 novel *Mansfield Park* and showed me the passage in which a group of young people plan an amateur home theatrical. One of them says, "And my father's room will be an excellent green-room."

So the word "greenroom" ("green-room" later lost its hyphen) has a history, but how did the word originate? There are several theories, but none has been proven, as columnist William Safire learned when he wrote a *New York Times* column about the greenroom, which was so named, he assumed, because of "the guest-relaxing color on its walls."

One reader assured Safire that the stage waiting area was originally called the "attiring room," or "tiring room," until shrubbery for stage decoration was stored in one. Then it became known as the "greens room" and later the "green-room."

Another reader wrote to Safire saying that green cloth was so widely used in English theaters on curtains, costumes, and even the audience seats, that it became associated with every part of the building. Other explanations, though plausible, were equally unverifiable, and Safire was forced to conclude that "the reason for the name remains obscure."

The suggested etymology in the OED is short, sweet and just as vague as any other I've seen. The dictionary says that the greenroom is "probably so called because it was originally painted green."

I suspect that's as close as we'll get to explaining these greenroom tales.

The Modem Tax Rumor

An electronic message that has been showing up on countless computer screens lately is headlined Mobilize!, and it's calculated to strike fear into the heart of every computer user who reads it. Widely distributed via electronic mail and computer bulletin boards, the message itself begins:

"Two years ago the FCC tried, and (with your help and letters of protest) *failed*, to institute regulations that would impose additional costs on modem users for data communications. Now they are at it again."

The warning then claims that "The FCC proposes that users of modems should pay extra charges for use of the public telephone network which carry their data. In addition, computer network services . . . would be charged as much as $6.00 per hour per user for use of the public telephone network."

Actually, a proposed surcharge on data transmission was rejected by the FCC back in 1988. But the scare-notice urging users to join the campaign opposing the plan refuses to die. Three years after the scheme was scrapped, the superfluous appeal is still being circulated.

In summer 1991, the warning raced through information networks that are widely used by university librarians—until a few savvy library folk spotted the false story and debunked it on the same nets. I won't mention any names, because some of my best friends, and a few family members, are librarians, some of whom were temporarily impressed by the story. (You know who you are!)

Anyone who relies on computers for communication with professional colleagues would understandably be concerned, since modems are the devices that "MOdulate and DEModulate" computer signals so they can be transmitted over the phone lines. (Please don't expect me to explain how modems work, though!)

Although the proposal was popularly called "the modem tax," in reality the idea was to impose a surcharge on using telephone lines to carry computer data. The plan was killed, as explained in a *Wall Street Journal* article on March 17, 1988, after "computer users around the country deluged the FCC with 10,000 letters opposing access fees, the most letters the agency has ever gotten on a telephone issue."

Fine and dandy—the voice of the people was heard. Now if only the people would realize that the issue has been settled, and would quit sending angry letters about it to Washington.

The memo urging people to mobilize against the modem tax has contained virtually the same text since it appeared in 1987, the year the surcharge was proposed. The notice summarizes the proposal, provides the text of a suitable protest letter, and lists three government agencies where signed copies of the letter should be sent. Those letters are still pouring in to the FCC and to the chairs of House and Senate subcommittees on communication.

That's understandable, since the message concludes with a challenge that's hard to resist: "Make it clear that we will not stand for any government restriction of the free exchange of information!"

The good news is that many people who regularly read computer bulletin boards and network newsgroups have been quick to debunk the modem tax story. Almost as fast as the mobilization notice appears on the wires, other computer buffs reply with comments such as "Cripes! This again?" and "This rumor is false!"

Often they post copies of the *Wall Street Journal* article, or punch holes in the logic of the memo. One hacker also checked out a piece of supposed verification that appears in the warning message, and he found it wanting.

Nearly all copies of the modem-tax message name a talk

show host on KGO radio in San Francisco who supposedly sounded the alarm about the new regulation and compiled the addresses to whom people should protest. But when a computer user got curious and called KGO, he learned that the discussion about the issue had been broadcast several years ago. Nobody at the station could remember the exact date or content of the program.

But once a rumor gets into print—or, in this case, into a computer bulletin board—it's very hard to kill.

Log-on Lingo and Other Net Takes

Even when I'm on the job writing about urban legends I've researched, a distinctive form of occupational folklore emerges right on my computer screen. A typical day in my life as an urban legend researcher may begin like this.

After breakfast I stroll into my study, set my second cup of coffee on the desk, turn on my computer and modem, and dial up the university's computer to see what's new on the net.

Net is short for network, and computer networks are simply electronic bulletin boards and mailing systems by which users can communicate with each other. Usually I glance first at the latest postings to two USENET groups called "alt.folklore.urban" and "alt.folklore.computers."

I've learned that you pronounce those periods in the net names as the word "dot"—it's "alt dot folklore dot urban," etc. Through browsing on the net, I've also become aware of how many computer users in business, industry, and academe are fascinated with the folklore of modern life.

On an average day there may be dozens of comments posted about subjects as diverse as birds supposedly exploding after eating rice thrown at weddings, contact lenses fused to corneas from effects of arc welding, and the Procter and Gamble logo as an alleged satanic symbol.

Favorite topics on the computer folklore newsgroup are stupid user stories, the oldest hardware still in use, the computer system with the most blinking lights, and nominations for the worst computer operating system ever designed.

Each question or example draws many responses from other readers, some of them living abroad, who share variations of the stories they've heard or give information to validate or debunk them.

Actually, not all of this material is folklore, strictly speaking.

But it's all slightly offbeat, and most of it is very interesting. I'm hooked on USENET newsgroups, though I seldom post messages of my own. (I get enough snailmail [see below] as it is.)

The computerized conversations within this modern folk group tend to use acronyms familiar to many hackers. For example, IMHO means "In my humble opinion," BTW means "by the way," and RTM (which has an off-color variation, RTFM) means "read the manual."

Readers often provide *e-mail* (electronic mail) addresses for follow-up information, but they sometimes refer to regular mail as *snailmail.* A discussion of possible backwards masking on rock recordings was headed *gniksam sdrawkcab,* and evidently everyone understood.

Also common is the ubiquitous sideways-turned smiley face of computer messages :-) with its "winking" variation ;-) and its variation showing a wearer of eyeglasses 8 -). Net readers have adopted the term *urban legend* enthusiastically, as well as FOAF (friend of a friend).

Perhaps an explanation of other terminology is in order:

"Alt" stands for alternate and refers to a large group of topics assigned by the net to rather informal electronic chitchat, as opposed to the more serious newsgroup topics that seem to cover every conceivable scientific and academic topic.

USENET is described in my university's computer center info sheet as "an electronic Bulletin Board System (BBS) that lets you subscribe to a wide variety of information categories, reply to articles written by others, and compose and submit your own articles."

For my purposes, "alt.folklore.urban" and "alt.folklore.computers" provide the best research service when the USENET community gets into an extended exchange of variations on a theme. For example, the "stupid user" topic elicited an amazing array of tales about misunderstood computer instructions, misused equipment, and mangled disks resulting from folding, disassembly, magnetization, or just shoving them into the wrong slot. Most of these stories seemed to come from hearsay rather than personal experience.

After one net reader asked about the "professional party school" rumor, a flood of responses arrived. The original note mentioned a rumor that a survey—supposedly published in *Playboy*—of the best colleges for partying had not listed the University of Wisconsin because "we don't rank professionals."

But other readers had heard the same story told about the Universities of Florida, Maryland, Kentucky, and Virginia as well as Boston College, Ohio University, Villanova, and West Virginia University. (I also have the University of Pennsylvania and Gonzaga University named in my own files as being the supposed "professional party school.")

The last time I checked the newsgroup, the list was still growing, and new topics appear almost daily.

5

Fun and Games

"Built in a Day"

A student in one of my recent American Folklore classes, Jennifer Shaw of Salt Lake City, proudly showed me her letter that was published in the August 1987 issue of the fashion magazine *TAXI.* Good for her! She had spotted an urban legend even before she studied folklore.

In the December 1986 issue of *TAXI,* the editor had told a story heard in Milan, Italy, from a taxi driver (which seems appropriate!). "Whether true or not," the editor wrote, "it's not bad."

The cabby claimed to have driven an American fashion buyer around the city to view the architectural highlights. At each one, the American asked how long it had taken to build; and the cabby said "two years," "three years," or whatever.

Each time the American would scoff, commenting, "Well, in the States we would have had that building up in two months (or three months, or whatever)."

Then the cab arrived at the Piazza del Duomo, where the magnificent cathedral of Milan caught the American's eye. "Now that is really beautiful!" he said, "How long did it take to build that?"

Exasperated, the cabby cracked, "For heaven's sake. It wasn't there yesterday!"

Jennifer Shaw wasn't fooled by that story, because she had heard a variation in one of her Italian classes here at the University of Utah. As she explained in her letter to the editor, her Italian professor had told it about a cab driver in Rome talking to a passenger from Texas.

In this Roman variation, the monumental buildings that caught the tourist's eye were the Pantheon, St. Peter's Basilica, and the Colosseum.

TAXI's editors admitted that the same story had gone the rounds of other countries. In a note following Shaw's letter they mentioned that when it was told in Paris, the landmarks were Notre Dame, the Louvre, and the Eiffel Tower.

Dr. Bengt Holbek of the University of Copenhagen Institute of Folklore wrote me:

I read that story many years ago in a collection of anecdotes from Scotland. It was about Edinburgh, and the actors were a bragging American and a Scottish taxi driver. I don't recall the first two famous buildings, but when they got to the Firth of Forth Bridge, the American asked "What's that?" The driver replied, "I don't know. It wasn't there this morning."
But is this an urban legend?

My reply: "It's probably more of a joke than a legend, but it's certainly urban."

A second northern European example appears in an article titled "Tales of America" by Knut Djupedal of the Norwegian Emigrant Museum in Hamar, Norway. (See *Western Folklore*, vol. 49, 1990, pp. 177–89.) This version, Djupedal writes, was told after he had once talked at some length at a party about his years in America:

There was a returned emigrant on the morning train from Bergen to Oslo. All day he talked to anyone who would listen about how wonderful things were in America, how much bigger everything was, and particularly, how quickly things got done over there. The train was so slow he said, and he let the conductor know, time after time, that things moved faster in America.

A few days later, the returnee was on the afternoon train from Oslo to Bergen, with the same conductor. As they were passing the town of Hønefoss, the emigrant asked the conductor, "What town is that?"

"I don't know," said the conductor. "It wasn't there this morning when we came from Bergen."

In a footnote, Djupedal adds:

I have heard exactly the same story told about an American tourist in Paris and his cab driver. After spending the whole day complaining about the speed with which the French finish their national treasures ("It's been 800 years and you haven't finished that cathedral yet?") the American finally sees the Eiffel tower and asks, "What's that?"

"I don't know," answers the cabby. "It wasn't there yesterday."

This story was told to me by Russell Boyer in October 1989. I was telling him my story, and when I neared the end, he stopped me with: "Don't tell me. Is the punch line, 'I don't know, it wasn't there yesterday?'" One wonders if this is a generic "American Abroad" joke.

My reply: OK, OK, I've admitted that it's a *joke* not a legend. Mark Twain was one of the godfathers of this brand of guide-baiting humor. In his best-seller of 1869, *Innocents Abroad*, Twain recounted several stories about American tourists who irritated their European and Middle Eastern guides.

His closest example to the "Built in a Day" story concerned the signature of Christopher Columbus, shown by a guide to members of Twain's party in Genoa. After scrutinizing the document, one traveler said to the guide, "I have seen boys in America only fourteen years old that could write better than that."

But we needn't go so far afield for a variation of the cabby's

story. Right here in Salt Lake City it's told about J. Golden
Kimball (1853–1938), a Latter-day Saints (Mormon) leader famous for his quick wit and salty speech.

According to the legend, J. Golden was showing some foreign dignitaries around the city, pointing out various imposing
structures that the Mormons had built. At each stop the visitors
would claim that in their country, people could have erected
the same building in half the time.

Kimball became angry at these put-downs, and when the
visitors noticed the big Latter-day Saints temple and asked
what that building was, the church leader scratched his head
and replied in his trademark high squeaky voice, "Damned if I
know. It wasn't there yesterday."

A footnote to this story: When I looked up the Kimball anecdote
in Thomas E. Cheney's authoritative collection of J. Golden
stories, *The Golden Legacy: A Folk History of J. Golden Kimball* (Salt
Lake City: Peregrine Smith, 1974), I found it credited to—of all
people—me! I'm not even a Mormon, and I didn't move to Salt
Lake City until 1966.

Have I become a source of folklore, not merely a collector?
Well, not quite. You see, Cheney did get the story from my files,
it's true, but a quick check there showed that I had heard it in
1967, from . . . of course, another student.

Where would I be without my students?

Tour Guide Stories

On the tour buses passing by former president Richard Nixon's beachfront property in San Clemente, California, the guides tell a funny story that they swear is true. I strongly doubt that the reported incident really happened, and so does Bryan Crimin of Layton, Utah, who heard it told recently.

This beautiful San Clemente beach, the tour guides say, was very popular with the local surfers, but during Nixon's presidency his portion of the shoreline was designated off-limits to the public.

Some evenings, the president liked to swim in the ocean by himself, and on one occasion he got caught in some big swells and was in danger of drowning. His cries for help were heard by two local surfers who were trespassing on the off-limits area, and they rushed over and were able to save a very grateful President Nixon.

The president told the surfers that he would repay them by granting each one any wish that was within his power to make come true.

The first surfer asked that the beach property be opened again to the public so everyone could enjoy it, and Nixon granted that wish at once.

The second surfer asked if he could have a burial plot for himself in Arlington National Cemetery. The president thought about this for a moment, and then said he thought it could be arranged. But he asked the young man why he had made such an unusual request.

"Because," the surfer replied, "when my father finds out that I saved Richard Nixon, he's gonna kill me!"

A great story, but its basis in fact seems suspect. Why were Nixon's Secret Service bodyguards not standing by during the president's solitary swims? And why did no journalist ever report the dramatic incident? Also, that wish-come-true line sounds like it was borrowed from a fairy tale.

But, as Mr. Crimin wrote to me, "When I challenged the guide about the story, he swore it was true. He had related it to thousands of tourists over the years."

I wonder if Utah tourists are extra skeptical of tour guides' "true" stories, since we have several popular but doubtful tales constantly circulating in our state.

The favorite local legend tells how Mormon leader Brigham Young, though weak from a bout with mountain fever, sat up in his wagon and spoke four simple but eloquent words when he looked over the Salt Lake Valley as the pioneer party entered the region on July 24, 1847. "This is the place!" are the words he spoke, according to the legend as well as a twentieth-century Utah folksong. An impressive This Is the Place monument and visitors' center stands at the spot where church president Young supposedly spoke the historic sentence, and every tour guide repeats some version of the story.

But no such statement by Young appears in contemporary accounts. The first published report of it many years later reads "This is the right place. Drive on."

The real nature of the "truth" lying behind historical legends is that even if the famous person did not say exactly what our favorite stories claim, then at least it's what that person *should* have said on the occasion.

The same idea applies to pioneer Ebeneezer Bryce, for whom Utah's Bryce Canyon National Park is named. Tour guides and park brochures relate that Bryce's first remark upon discovering this wild area full of convoluted rock formations was "That would be a hell of a place to lose a cow!"

If he didn't say it, he should have! But the same remark is credited to other pioneers gazing at different stretches of rough terrain in several other western states, and the comment really is appropriate, if not literally true, for each region.

The best recent Utah tour guide story, I think, turns the tables on a naive visitor who expects the Latter-day Saints to have horns or to be dressed in some kind of dark conservative sectarian costume.

This tourist, according to the story, asks the guide as he boards a tour bus, "When we're on this tour, would you please point out to us one of those awful Mormons?"

And the guide, without a word, smiles and points to himself.

Note: Maybe these "recent" tour stories are not so recent after all. Following the publication of the above column, I heard from two readers who knew earlier versions.

Professor W. Edson Richmond of Indiana University wrote that he had heard the "My Father's Gonna Kill Me" story told repeatedly about Finland's president Urho Kekkonen when Richmond was living in Helsinki in 1959 and 1960. The only difference was that President Kekkonen was said to be ice-skating off his shoreline property just outside Helsinki on the Gulf of Finland when he fell through the ice and was rescued by two boys skating there illegally.

Pleasance F. Skinner of Salt Lake City wrote telling how she used the "I'm a Mormon" line in 1943 after driving four businessmen around the city before they boarded their Pullman car heading for the East. After listening to their banter about how easy it was to recognize Mormons by their wild eyes, weird manner of speaking, etc., Skinner introduced herself to the businessmen thus as she let them off at the train station, "I'm Pleasance Furse Skinner, better known as 'Jackie.' I was born of Mormon parents, was baptised a Mormon when I was eight, and am still a Mormon. Please come and visit our city again, since I'd love to tell you more!"

One final word on Utah "legends." On July 4, 1991, the *Salt Lake Tribune* carried a front-page story about misinformation passed on by tour guides in Utah's state capitol. Among other things, the guides have been telling tourists that the Great Salt Lake is saltier than the Dead Sea, that Ogden is Utah's second largest city, and that State Street in Salt Lake City is "the longest, straightest street in the world."

The facts, said the *Tribune*, are these: Ogden is the fifth largest city in Utah (West Valley City is Number Two), the Dead Sea is saltier than the Great Salt Lake, and there's no definitive data on length and straightness of city streets.

Golf Stories

Dear Professor:

My husband and I are golfers, and we know lots of golf stories. Like the one about the player who, on a par-three water hole, hits repeatedly into the water and finally throws his bag in the water and storms off.

Fifteen minutes later he sheepishly returns, fishes out his bag, gets his car keys from the zippered pocket, and returns his bag to the water.

How many times have you heard this told? Do you know any golf legends?

> *Mary Powell*
> *New Braunfels, Texas*

"Dear Mrs. Powell," I replied, "I'm not a golfer, but I love your story, which I've *never* heard before. I suppose it's just the kind of anecdote that duffers must tell as true stories at the nineteenth hole."

The only bit of golf folklore I could think of was just a rumor, not a legend. It was the notion we all heard as kids that if you hammered a nail into a golf ball or cut the ball apart, it would explode. Sometimes kids referred to "Atomic Golf Balls" as the kind with the potential for the biggest blast, though I've never heard of this brand of ball.

A good debunking (sounds like a golf term, doesn't it?) of the exploding golf ball rumor is found in Hal Morgan and Kerry Tucker's book *Rumor!* (New York: Penguin Books, 1984, pp. 37–38). In the version they heard, every golf ball contains an explosive ingredient. Sometimes the fluid inside the ball is a strong acid that could blind a person, or it's simply a gob of honey or Karo syrup.

Some people fear that their pet dogs will die if they chew a golf ball apart and swallow the liquid center. However, representatives of the golf ball industry told Morgan and Tucker that over the years the fluids used inside golf balls have included a mild oil, a saline solution, or glycerine, but never an explosive or poison.

Eventually I heard other golfers tell the lost-keys story, and then I received a new golf story in a note from Jim Jones of La Jolla, California. Jones had heard the following as part of a pep talk he attended for teachers, from a woman promoting the values of positive visualization:

"An American serviceman, an avid golfer, was taken prisoner during the Viet Nam War and subjected to ghastly, inhumane conditions. While many of his fellow prisoners suffered grave emotional disorders and mental breakdowns, he was able to cope with the misery of his existence by visualizing eighteen holes of golf every day.

"He visualized all the drives, the putts, the fairways, and the greens. As he imagined himself playing each daily round, he kept refining his game.

"When the POW was eventually released, back home one of the first things he did was grab his golf clubs and head for the course.

"He played the best round of his life!"

I didn't recognize this story either, and I began to think I ought to take up golf to keep abreast of such tales. But when I mentioned it in class, a student of mine remembered reading it in an inspirational book called *One Minute Messages* (Salt Lake City: Sunrise Publishing, 1986), by Dan Clark and Michael Gale. Clark turned out to be another student of mine whose name I'd forgotten, though he has, since taking my class, become a very successful motivational speaker and consultant. On page 152 in the section called "Practice in Your Mind," Clark identifies the prisoner as "Major Nesmeth." He reports that Nesmeth spent seven years in captivity, and that he shot a 74 the first time he played after his release, even though his best scores previously had been in the low 90s. Clark's source, he informed me, was Zig Ziglar's book *See You at the Top*, but just as I was about to look up that reference, a letter arrived claiming that an account of the same incident had been published in *Reader's Digest*. It seems likely, but so far I haven't found it.

Come to think of it, I do have a great story with a golf ball in it that actually happened to me and my family years ago when we were on a camping trip here in Utah. We had parked our car a hundred yards or so from where we were fishing, a good distance away but still in plain sight on a bank above the stream.

Returning to the car disappointed after a couple of fishless hours, we were further dismayed to find that someone had broken a window on the side of the car facing away from us and stolen some of our food and supplies. Nothing valuable was missing, as we had left most of our gear back at the campground, but we stopped at the nearby Forest Service ranger station to report the incident.

A serious young ranger listened to my account of the incident and wrote it up. As he inspected the car, he spotted a golf ball on the floor.

"Do you play golf?" he asked me.

"No, I don't," I replied.

The ranger carefully picked up the ball, holding it in his handkerchief. "This may be an important clue," he told us. "It looks like the blunt instrument used to break your car window."

It seemed unlikely to me that anyone could break auto safety glass by pounding it with a golf ball, but the ball was pretty beat up, and the ranger seemed sure of himself. I had no recollection of a golf ball being in the car.

As I signed the complaint, my young son tugged at my sleeve.

"Just a minute, Erik," I said. "We're filling out the crime report."

"But Dad. . . ." he said.

"Just a minute, son."

The ranger finished the paperwork and promised to contact us if he apprehended the thieves. After he drove off I turned to my son and asked him what it was he had wanted to say.

"That golf ball, Dad. That's the one the dog always chews on, and she dropped it in the car the last time we took her to the vet."

That story's true, I swear, but it may be on the road to becoming a legend. The last time I heard one of the kids recounting the story, they had the ranger taking fingerprints from the golf ball, the dog whining all night looking for her lost toy, and all of us catching giant trout.

These Creative Tales Age Well

Imagine this scene:

A barbarian swaggers up to the counter at a Burger King. I mean a REAL barbarian who looks as if he just stepped out of the Middle Ages. He's wearing a leather tunic, sandals, a bearskin cape and a war helmet, with dark flashing eyes and a bushy beard. He carries a battle-ax in one hand, and a sword hangs at his side.

He pounds a huge fist on the counter and demands, "Meat!"

The Burger King counter clerk, terrified, asks nervously, "How would you like that, sir?"

The barbarian looks puzzled for a moment, then extracts a coin from his belt pouch, flips it, and squints at it.

"Cooked!" he thunders, as the clerk quickly serves him a stack of burgers.

In a variation of the story, as you might expect, the barbarian orders his meat "Raw!" The incident is attributed to different fast food restaurants in various cities, and it may actually have happened at some time.

These guys are not madmen or movie actors; instead, they're time travelers, in a sense. The explanation is that the barbarian in the Burger King is a member of the Society for Creative Anachronism (SCA), and this is a favorite SCA legend. According to the story, a member dressed as a barbarian, while wearing his full regalia on his way home from a meeting of the group, decides to play a prank.

The SCA, founded at Berkeley, California, in 1966, is devoted to re-creating characters and activities typical of life in the Middle Ages. Members choose a medieval persona and adopt that character's language and lifestyle during SCA events like jousts, tournaments, revels, investitures, and staged battles.

SCAers assume the roles of knights or ladies, royalty or commoners, and they create highly authentic costumes appropriate to their characters. They take names like Queen Carol of Bellatrix, Corwin of Darkwater, Kevin Perigrynne, and, for a barbarian, Erdic Two-Tails of the Hoard.

Supposedly the SCA was investigated by the FBI who confused the word anachronism (time displacement) with anarchism (opposition to all forms of government), and they thought this was a subversive organization.

Most of the legends I've heard about the SCA, like "The Barbarian in the Burger King," describe an SCA member wearing a costume who surprises someone in a modern setting. Another popular story of this type is "The Knife in the Chainmail," which tells of an SCA "knight" wearing realistic armor who has slipped a coat on over his costume. On the street, or in a bus or a subway car, an assailant stabs the disguised knight, unaware of the chain mail. The knife either breaks or becomes stuck in the mail, and the panicked attacker flees.

In a similar story the mugger sneers, "I've got six inches of steel that says you're going to give me all your money." The anachronistic knight pulls his sword from under his coat and replies, "I'll see your six inches and raise you thirty." The mugger flees. A similar scene occurs in the film *Crocodile Dundee* when a New York City mugger threatens the visiting Australian crocodile hunter with a knife. "You call *that* a knife?" Dundee says as he draws his much larger weapon.

Another cycle of SCA stories deals with a woman saved from an attacker by a band of knights in shining armor who rout the enemy, then leave without identifying themselves. In some versions of "The Knights and the Lady" the SCA defenders are mere commoners armed only with quarterstaffs. They are subsequently knighted by the ruler of their "kingdom" for their bravery in defending a lady's honor.

The Society for Creative Anachronism is popular with military personnel, and one story is based on that connection. Supposedly when the aircraft carrier USS *Nimitz* was being observed by a Russian spy ship, the SCA group aboard was called into action.

The captain of the *Nimitz*, it is said, ordered all off-duty SCA fighters to don their armor and report to the deck. There they engaged in two hours of fighting practice while the spy ship edged closer and took pictures.

I got all of these SCA stories from a recent exchange on a computer newsgroup devoted to urban folklore. Now that's an anachronism!

Biker Legends

"Some of your urban legends reminds me of biker legends I've heard," Eileen Bradford of Lemon Grove, California, wrote to me. Here's an example:

"The story about Burt Reynolds giving out his credit card number jibes with a tale about Malcolm Forbes at a Harley shop. Supposedly he told everyone his telephone credit-card number so they could make free calls, since he was such a bitchin' biker dude."

Bradford also sent the biker version of "The Bargain Sports Car" legend. She wrote, "This one involves a 1953 Panhead or some similar righteous Harley-Davidson motorcycle advertised in the paper for $100."

According to the story she sent, a reader of the ad can't believe his eyes. He assumes that the figure in the paper has to be a typo, but he responds to the ad anyway, just to check it out. Sure enough, everything is just as the ad stated. The bike is a shiny, chrome-plated beauty, and when he kick-starts it, it runs like a dream."

But it turns out that the guy who owns the bike is in the process of divorcing his wife, the person who placed the ad. He had called and instructed her to sell it and send him the money. And that's exactly what she did.

Bradford added, "I've also heard a version where the husband, son, or brother was killed on a vintage Harley, but the bike survived the death crash with nary a scratch and was sold to an eager biker for a song."

I didn't realize that there were distinctive biker legends like these until Bradford wrote. She, in turn, learned how they fit into the larger category of urban legends when reading my latest book.

Seems like a fair trade to me—story swapping via print and

mail—although it would certainly be more exciting to hear the biker stories firsthand at a Hell's Angels or Sundowners rally.

Bradford's letter surprised me in another way too: It was detailed, witty, neatly typed, and five pages long. Somehow that didn't seem to me to fit the writer's description of herself, "a member of the biker community for years, and married to a biker for the last ten."

What did I expect, a letter scrawled on the back of a beer carton with a bloody finger or an oil dipstick? Shame on me for harboring such a stereotype!

My assumption that all bikers must be crude clods was challenged by yet another of Eileen Bradford's biker legends. She explained, "This one is a variation on your story about the scuzzy hitchhiker and the clean-cut one."

This biker legend involves a storekeeper in Sturgis, South Dakota, during Bike Week which is held there every year in August. Thousands of bikers converge on Sturgis in their annual "run" or "rally." According to the story, when they come in to shop they make the storekeeper nervous.

About 25 long-haired, dirty, dangerous-looking bikers and their women barge into the store, buying truckloads of beer, whiskey, soda, bread, baloney, etc.

The storekeeper is terrified the whole time that they're in his store, but when several clean-cut young jock-types come in, the owner calms down a bit, figuring these all-American youths will protect him from the biker trash.

The bikers pay for their stuff and leave. The storekeeper turns to the college boys and says, "Wow! I'm sure glad they're gone!"

The college kids all holler, "Yeah, so are we!" and they pull out guns, stick up the store, taking all the money that the bikers had just spent.

Another rally legend is about a biker trying to pump gas into his motorcycle while drunk. The bike tips over on top of him, spraying gas all over, and the trapped man calls to the cashier for help.

The cashier, however, just laughs at his predicament and says "You can help yourself, biker trash!"

Supposedly, the downed biker pulls out his cigarette lighter, holds it up, and screams, "I've got nothing to lose, so if you don't pull this bike off me right now I'll blow you, me, and this station to kingdom come."

The cashier hurries to his rescue.

Somehow, I get a bang out of that one!

A BIKER VERSUS A SMOKER

You have to be a very bright North Carolinian to receive M-Blem, which is described on its masthead as "the regular newsletter of Mensa of Eastern North Carolina." Mensa, of course, is the organization for people with unusually high IQs.

Since I don't qualify to subscribe to M-Blem, I would have missed a good tale if John E. Maroney of Chapel Hill, North Carolina, had not sent me a story that was published in the February 1990 issue of the newsletter.

The part of the anecdote that I found so interesting had nothing to do with intelligence; it was about nonsmokers' rights. "This little piece," reported M-Blem concerning the story, "has been around Mensa a few times." The editor, Karen Tiede, wrote that she found the story in 1988 in another Mensa chapter's newsletter where it had been credited to a third such periodical. (The story is told frequently outside of Mensa circles, and I've heard it several times myself.)

The M-Blem version, told in the first person, involves a diner in a restaurant who asks another patron, who is smoking while seated in the no-smoking area, to put out his cigarette. The waiter also prods the smoker either to quit smoking or change tables. The story continues, "Of course he didn't leave until he had finished that cigarette and lit another. But at least he did finally go."

This is where the story takes a surprising turn:

Apparently he had noticed the motorcycle helmet and jacket I was wearing when I came in, because in a minute or so I noticed him eyeing the Harley parked by the front door. He took out a small notebook, wrote something on a leaf from it, tore off the note, and placed it between the seat and the gas tank.

His next action took me completely off guard. He looked straight in the window at me, then put his foot against the gas tank and shoved the motorcycle over on its side. He then spun around and ran smack into a very large bearded fellow, who apparently owned the Harley.

That which ensued netted him at least one broken bone and hopefully at least a little jail time. After the police had come and gone, I helped the bearded gentleman right his bike, and noticed the note the man had left. I unfolded it and read:

"This will teach you to mess with a smoker's rights."

I laughed and handed the note to the cigar-chewing biker. I then went around to the other side of the building, got on my Honda, and went back to work.

The same story has been attributed to restaurants in various cities, so I've heard some variations in the wording of the note. One is, "You mess with my rights, I mess up your bike!"

The general themes of a mistaken identity, an insulting note, and a misdirected attempt at revenge are found in other urban legends, although not together as in this one.

The flip-side of the cycle-revenge ploy is revealed in another story that is told about a trucker who is harrassed by a group of motorcyclists while he's eating lunch at a truck stop. A variation of this one was used in the movie *Smokey and the Bandit* when Jerry Reed's character is roughed up at a southern greasy spoon.

The bullies shake pepper into his chili, steal his french fries, and put salt in his coffee while jeering him. But the trucker calmly finishes his meal, pays his check, and then leaves the café without saying a word.

The bikers laugh uproariously, and one of them says to the waitress with a sneer, "He sure wasn't much of a man, was he?"

The waitress, according to the story, replies "No, and he's not much of a driver either. He just ran his truck over a whole row of motorcycles and crushed them flat!"

It sounds like that trucker may be smart enough to join Mensa.

TWO MORE BIKER LEGENDS

A woman in Los Gatos, California, named Mary Martin sent me the following story that was told to her by a British citizen living in Tucson:

A man was taking a test to get a motorcycle license in England. Part of the test was to see how quickly he could stop in an emergency.

He was told to ride around certain streets and return; the examiner would jump out in front of him unexpectedly, and he was then to stop immediately.

Well, he drove around as directed, and after a while went back past the motor vehicle department expecting to see the examiner waiting for him.

It turned out that the examiner had jumped out in front of the wrong motorcycle and had been taken to hospital with serious injuries.

The Brits call this urban legend "The Unlucky Examination," telling it about both cycle and auto exams. (See, for example, Paul Smith, *The Book of Nasty Legends*, London: Routledge & Kegan Paul, 1983, p. 77.)

Only the phrase "to hospital" betrays the British origin of Martin's version. As the English tell it, you usually get dry understatements like "The driving examiner, you see, had made rather an error."

But to convey the genuine flavor of urban legend style in England, you need an entire text. Here's a similar story quoted verbatim from Rodney Dale's 1978 collection of "modern myths" *The Tumour in the Whale:*

> *A foaf ["friend of a friend," Dale's coinage] had a vintage Austin—mechanically immaculate, but bodywork tatty. Well, he was driving along—outskirts of Nottingham actually— when he was stopped by the police.*
>
> *They had a good look at his car: tyres OK, steering good, lights working, nothing falling off—couldn't find anything wrong.*
>
> *"Right," they said, "We want to test your speedometer and brakes. Drive along at a steady thirty and we'll follow you. Then when we blow our horn, you do an emergency stop."*
>
> *So the foaf did as he was bid, and hearing an almighty blast on the horn stepped on the anchors. There was a most tremendous crash as the police car ran into the back of his Austin.*
>
> *It was, of course, another vehicle which had blown its horn. (Pp. 124–25.)*

Let me contrast that one with a motorcycle story sent by Carl B. Rexroad of Bloomington, Indiana, who heard it "in a barracks sometime during World War II from one of the fellows in our artillery battery."

This was supposed to have happened in the storyteller's hometown to some fellows he knew:

> *These three young men about to be drafted were cruising around town on their motorcycles one evening and they decided to go out on the highway passing through town.*
>
> *Although they were already going at a pretty good clip, one guy really stepped on it and roared out way ahead of the other two.*
>
> *Then he turned around to rejoin them, and as he approached the other two bikers he decided to give them a thrill by riding between them.*
>
> *He veered over into their oncoming lane, but what he*

didn't realize until it was too late was that a truck with its
lights fairly wide apart had passed them.
   He had a funeral rather than a draft call.

   Mr. Rexroad asked me if this is an urban legend.
   My answer: Of course it is!
   Not only have I heard the story before, but I can't believe
that a couple of young bikers out cruising would ever allow a
truck to pass them on the highway.

Generation Gap Lore Moves with the Times

In 1989, the twentieth anniversary year of Woodstock and of man taking his first steps on the moon, I wondered, "Does the generation gap still exist, or is it just a nostalgic memory?" I hadn't heard much about the generation gap lately, except in the form of what sounds like an urban legend alluding to the first moonwalker.

According to the story, two friends got into a conversation with their dinner partners about the generation gap. As a test, one of them turned to some young people dining at the next table and asked, "Do you know who the first man to set foot on the moon was?" And in each case, the young people were said to have answered, "Neil Young."

Joan Golden of Denver passed the story on to me. She heard it from two friends, each of whom swore it was true. The friends' matching stories supposedly occurred when they were dining out, but, Golden noted, "not with each other, not at the same eatery, and not even on the same day." Yet, the two stories are identical, and each teller stuck by it.

How can I say that the story may be a legend, when the tellers say it's true? I need some evidence of wider distribution, variation, and perhaps other stories on the same theme.

I tried asking the same question to several people of different ages, and they either got the answer right (Neil Armstrong), or they made an obvious joke ("I know, Jack Armstrong!") or they simply got confused ("Was it John Glenn?").

But I do have a very similar generation gap story, and it also has a first-person claimant to being true. When I first heard it from readers in Oklahoma and Indiana who had *not* witnessed the incident, I dubbed it "The Youngest Fans":

Two young girls in a record store were browsing through rock albums under the letter *B*. One of them pulled out a Beatles album, turned to her friend, and said, "Oh, look! Paul McCartney was in another band before Wings."

My mention of that story in a column prompted a response from Liz Goudy of Syracuse, New York, who said that nearly the same incident happened to her in a local record store in 1980. She was browsing through the *S*'s looking at Barbra Streisand records. The bin was located near the *W*'s where someone had misfiled a Beatles record next to records by McCartney's group Wings. (That's the kind of specific detail I love to get!) Wings was the band formed by McCartney after the Beatles broke up. Anyway, in Goudy's version it was a young boy who spoke up to his friend, saying, "Look, Paul McCartney was in another band!"

Liz wrote that she was thrilled to have started an urban legend, and I'd like to think she's right. But Steve Allen tells the same story in his book *Dumbth* (Buffalo: Prometheus, 1989, p. 92) and credits it to "Bill Hertz, the magician" who said that he overheard the teenagers in a New York City record store. In any case, I expect someone else to write saying that they heard the same story told earlier, or told about another singer.

Maybe both of these generation gap stories stem from hoaxes. Could young people be going around saying outrageous things just to bug their elders?

I have yet another example of this genre, one that kind of bugged me at the time I collected it. I heard this piece of generation gap lore about twenty-two years ago from my then nine-year-old son who was singing some parodies with a playmate. He sang one real gem, which I tape-recorded on the spot, and subsequently heard in different versions from other kids. It was a set of new words for that old round that schoolkids are taught to sing, either in French as "Frère Jacque, Frère Jacque. Dormez vous? Dormez vous?" or in English as "Are you sleeping? Are you sleeping? Brother John, Brother John. . . ." The kids' version graphically demonstrated a gap between the generation's behaviors. Their words went like this:

Marijuana, Marijuana
LSD, LSD
Scientists make it. Teachers take it.
Why can't we? Why can't we?

It's not exactly an urban legend, but it is a powerful piece of modern folklore!

Messin' with Jazz

Jazz historian Marshall Stearns in his 1956 book, *The Story of Jazz,* begins with a well-known anecdote:

"In reply to the sweet old lady's question, 'What is jazz, Mr. Waller?' the late and great Fats is supposed to have sighed: 'Madam, if you don't know by now, don't mess with it!' "

Jazz pianist Thomas "Fats" Waller, composer of classic songs like "Honeysuckle Rose" and "Ain't Misbehavin'," died in 1943 at the age of thirty-nine. The words "Don't mess with it" fit his effervescent personality perfectly, even though he may never have uttered them.

This story of his clever response circulated during his lifetime, though, and variations have been repeated in jazz histories ever since. For example, Dave Dexter's 1946 book, *Jazz Cavalcade,* gives this version:

"A young woman approached him to ask his definition of jazz. Fats's massive hands struck a discord as he turned to the inquiring dilettante. 'Honey,' said Fats obligingly, 'If you don't know what jazz is by now, then you've got no business messin' with it.' "

As far as I know, the story, which I regard as an urban legend, was never verified by anyone present during the incident. Two jazz histories of the early 1950s disagreed on whether Fats had said "Lady, if you has to ask, you ain't got it!" or "Lady, if you got to ask, forget it, give it up!" A 1959 article in *Downbeat* magazine called it "an oft-told tale," then rephrased Fats's comeback slightly as "Lady, if you don't know, don't mess with it."

Robert Paul Smith, writing in *Saturday Review* in 1966, seemed to know something that other historians didn't. He claimed that he was unable to quote Fats exactly "even in this non-family-type magazine," so he settled for paraphrasing the punch line as "Lady, don't mess with it!"

Apart from writings about jazz, the Fats Waller story has been used to illustrate the general problem of defining the indefinable. In a 1978 London theater review I found this:

"Style is difficult to define, for the same reason Fats Waller gave when someone asked him what swing was—if you got to ask, you ain't got it."

Now the question has become "What is swing?" Fats must have turned over in his grave at that!

Even worse, a rival jazz pianist sometimes gets credit for the witty reply. For example, in a 1959 symposium concerning American leftist politics, one speaker said, "In the words of the late Jelly Roll Morton, 'If you gotta ask what it is—don't mess with it!' "

It appears that the story of the nondefinition of jazz was originally told about Fats Waller; he certainly was the person most often credited with it, even though never with identical wording.

Yet Louis Armstrong eventually became the jazzman most closely associated with the story. Many interviews and feature articles attributed the saying to Satchmo, either giving it as "Lady, if you got to ask, you'll never know" or the familiar "Don't mess with it." So common was the link to Louis that *Time* magazine once captioned a photo of Armstrong, "Don't mess with it," and offered no further explanation.

A different anecdote about a jazz musician appeared in a 1959 *Downbeat* article that was headlined "If you gotta ask. . . ." The story told of a high school student yelling at clarinetist Jimmy Giuffre during one number, "Where's the rhythm?" Giuffre's answer was said to be, "It's understood." The typical mechanism of folkloric variation is illustrated by the fact that when retelling this story I've sometimes inadvertently given the question as "Where's the melody?"

Semanticist and the late U.S. Senator S. I. Hayakawa attached a deeper meaning to the "Don't mess with it" reply. Referring to the Louis Armstrong version, Hayakawa once said (or, at least, so I once read), "It's a beautiful proper non-Aristotelian rebuke to an asker of an Aristotelian nonsense-question."

If you have to ask what that statement means, then don't mess with it.

6

Foreign Relations

Culture Clash Legends

Readers often write me saying that they've been doing as a hobby what I do as a profession—collecting urban legends. Though they're usually unaware of the term "folklorist," that's what they are, nevertheless, and typically they're eager to share stories.

I get some great legends this way!

For example, Robert Goldfarb of Studio City, California, wrote, "Long before I encountered your works and discovered the urban legend, I collected 'true' stories that demanded attribution to be effective and which I had to hear more than once to admit to my collection."

Let's see: Stories that are said to be true, attributed to specific someone or someplace, and told repeatedly. Yes, they're quite likely to be urban legends.

Goldfarb dipped into his collection and sent a column written by the late poet John Ciardi in the November 27, 1965, issue of *Saturday Review*. It began, "The strangest thing happened to a friend of mine. . . ." Ciardi's friend, said the poet's column, "launched his story as a straight account of something that had happened to someone he knew."

In this case, Ciardi was also operating as a folklorist, since he knew the story was a traditional one. He wrote, "Storytellers have become oddly sneaky these days; they think nothing of claiming to know a person to whom the oddest thing happened to happen." In response to being told such allegedly "true stories," Ciardi observed, "We pretend to believe lightly what none of us would be caught believing seriously."

His example was a classic culture-clash legend in which an expression written in a foreign language is misunderstood, with comic results. My dry summary of the gist of the story was a typical professional folklorist's approach; Ciardi's actual example was much more lively.

His friend had told him about a friend of his, whom he described as "a well-designed dress designer who liked to knit." The designer copied some Chinese characters from a menu in a Chinatown restaurant to use as the pattern of a colorful sweater which she then knitted.

Ciardi's friend claimed that this is what happened the first time she wore the sweater:

"Someone (the friend of a friend) who had been brought up in China as the son of a missionary and who had studied Chinese, took one look and let out the guffaw that always comes. The characters, in their well-designed row across the designer's well-designed breast, read: 'This dish cheap but unmistakably good.' "

Goldfarb, Ciardi, and I (plus probably many readers) have heard this story, or others much like it, many times before. But most of us have never met the knitter, nor seen the sweater, nor spoken to the person who provided the translation. We've only met the friend of a friend who said it was a true incident.

Another part-time folklorist wrote to me and sent a different culture-clash story. Dr. Nancy J. Frishberg of the IBM User Interface Institute in Yorktown Heights, New York, wrote, enclosing a clipping from the "Metropolitan Diary" column in the *New York Times* for August 29, 1990.

The item described a foreign student, "unfamiliar with our customs," who was seen to open a tea bag and sprinkle the leaves into hot water. Someone demonstrated for the student how to dip the bag up and down to properly make tea the American way.

Later, the writer claimed, "I noticed an unopened packet of sugar floating in his tea."

But Dr. Frishberg commented, "I've been telling this same story for years, after I heard it from someone who studied at Cornell and who told me it had happened to a well known professor there and a graduate student from India."

In the spirit of modern folklore, I responded with this electronic-mail message:

"Well, Dr. F., the way I heard it—MANY years ago—a group of Americans at an international conference hoaxed some Russians during a tea break by putting their tea bags into their mouths and drinking hot water through them.

"The Russians followed suit, both then and later on at a fancy official reception."

I vaguely recall that this tea bag confusion story used to be told about specific foreign officials attending a formal White House function, but the details escape me.

Did the story go that the president of the United States himself sipped hot water through a tea bag at the reception so as not to embarrass his foreign visitors?

At any rate, a second reader who clipped the *Times* "Metropolitan Diary" torn tea bag, floating sugar-packet story for me also found the incident described in Roger E. Axtell's book *Do's and Taboos of Hosting International Visitors* (John Wiley and Sons, 1990, p. 37). Axtell credits this "true story" to a former marketing executive for the Johnson Wax Company who was hosting a visitor from Pakistan in the company cafeteria.

Refugees Adapt to Life Hmong Strangers

An article by Spencer Sherman in the October 1988 issue of *National Geographic* titled "The Hmong in America" tells how these Southeast Asian people, having come to the United States only recently, are still unfamiliar with western comforts. The Hmong have been mystified by light switches, tried to wash rice in their toilet bowls, and lit cooking fires on their apartment floors.

Herman R. Bininda of Calgary, Alberta, called my attention to the article and suggested that these claims resemble the urban legends often told about refugees thrust into advanced cultures.

Bininda's experience with refugee stories, it turns out, goes back fifty years or more. "I was born before WWII in what is now the Federal Republic of Germany and witnessed the influx of refugees from the former German Provinces of East Prussia, Pomerania, and Silesia," he explained.

"Many of the stories I heard then about refugees are now being echoed in the stories of recent immigrants to North America, such as the Hmong people."

Bininda remembers that some Eastern European refugees, not yet accustomed to Western plumbing, washed potatoes in the toilet bowl. When they moved from refugee centers to permanent homes, they tried to take their light switches with them to provide illumination in their new surroundings.

Supposedly the refugees raised pigs and rabbits in their bathtubs. And Gypsies were said to have made campfires in their apartments, using the floorboards for fuel. While some such incidents may actually have occurred, it seems likely that other reports are merely based on unverified hearsay—rumors and urban legends, that is. The continued telling of similar stories also suggests that their source is folk tradition rather than reality.

Such stories become widespread in any developed country when there is a heavy influx of refugees arriving from less-developed regions. Swedes, for example, tell of Turkish immigrants who grow potatoes in their living rooms. Australians report that aboriginal families, given "a beautiful home" in a city, eventually burnt it all up for firewood.

In England, Pakistanis are the targets of refugee horror stories. In one tale they are said to have rented a single unit in a series of row houses on a London street. Then they burrow through the walls and spread from attic to attic down the row, packing friends and relatives into the confined but habitable (and *free*) living space.

The rightful residents, invariably native British, eventually discover the unwanted foreigners, of course. Either they hear noises coming from the attic, or they smell a terrible odor—the result of unsanitary living conditions, or of a garden that the Pakistanis have planted on the attic floor.

When settlers go the other way—from more advanced cultures to places with a lower standard of living—a reverse form of immigrant story may develop. I got this report from Istanbul:

"Here in Turkey the Japanese are very much admired for their efficiency in business and their wizardly technical achievements. So we have many urban legends about them.

"For example, they are supposed to have developed a special kind of spectacles that show the people around you stark naked. The Japanese are also credited with developing dwarf ponies and even dwarf people—something like the dwarfed trees and shrubs in Japanese gardens."

Do you remember the similar scenes in the film *Star Trek IV* in which advanced visitors from afar had problems coping with "backward" twentieth-century life? In one sequence engineer Scotty tried to give voice directions to a Macintosh computer by speaking into the "mouse" pointing device.

My Mac, on which I'm writing this, shows a smiling face when I turn it on, but it won't obey when I talk to it. At least, not *yet*.

British Travel Troubles

I'm always interested in urban legends that seem unique to a particular region or country, and I've found a couple of beauties that seem distinctively British. These stories concern customs that the English call "day trips" (group holiday excursions of one day's duration) and "mystery trips" (day trips organized by travel agents for clients who are not told where they will be going).

To get the full flavor of a legend called "The Day Trip" you need to hear an Englishman telling it. Here's how they tell it in England, from a book I've quoted before, Rodney Dale's 1978 collection, *The Tumour in the Whale: A Collection of Modern Myths*.

Talking of trippers, a party of Cambridge people on a gasworks outing to Yarmouth had to help one of their number back to the coach because he was helplessly drunk.

On reaching Cambridge, they took him home and put him to bed to sleep it off. When he woke, he was astonished to find himself at home in Cambridge because he hadn't been a member of the coach party but was in the middle of a fortnight's holiday in Yarmouth and had merely fallen in with the crowd of his workmates who happened to be on the works outing.

Meanwhile, his wife [who was with him in Yarmouth] had reported him missing to the police.

In variant versions of this legend, day-trippers from Derby become friendly with a stranger in a pub in Blackpool. When the man passes out drunk, they check his wallet, find his address, bundle him onto the coach, and deliver him to his home in a nearby town.

But it turns out that the man was on his honeymoon. His mother is surprised to find him back on her doorstep in Derby, while the bride, alone in a Blackpool hotel, wonders what has happened to her husband.

Rodney Dale deserves a place in the Urban Legend Hall of Fame, because (as I point out at every opportunity) he coined the term FOAF for friend of a friend, which is the typical source that's credited for legends. Here's how Dale tells the second British travel trouble story, "The Mystery Trip":

"A FOAF and his wife went on holiday [understood: to another town] and thought it would be rather fun to spend a day on an advertised mystery coach trip.

"So they bought tickets and set off in high hopes, only to find that the mystery destination was their home town.

"Rather than paying exorbitant rates for the local food, they decided to pop on home and cook themselves a meal there. But somehow they managed to miss the coach back."

Legends about travel mishaps seem to be a specialty of the English. Here's one more I heard recently from English folklorist Paul Smith:

A man boarded the last train of the day out of London to travel up to Doncaster, but conversing with another passenger he discovered that he was on an express going straight to York.

He decided that if the train slowed down sufficiently at Doncaster, he would try to jump off. Approaching the Doncaster station, the train did slow somewhat, and the man grabbed his bag, jumped to the platform, and ran alongside the train in order to reduce his speed.

But when the following coach caught up with him, another passenger reached out an open door, grabbed his arm, and yanked him back into the train, saying, "You're lucky I saw you running. Don't you know that this train doesn't stop at Doncaster?"

It sounds like something out of Monty Python, but Paul swears it happened to a FOAF. And I know that a fellow folklorist would never lie about a story.

Good on You, Australians

"Practically all the urban legends you write about are current in my part of the world," writes Adrienne Eccles of Unley, South Australia. To prove her point, she sent me four typewritten pages of story texts and synopses. Probably only the cost of international postage restrained her from sending even more stories; for, as my mail shows, Australians love urban legends.

The plots of these versions should be familiar to American legend buffs, for all of them are here as well. But the details differ, and the Aussie style of telling them is inimitable. Here are three of Adrienne Eccles's stories having to do with travel.

"AUNTIE IN HER PANTIES"

A friend's aunt and uncle, of retiring age, were travelling across the Nullarbor Plain, a long dull trip—dead flat—featureless, treeless, uninhabited semi-desert for hundreds of miles.

Uncle was driving, and as the car was not air conditioned, he suggested that his wife might lie down in the caravan [camper-trailer] as they travelled. She stripped off her clothes down to her panties, and slept.

After some hours, Uncle stopped the car and went to relieve himself by the roadside. There was no sign of habitation, and no other traffic. Aunty woke up and decided to do likewise. But uncle, unaware that she was out of the caravan, climbed back into the car and drove off.

So there was Auntie, stranded in the middle of nowhere in her knickers. A young man on a motorcycle came along, travelling in the same direction. He was amazed to see this middle-aged overweight woman in a state of undress by the

roadside, and even more amazed to hear her explanation.
He put her on the pillion seat, and they gave chase. A short
time later, Uncle was astounded to be overtaken by a
motorcycle ridden by a leather-clad bikie and his nearly nude
wife.

In the American versions, it's the husband who's asleep after
a long day of driving. But the Aussie version is more colorful,
don't you think?

"THE WRONG REST STOP"

A semi-trailer driver—a truckie—was taking loads between
Melbourne and Adelaide. Just outside Adelaide the highway
descends a range of hills, including a notorious hairpin bend
called "The Devil's Elbow."
Scattered all through this part of the hills are short uphill
safety ramps where a truck with failed brakes can roll in for an
emergency stop.
One day a truckie was just approaching Eagle on the Hill, a
couple of miles above The Devil's Elbow, when he lost his
brakes. It's a busy road, and he had a full load on board.
Unable to slow down, he careered along, flashing his lights
and blaring the horn, swerving all over the road as he wrestled
with the truck.
Miraculously, he kept on the road, and cars cleared out of
his way. If he could keep the truck upright and get around
The Devil's Elbow, there was a safety ramp a few hundred
yards beyond.
By a miracle, he made it around the bend without rolling
over, and turned the speeding truck off onto the safety ramp.
There, halfway up, was a family having a picnic.

And you thought ants on your picnic blanket were a problem!

"THE BUMPKIN BUYS A CAR"

A well-to-do outback station owner turned up in Adelaide, and, still dressed in his hat, moleskin trousers, and elastic-sided boots, went into a luxury car dealer's to test-drive a Porsche.

The salesman, a young cheeky fellow, thought the customer couldn't possibly have any money, and he decided that here was a country bumpkin who just wanted to have a drive in a smart car.

He allowed the station owner to have the test drive, but could scarcely suppress his mirth and derision when the man said, "Yes, I like it. I'll buy it."

The salesman scoffed, "What do you propose to pay for it with?" and the taciturn gentleman answered, "Cash."

At this, the young salesman burst out laughing. Annoyed, the customer put on his hat and left. He went down the street and bought a Mercedes.

Great storytellers, these Australians! Or, as I learned to say when I visited Down Under, "Good on you!"

MORE ABOUT AUSTRALIAN LEGENDS

When I heard about *The Gucci Kangaroo* I thought it might refer to an expensive stuffed toy, or perhaps a chain of boutiques selling Australian imports. It turned out to be a book of Australian urban legends compiled by Amanda Bishop (Hornsby, NSW: Australasian Publishing Company, 1988). Reading it, I really had a chance to see how similar urban legends from Down Under are to our own. That was not a total surprise, though, since I've reported on several Australian stories in my columns.

The book's title, for example, refers to a story about tourists driving in the outback who hit a kangaroo. Thinking the animal dead, they prop it against a fence and dress it in someone's jacket, intending to take a gag photo.

But the stunned 'roo revives and bounds away with the jacket

THE GUCCI KANGAROO

&

Other Australian Urban Legends

AMANDA BISHOP

Illustration: Peter Fairlie

containing the driver's passport, money, return ticket, etc.

During the 1987 America's Cup competition, which was held in the waters off Perth, in western Australia, a Sydney newspaper reported that this adventure happened to the Gucci-clad crew of the yacht *Italia*.

I've also heard it told about the U.S. crew wearing designer jackets, and earlier the story was told on the Kingston Trio when they were touring Australia.

Bishop traces the story's "50-year transformation from a bush yarn to an urban legend" but doesn't mention that the same story with different animals as tricksters—and with variations on the items stolen—has circulated almost as long here in the States.

"The Gucci Kangaroo" may be an original Australian story that changed as it spread to other countries. Or, Australians may have grafted their "bush yarn" onto a recently imported urban legend told about a different animal that revives and runs for it.

As with most parallel stories, it's difficult to say which came first. For example, "The Animal's Revenge" legend in both the United States and Australia is about a cruel man who ties dynamite to a coyote, rabbit, or dingo dog.

The prank always backfires when the man lights the fuse, releases the animal and it runs under the man's house or camper, destroying it. Australian author Henry Lawson used that legend in his 1899 short story called "The Loaded Dog," and Jack London told a slightly different version in his 1902 story titled "Moon-Face."

All of these tales, however, were anticipated by a medieval legend about birds used as incendiary missiles against a besieged village, and by Samson's trick, described in the Old Testament, of setting foxes' tails afire and releasing them into his enemies' fields.

Amanda Bishop, wisely, is not about to claim the Australian origin of any urban legends. She writes, "as to stating categorically that even one of them is a 100-percent fair dinkum Aussie tale, you'll have to stake me over an anthill first."

I usually follow the same cautious approach, though I wouldn't use those words. Maybe I'd say, "You'll have to force me to watch reruns of *Green Acres* first."

One story in *The Gucci Kangaroo* that does sound like an Aussie original is about a stockman who is thrown from his horse and breaks his leg. He sends his dog—one much admired for its intelligence—back to camp for help. Tied to the dog's collar is his hat with a rescue note stuck in the hatband.

But when the dog gets back to camp, he goes straight to the stockman's bunk and curls up for a nap, proving how smart it really is. The man is rescued only when his mates follow the horse's tracks back to the accident scene.

I suppose I'll eventually find that one also told in Death Valley or on the high plains of Mongolia or even in Siberia.

Bishop describes herself as "an amateur enthusiast," and says her small paperback collection contains, "all the stories I know." Like me, she solicits further urban legends from her readers.

I hope she receives floods of mail containing legends, just as I do. I'm looking forward to a series of Australian urban legend books by Bishop.

To get her started, I've sent Amanda Bishop several of my recent columns dealing with hot new American urban legends.

G'Day Mate, and happy collecting!

Tall Tales from the Low Countries

I learned some of the latest legends from Leiden and Leuven, and they have a distinctly Low Country flavor. This proves once again that urban legends are truly international.

Peter Burger, a writer from Leiden, the Netherlands, and Stefaan Top, a folklorist at Leuven University, Belgium, recently sent me some samples of current urban legends from each country.

Not surprisingly, many of the same stories known in the United States are told there as well. Among others, Burger mentioned the legends I call "The Exploding Toilet," (from *The Vanishing Hitchhiker*) and "AIDS Harry" (a variant of "AIDS Mary" that's reported in *Curses! Broiled Again!*) as known in the Netherlands; while Top listed "The Choking Doberman" and "The Runaway Grandmother" as being current in Belgium. (See Stefaan Top, "Modern Legends in the Belgian Oral Tradition," *Fabula*, vol. 31, no. 3/4, 1990, pp. 272–78.)

But each of my Low-Country correspondents also included a few stories that I've never heard in this country, legends that are possibly unique to their nations. For example, from his brother Peter Burger heard the following legend that could be titled "The Contaminated Comforter." It contains a familiar general theme of infestation, but here it concerns a typical European item, one of those large fluffy down comforters often used over there as bed coverings.

According to the story, a woman was able to buy a down comforter at a bargain price, and she put it onto her bed as soon as she returned home. But when she entered her bedroom a short while later, she found that the new comforter had slipped to the floor. She put it back on, but soon saw that it had slipped off again.

That night she slept under the comforter, and again it

slipped off her bed. The next morning she opened a seam in order to check the stuffing. Inside, rather than the delicate ei-derdown of a fine comforter, she found common chicken feath-ers with dried blood still stuck to their ends. These bloody feather ends were thickly infested with maggots.

The squirming of the thousands of maggots was what had caused her contaminated comforter to crawl to the edge of the bed and fall to the floor.

That was certainly no Dutch treat!

Since down comforters are less common in the United States, this story is not told here, to my knowledge. But we do have plenty of other contamination legends, some of them in-volving snake-infested sweaters, coats, and even electric blan-kets.

Turning to the Belgian legends, along with the stories he sent, Professor Top commented that many of their stories "have three shades of meaning: bad, worse, and worst."

As an example, he included a grisly tale about a farmer who started up his combine when preparing to drive it into the fields to harvest a crop. Unfortunately, he found out too late that his children were hidden inside, hoping to hitch a ride to the field.

Not all Belgian legends are so gory. To demonstrate the humorous side, Top sent me a story that could be titled "The Stolen Cobblestones." Supposedly, this happened in the city of Berchem in the province of Antwerp, and it was told by a Leuven University student.

On a certain street, a heap of cobblestones had stood for some time, part of the material being used to repair the pave-ment. A man from Berchem happened to be paving his own courtyard with similar cobblestones when he ran short by about ten stones. So he drove over to that street and loaded the stones he needed from the pile into his van.

Just then a policeman came along, catching him in the act, and asked what he was doing.

"Oh," said the man, "You see, I had a few too many cobblestones for paving my courtyard, and so I thought I'd just add the extras to this pile."

"Nothing doing!" said the policeman, "You keep those stones in your van and get out of here before I run you in for littering a public street."

There may be an American counterpart to this story that involves another kind of building material, but I don't expect to hear the cobblestone version repeated in this country.

At any rate, now that I have examples of urban legends from two of three of the Low Countries, all I need to complete the set is a legend from Luxembourg.

Finnish Urban Legends

Professor Leea Virtanen, folklorist at the University of Helsinki, sent me her new legend collection. It's titled *Varastettu Isoäiti* (Helsinki: Kustannusosakeyhtiö Tammi, 1988). I know that must refer to "The Runaway Grandmother" legend, because the cover illustration shows a car with a body rolled up in a rug on the roof. (Unfortunately, I don't speak Finnish.)

This legend tells of a vacationing family who stow their grandmother's corpse on the car roof after she dies during a trip. Then their car and the corpse are stolen when the family stops for a meal on their way home. I wonder what kind of twist the Finns give to the story.

Virtanen also sent me a handy summary of her book's contents—but it's in German. Let's see now; the first story is listed as "Die gestohlene Grossmutter." That's "The Stolen Grandmother" for sure.

Combining my somewhat shaky grasp of German with the cartoon illustrations scattered throughout the book, I worked out the titles of quite a few of the Finnish legends.

Some are easy: for example "AIDS Mary," the legend about a man and woman who meet in a bar and decide to spend the night at his place making love. He awakens in the morning to find—as the illustration in the Finnish book shows—that the woman has left a message written in lipstick on his bathroom mirror: "Welcome to the AIDS club."

The Finnish version even has its punch line in English!

I can also recognize from the pictures in the book the urban legends that American folklorists call "The Hairy Armed Hitchhiker," "The Dog's Dinner in Hong Kong," "The Boyfriend's Death," and several others.

"The Tarantula in the Yucca" is a giveaway, since not only does the illustration show a spider's face peering out from the hollow stem of the houseplant, but the Finnish title is *Tarantella jukkapalmussa.* Just try saying it out loud, and you'll understand it. (See chapter 7 for the recent American counterpart of this story.)

But several of the Finnish stories baffle me. What's going on in the illustration of a punk rocker sitting next to a little old lady on a trolley car?

I can see the cat exploding in the microwave oven in one picture, and the laughing paramedics dropping the stretcher in another, and I know that both refer to well-known legends. But what's the point of the drawing that shows a man being hit on the head by a candelabra? And who is the man wearing the funny hat serving coffee to someone in yet another illustration? I've just got to learn some more Finnish, or at least improve my German.

When Virtanen gave a paper on her collection at a Texas meeting we both attended, she sadly admitted that only one story, so far, of her Finnish urban legends lacked parallels in other countries. This one told of a boy whose brain froze after he disobeyed his mother's instructions to wear a cap outside in the winter.

"This may be Finland's only original contribution to contemporary legends," she said.

I tried to cheer her up with an impromptu story about somebody cooking his insides in an overheated Finnish sauna, but another folklorist gave it away by saying, "Oh, that's just the tanning salon story!"

I wonder how the Finns say "tanning lamp."

My Man in Silesia

I know that Dr. Dionizjusz Czubala and I are kindred souls—fellow urban legend scholars—although I'm not sure how to pronounce his name, nor can I read a word he's written. It's all in Polish.

Czubala is a folklorist teaching at the University of Silesia in Katowice, Poland. He and his students collect contemporary folktales. Recently he sent me a copy of his 1985 book *Opowiesci Z Zycia*. The title translates as "Tales Taken from Life," according to its frustratingly short and sometimes strangely phrased English summary. The summary also explains that one of the chapters is "devoted to some sensational events and gossips treated as a manifestation of verbal folklore different from the recollecting stories."

Not too clear—but heck, I can't say "Boo" in Polish. Still, this statement, plus another saying "The author assumes that folklore is still living," made me want to know more about his findings. So I asked a Polish graduate student named Zibignieuw who works in our university library to translate some of these Polish modern legends for me.

I learned that many of the stories in Czubala's book deal with what he refers to as "Polish crisis conditions," especially fighting against Germany in World War II and becoming a Communist country after the war.

One example of a wartime legend tells of Polish partisans surrounded in a forest by German troops. Supposedly, the Poles succeeded in annihilating a whole unit of the Germans. Then the Polish commander ordered his men to put on the uniforms of the slain enemies. The disguised Polish soldiers were able to pass through the German lines, turn around, and attack the enemy from behind.

Another Polish wartime tale of trickery describes German

troops searching a village for someone referred to as "peasant X" (I'm glad I don't have to grapple with another long Polish name!).

By sheer chance, the Germans met X on the road into town, but he didn't admit to his correct identity. When they questioned him, he told them his name was Y, and he offered to point out X in the village. They drove around the village all day searching for X, who was never located, since he was already in the car.

An example of a postwar Polish legend is "The Two Smugglers." In this story several people were in a compartment of a train returning from Russia. A young lady in the compartment mentioned that she was frightened that the customs officials might find a gold ring that she was smuggling to Poland.

When the officials entered the compartment, another passenger, a man, told them that the lady was smuggling a gold ring. The officials took her ring, scolded her, and left the compartment without searching any other passengers.

After the train began moving again, the man opened his coat and displayed a large number of gold rings that *he* was smuggling out. He apologized to the young lady, and offered her any ring from his hoard as compensation for her loss.

As an example of a recent horror legend, Czubala included "The Black Limousine." According to rumors, this threatening vehicle was seen in many places, although these reports were always attributed simply to friends of friends, never as a first-hand experience.

Someone dressed as a priest or a nun would supposedly lure small children into a black limousine by promising them candy. The unfortunate children were never seen alive again. Supposedly the kidnappers drained the blood from their victims to sell abroad, and then disposed of the children's bodies in garbage cans.*

---

*In a report published in English about "The Black Volga" story in *FOAF-tale News* no. 21, March 1991 (newsletter of the International Society for

This story is similar to legends circulating recently both in Western Europe and the United States. The claim is made that children in Third World countries are being kidnapped or bought and slain in order to provide organs for transplant operations in wealthier countries. (See also "The Kidney Heist" in chapter 3.)

I'll keep in touch with my man in Silesia to see what else is being talked about on the Polish urban legend circuit. The Poles are doubtless telling some beauties based on events there during the the past few years!

Contemporary Legend Research), Czubala summarizes four Polish and six Russian variants of the tale and mentions, "I have never met with a more widely circulating story. The distribution was so intense that you could hardly meet a Pole who was not familiar with the story."

Hold That Taiga Tale

I never expected to find an urban legend told as a taiga camp story deep in the heart of the Soviet Union. In fact, I even had to look up the word *taiga* when I read Russian author Yevgeny Yevtushenko's 1981 novel, *Wild Berries* (translated by Antonina W. Bouis. London: Black Swan, 1984).

According to my dictionary, *taiga* refers to the "swampy coniferous forest of Siberia beginning where the tundra ends." That seems like a good setting for stories about bears, wild rivers, earthy peasants, old war heroes, petty government officials and the like—and the book's full of such things—but it's hardly a region where you'd expect to find an international big-city yarn.

Yet, there it was, a fine version of a classic urban legend involving a dead cat and a switched parcel. Yevtushenko retold the story in a scene of the book in which a group of prospectors are sitting around their camp telling tales about cats.

(I immediately became interested at the point where one man tells a story involving a dead cat, because one of the basic rules of urban legend spotting is "Never trust a dead cat story.")

After one storyteller finishes, the next begins, "I'll tell you about Ruslan and Ludmila," and a third character interrupts, "Don't get sidetracked from cats." But there is a cat in the story, and Ruslan and Ludmila, the man explains, is a kind of cake made in Leningrad that's named for two characters in a Russian fairy tale. It's as if we had a dessert called Hansel and Gretel's Gingerbread.

In his story, the narrator describes how he once rode on a commuter train in Leningrad, and sat near an old lady who had a cake box, wrapped and tied, that had a Ruslan and Ludmila label on it. A group of long-haired young people boarded the same train car, carrying some packages and bottles and playing

loud music on their tape recorders. The quiet old lady closed
her eyes in disgust until the intruders left, then opened them
again and began crying.

She had immediately noticed that the young people had
taken her box and left one of their own in its place. The new
box said only Fruit and Berry on its label. The storyteller says
that he tried to comfort her by saying, "At least you still have a
cake. You won't come visiting empty-handed."

But the old lady explained through her tears, "I wasn't going
to visit anyone. I was on my way to bury Vasya, my cat. I had
him for eighteen years. I was carrying poor dead Vasya in the
box. I wanted to put his body to rest somewhere in the country,
near birch trees."

If you don't recognize in the old lady's story the legend called
"The Dead Cat in the Package," then you must not be a regular reader of my column or books. It's one of the oldest, most
widespread, and variable urban legends of all time. Whatever
twists and turns the dead-cat plot takes, it always involves some
unwitting person who steals what he or she thinks is a valuable
package and ends up with a cat's corpse.

I'm sure from the discussion of the story by characters in this
terrific novel that Yevtushenko was aware that he was using an
apocryphal story. Mike Corrick of Salem, Oregon, who sent me
a photocopy of the excerpt and inspired me to read the book,
added, "I particularly like the author's comments here concerning the life and growth of urban legends."

Referring to one of the geologists who heard the story, Yevtushenko wrote, "He had a feeling that he'd heard this story
somewhere else. It seemed to be something perilously close to
an old chestnut." The geologist decides not to challenge the
story, however, because, as Yevtushenko wrote, "There is a
peculiarity of the taiga camp story: Even the storytellers themselves don't know exactly where the truth ends and invention
begins."

It sounds to me that the taiga tale as a genre has a lot in
common with the urban legend, and in this case the two over-
lap.

The Latest Legends from Italy

Phantom black ambulances supposedly used by kidnappers, legendary panthers roaming the suburbs of Rome, and unreliable prophecies of earthquakes—these stories and more, all rampant in Italy recently, are discussed in the first number of a newsletter called *Tutte Storie,* or "Nothing But Stories." It's published by the new Italian Center for the Collection of Rumors and Contemporary Legends. In Italian the last phrase reads *Voci e Leggende Contemporanee.*

The newsletter, edited by Paolo Toselli of the city of Alessandria, in its first issue (dated March 1991) runs sixteen pages, providing short English and French summaries of its articles. Although I can figure out a few phrases like *all'amico di un amico* (friend of a friend), it's handy to have the English explanations of Italian stories, such as this one:

"The Black Kidnapping Ambulance. 'There is a black ambulance driving in town to kidnap our children.' That's the latest rumor, persistently circulated throughout Southern Italy in November 1990. A phantom gang is said to kidnap children in order to feed a terrible trade of human organs." (See "My Man in Silesia," for Polish and Russian variations of the same legend.)

Though the English could be more proper, this concise summary at least tells me that a legend similar to "The Kidney Heist" story which swept the United States recently (see chapter 3) has also been told in Italy.

The urban panthers, also referred to in the newsletter as *felini misteriosi* (mystery cats), are given the most detailed treatment. The newsletter includes a map marking forty-five separate places where the phantom beasts were supposed to have been sighted between December 1989 and May 1990, and details of each of the sightings are described.

This survey of panther reports concludes, in the English

summary, "Dogs were found torn to pieces, as well as some paw prints, but the black beast vanished into thin air." (Compare the "Motown Panthers" stories in chapter 7.)*

The faulty earthquake prophecy *(terremoto annunciato)* receives this description in the newsletter: "In the afternoon of January 4, 1991, a rumor was circulating in Turin that the whole town would be destroyed by a terrible quake in the night. Everybody talked about it, nothing happened."

This incident is compared to another that occurred in February 1990. At that time, the newsletter reports, "An announced, unexisting tornado coming from France created a great concern in schools and offices." The article concludes that "rumors of impending catastrophes are originated from unconscious fears unchained by some trigger."

The metaphor may be a bit mixed, but the idea is clear enough.

Other articles in this issue of *Tutte Storie* describe Italian variations of well-known international legends. For instance, an item titled *Vecchia Leggenda, Nuova Versione* (Old Legend, New Version) is about the story I call "The Mexican Pet." Rather than the plot concluding when the couple's new dog is identified as a rat, as in the typical American version, the Italian version ends this way:

"A veterinarian identifies the pet adopted from the street as a dog/mouse crossbreeding and orders its owner to kill the animal and burn all furnitures in their home."

I'm sure that should be "a dog/*rat* crossbreeding," unless the mice grow to truly monstrous size in Italy.

I'm also sure that there's much more good data for my urban legend studies in the newsletter. For example, one article titled "Rumors Are Running in Italy" summarizes recent progress in legend studies, but about all that I can recognize in it are a few

---

*The third issue of *Tutte Storie* (November 1991) announced "Alarm in Tuscany: The Panther Appears Again." Despite a recurrence of the rumors, the newsletter reported, "fifteen days of searches passed in vain."

book titles. Another one titled "One Town, Many Legends" surveys the stories current in Alessandria, but I'm puzzled by most of the examples cited.

A headline on another article took a little thinking, but I eventually translated *Per Favore Informate i Vostri Bambine* as "Please Inform Your Children." Then I recognized the allusion to the "Blue Star Acid" legend. With that clue, I could easily match up the English-language versions of anonymous fliers warning people about LSD-laced stick-on tattoos with the corresponding version circulating in Italy. Evidently, this piece of photocopied folklore has migrated from the United States to southern Europe.

Urban Legends in Japan

As with cars, electronics, and Disneyland, the Japanese have their own versions of legends we consider American. I discovered this when Issei Kasai of Tokyo, who had just read the Japanese edition of one of my books wrote to recount a few familiar legends the way they're told in his country.

Among the stories enclosed was the following:

A girl student of Doshisha University went on a travel to Thailand. She went shopping to a first class department store to buy a beautiful ethnical blouse.

So she took one and went into the dress room. When she became naked, suddenly the floor downed. It was set by the kidnappers' group.

The floor was introduced into downstairs. Some men waited her there. They caught her and sold her to a prostitution inn.

Eventually, the Japanese girl is rescued and brought home, but people said "she has become crazy." She is said to be still alive and living in Shiga Prefecture, Kasai added.

There are many Western variations of abduction legends like this one. In the United States, they're usually concerned with the so-called "white slavery" racket of enforced prostitution. In France, they were so prevalent at one point that an entire book, *Rumour in Orleans* (published in French in 1969; English ed., New York: Pantheon, 1971) chronicles how several dress shops in that city became the targets of this abduction legend.

Written by a team of French sociologists, the study describes the spread of rumors that young girls had been abducted from six dress shops there and forced into prostitution. All the shops were operated by Jews, and the rumors took on distinctly anti-Semitic overtones. Yet, the authors noted, "not one disappearance was actually reported to the police."

While the sociologists merely paraphrase the rumors themselves, their flamboyant analysis and writing style makes the spread of a rumor sound like a forest fire or some other awful disaster. Take the following passage, for example:

"A rumour, a wind of fantasy . . . a cyclonic depression . . . the turbulent encounter between a fully-fledged rumour and the various repressive elements which it set in motion, a maelstrom which, by a series of chain-reactions (and counter-reactions) shook every filament in that mysterious entity which constitutes a town."

In other words, "Rumors were flying." But, ooh la la, what purple prose!

Mr. Kasai also sent me a Japanese version of "The Vanishing Hitchhiker," the classic legend about an apparition who hitches a ride, then disappears.

Like the ghostly hitchhiker in many American tellings of the story, the Japanese spirit who hitches a ride in Kyoto is the image of a beautiful young woman who lost her life in a gruesome incident. But this ghost is not the teenage victim of an automobile accident on prom night who is trying to return home. Instead, she represents someone who died in Hakuaikai Hospital, and whose body was sent to the University of Kyoto medical school to be used as a dissection cadaver.

The spirit has the appearance of a living woman when she enters a taxi near the hospital and asks to be taken to the University. But when the cab arrives at its destination, she has vanished.

Hakuaikai Hospital is near a place called Midoro pond, so the taxi driver supposes that the pond is the ghost's permanent residence—especially after he looks into the back of the cab and sees that "there is a wet seat where she sat."

An analogous motif—wet footprints in the car—is often mentioned in connection with American vanishing hitchhikers. Many of these spirits are said to have been picked up on rainy nights. Why, or how, a spirit would get wet feet is not explained, though.

7

Animal Legends

Sad Animal Tales, and Why There Are No Cats in Solvay, New York

"Lost Dog," reads the headline on a photocopy of a home-made flier that readers often send me. Sometimes there's a drawing of the supposed missing mutt, followed by this description:

"Three legs, blind in left eye, missing right ear, tail broken, accidentally neutered. Answers to name of 'Lucky.' "

I always get a kick out of seeing yet another version of this piece of photocopied folklore—or Xeroxlore, as folklorists call such material. But, please, animal lovers, don't jump on me for finding this one funny: I just enjoy the irony of the imaginary dog's name, certainly not the description of its pitiful condition.

Of course, there's no such dog. This flier describing Lucky the unlucky dog is merely a piece of urban folklore, and for me, at least, it still raises a chuckle.

Herb Caen, the venerable *San Francisco Chronicle* columnist, doesn't agree. In 1989 he begged readers to quit sending him any more such parody ads, saying "They arrive weekly at my desk in batches of half a dozen or so. They aren't even funny, but maybe I'm just tired of seeing them."

Like it or not, sad animal tales are a staple of modern folklore. Furthermore, the unfortunate animals' suffering is often the result of human negligence ("accidentally neutered"). So the stories warn against the possible consequences of our actions.

Here are a couple of other examples of this type of tale, as reported in the press.

"Holiday Party Spawns a Sad Little Fish Story" was the headline on a story published on January 7, 1990, in the *Los Angeles Times*. Writer Zan Thompson reported on a goldfish tragedy that supposedly happened during a series of Christmas parties given for a visiting celebrity:

"One woman hit upon an idea that must have sounded wonderful when she ran it by the florist.

"She decided to have tall clear cylindrical vases, each one artlessly filled with sprays of flowers. But how would that be different from every other flower arrangement?

" 'Ah,' she thought, 'I will put goldfish in the vases. They will make darting streaks in gold through the crystal water and among the green stems.' "

The sad result of her decorative inspiration, however, was that every goldfish died in the water from lack of oxygen and, to the guests' discomfort each fish was soon floating belly up in the vases.

Did it really happen? Was the story embellished as it passed through the L.A. rumor mill? Thompson doesn't make this clear, though he does raise several questions about what he calls the "finny debacle."

I sniff an urban legend here, if not a well-established one, then one in the making.

I'm more certain of the legend status of a story in the *Greenwich* (Connecticut) *News* for February 22, 1990. It appeared under the headline "Do Birds Really Blow Up When They Eat Raw Rice?"

Writer Ina Bradley explains that birds supposedly eat the rice thrown at weddings, which then "ferments in their stomach, rapidly expands, and BOOM!—an explosion and the birds' innards and feathers splat all over the guests."

Bradley notes that nobody ever reports a firsthand experi-

"Mother Goose and Grimm" reprinted by permission: Tribune Media Services

ence with birds exploding like this, and that many birds apparently eat plenty of raw rice, both wild and cultivated, with no ill effects. Nevertheless, the exploding-bird story remains a genuine concern of brides-to-be. One "Donna in Atlanta" wrote Dear Abby about it in a letter published in Abby's January 22, 1992, column. Donna hoped to have rice thrown at her wedding, but she worried about its potential for killing birds. She had also heard that birdseed distributors had started the rice story, hoping to promote the throwing at weddings of their product instead.

Abby's reply quoted her "current bird expert," the associate curator of birds at the Los Angeles Zoo, who explained that birds have good digestive systems, and that in most birds that eat seeds and grain their gizzard grinds up the hard items before they enter the bird's stomach. "If a bird were to die from eating rice," he concluded, "it would be a freak accident."

And finally, in an effort to get to the bottom of another potential sad animal tale, I turned to the readers of this column around Syracuse, New York. A reader in Liverpool, New York, wrote saying that if I queried readers of the Syracuse *Post-Standard* about why there are no cats in the nearby town of Solvay, they would supply the answer.

So, readers, I asked, why no cats in Solvay? (And are there other towns around the country that are supposedly catless?)

I feared there was another sad animal tale behind the question.

WHY THERE ARE NO CATS IN SOLVAY

The man from Liverpool, New York, had written saying that
the town of Solvay (near Syracuse) had three claims to fame—
Allied Chemical, the New York State Fair, and no cats. Why
are there no cats in Solvay? I asked my readers. Now I know,
and it's not a pretty story, though I believe it's merely a legendary one.

"Cat eaters reside in Solvay," one reader of the Syracuse
Post-Standard printed in red across a clipping of my column.
Other people were more specific; one person wrote, "The
Tyrolians use them as snack food."

How's that again? I thought Tyrolians went around in cute
leather shorts, yodeling, and chortling like Heidi's grandfather,
and that they ate things like bratwurst. Or is that the Bavarians
I'm thinking of?

Another Syracusian, who says she did research on the allegedly catless Solvanians, explained, "It seems that during
WWII the Austrians were starving and had to resort to eating
cats for survival. Solvay has a rather large population of Austrian immigrants, and some locals believe that cat eating continues to this day."

Others who wrote attributed the story's genesis as the WWI
period when starving Austrian soldiers were supposedly reduced to eating cat meat. "Did they really?" one reader mused.
"I don't know, but Solvay got the reputation of being cat free
because of its Austrian residents."

A typewritten postcard expanded on the topic: "Tyrolians
have various methods of serving cats—broiled, fried, baked,
and the all-time favorite, the Tyrolean/Europe style, which they
will not divulge."

Nor would this writer divulge his or her identity, explaining,
"I can't give my name, because I live in Solvay. . . . [signed] *One
Who Knows.*"

The most detailed explanation came in a letter signed M.P.

from Syracuse. The writer was "born in Solvay and old enough to know all about the subject."

M.P. first heard the story in 1920 when he or she was ten years old. "We were taught never to eat a meal at an Austrian's, Tyrolese, or Piedmontese home if they were having polenta (corn-meal mush) and rabbit.

"People claimed the meat was really cat, not rabbit, and boy did that turn us off."

But even M.P. was unsure if cats were actually eaten, and added, "As far as there being no cats in Solvay today, that's a lot of baloney."

My question: Are we really sure what's in that baloney?

Just so nobody reading the above will think that the residents of Solvay are unique in telling cat-eater legends about a particular ethnic group, consider some prototypes and parallels to the story that I've found:

In Charles Dickens's classic work *The Pickwick Papers,* published in 1836–37, Sam Weller tells Mr. Pickwick that he's heard about pies made from kittens being sold on the London streets as ordinary meat pies.

In 1885 an English newspaper reported on a woman convicted of trapping and butchering cats and selling them to people as rabbit meat. And in 1888 a poem by an Australian writer told about a Chinese cook who made "rabbit pies" out of tender puppies. (See *The Mexican Pet,* pp. 99–103.)

For decades Chinese, Indian, Yugoslavian, and other ethnic restaurants located in England, Germany, Scandinavia, and elsewhere have been the targets of dog- and cat-cooking stories, and these tales have carried over to the United States.

Since the late 1970s, when Southeast Asian refugees began arriving in the United States, stories have circulated about Americans' missing pets being served at the tables of Vietnamese, Hmongs, Laotians, etc.

In February 1989 the restaurant reviewer of the New Orleans *Times-Picayune* devoted a column to denying the story that "a certain restaurant was shut down by health inspectors after they found skinned cats in the kitchen freezer."

So, good people of Solvay, you are not alone with your reputation for harboring cat eaters.

Probably few, if any, of these stories are true, but as I've written before, the truth never stands in the way of a good story.

Why Your Pet Hates the Vet

Does your pet hate to be taken to the vet? Does it almost seem that Rover or Fluffy can tell when you're taking them in for their shots instead of just out for a ride in the car? If so, maybe your pets have heard some of the stories I have about bad things that happen to creatures great and small when they visit the animal doctor. Fortunately, I believe these horror stories are just legends.

First, an incident reported in a small-town Texas newspaper that supposedly happened to a local veterinarian. The vet had just added to the staff of his animal clinic a new graduate from a nearby college who was eager to please but short on experience.

One weekend, when the older vet left the younger one in charge, a man came in with a doddering, wheezing old mutt that seemed to be on its last legs. The man asked the young vet to "put old Rover to sleep." So the vet administered a lethal injection of doggie tranquilizer, and old Rover soon closed his eyes and breathed his last.

The owner asked the vet to help him load the dog into his car, explaining, "We're awfully fond of our dog—especially the kids are—but we're driving all the way across the country and Rover just can't travel that far without being sedated."

The owner continued, "Old doc so-and-so, your new boss, always gives Rover a little sedative so he'll sleep comfortably when we take him on a trip; so thanks for giving him his shot this time."

The young vet gulped and said "You're welcome," as he closed the door on the remains of old Rover, hoping the family would just assume the dog had died in his sleep.

I might almost have believed that story if the Texas newspaper had furnished any names, or if the article had explained how one sedative shot could have worked on Rover during an entire cross-country trip.

Further proof that it's an apocryphal inept-vet legend is that I've heard other stories on that same theme. For example:

An elderly woman brought her beloved pet canary in to a student-run free clinic at a veterinary college for treatment of its seriously broken wing. The students decided they should cauterize the region as part of their treatment.

First they anesthetized the bird with ether, then they reached for an electric cautery, forgetting that a bird's bones are hollow. The highly flammable ether had entered the broken bones, and when the tool was applied to the bird's broken wing, the entire bird burst into flames, leaving nothing behind but a small pile of scorched feathers.

I might even have believed *that* story, except that I've heard other versions involving veterinarian students treating parrots or parakeets with injured beaks. The birds are supposedly given gas rather than ether, and they too catch fire around the mouth, or explode, when the cautery is applied to the wound.

Similar stories of pets and vets are told in other countries. Here's one I got from an English reader:

There was this bloke who had a budgerigar (parakeet) which broke its leg. He took it to the vet who put it in a splint, but the budgie broke the splint shortly after it was brought home.

After several trips back to the vet—at six pounds per visit—to have the splint replaced, the next time the budgie broke its splint, the bloke decided to replace it himself.

He took a wooden non-safety match and taped it to the bird's broken leg.

As you probably know, budgies like to scratch, and there's often a piece of sandpaper in the bottom of the cage to scratch on. The newly-splinted budgie soon began scratching with its broken leg, and the match caught fire, burning the bird to a crisp in a few seconds.

The bloke had forgotten to remove the head from the match.

"Stupid Pet Rescues"

My family used to have a sweet, gentle Norwegian elkhound named Sonja. She didn't tend to stray; nevertheless, we kept her on a leash whenever we let her out in the yard or took her for a walk.

Once, after we had been gone for the day, we returned home to find that Sonja had somehow got loose. A neighbor boy had caught our pet, and he had snapped her by the collar onto her exercise line in the backyard.

But this dog, though a gray elkhound, wasn't Sonja; in fact, it was a somewhat larger male dog. Our own pet was safely inside the house where we had left her, now barking wildly.

We released the confused canine stranger—who took off for home—and we calmed our riled-up Sonja—who must have heard and scented the other dog tied up in "her" yard. We thanked our young neighbor for his good intentions, but also explained to him about girl dogs and boy dogs.

That's a true story, yet something very similar happened to a reader in Salt Lake City.

The reader came home once from work to find a strange dog inside her house, scratching eagerly at a door leading outside. The woman's son said he had let the dog come in when he opened the door for his own pet, Duke, thinking the other dog belonged to a friend of his mother's who was boarding it with them while out of town.

The reader had made no such arrangement, and she had never seen the dog before in her life. She sent me her story after reading a closely similar item in the "Life in These United States" section of a recent *Reader's Digest*, yet another "Stupid Pet Rescue."

The major difference her version and the *Digest*'s, which had been sent in by a reader in Arizona, is that in the magazine's version the rescued pet is a cat. This story too is a first-person report of something that presumably really happened.

In this variation, a couple with their home up for sale have a beautiful Persian cat that comes into heat just when real-estate agents are beginning to show their house. While the owners are at work, they post a note to the realtors on the front door: "Please do not let cat out."

Returning home that night, the owners find a neighbor's male cat inside their house consorting with their purebred kitty. There's a second note on the door:

"Another agent must have let your big tomcat out, because he was waiting at the door when I showed your home. I let him back in."

In all three instances, the families must have told and retold their stories of the "Stupid Pet Rescue," starting it on its way toward legendhood.

Yet another story about a bungled pet rescue appeared on a computerized bulletin board, nowadays a common medium for the circulation of urban legends. The story was supposed to have happened in Fairbanks, Alaska, to a friend of the person who had added it to the "net."

The man owned a cat that was a constant nuisance—she refused to use the litter box, scratched the furniture, yowled at night, and so forth. Finally, tired of the aggravation, the man conned a friend from the other side of town into taking the cat off his hands.

The next day the friend called to say that the cat had run off. The two men spent a day out in twenty-below weather searching for her without success. Returning home, the man found Puss huddled by his front door shivering in the cold. He was overwhelmed that the cat had missed him enough to find its way home across the snowy wastes in sub-zero temperatures, so he took her in again, vowing to cherish her forever.

He told the story about his wonderful returned cat to all of his friends, and, finally, a friend admitted the truth: He had recognized the cat across town, thought she was lost, and brought her back home in the heated comfort of his pickup truck.

The cat had yowled in protest every foot of the way, but the friend persisted in delivering her back where she belonged.

And that's how the cat came back.

(Following the publication of the above column, I heard from a man in Delaware who once, late at night, buried the neighbors' dog, mistaking it for his own, and also from a woman in Maine who once chased three stray pigs back into her pen, where she found her own three still safely locked in. Seems these Stupid Pet Rescues are fairly common, and there's more below.)

Talk about coincidences! Here are a couple of stories chock full of them.

A small news item headlined "A Coincidence" was sent to me by John Lafferty, librarian at the Preston School of Industry in Ione, California. The news story is dated January 27, 1928 (which happens to be the same month and day I began writing my column "Urban Legends" in 1987).

The long run-on sentence at the beginning of the clip summarizes another news item and then describes a local incident:

The story written by Mrs. Davis in the Stockton Record, *of an automobilist who picked up a man on the road, and feeling for his watch and finding it gone, drew a pistol and demanded his watch which, when handed over, ordered the man out and when arriving home found his watch where he had left it on the bureau, is the reminder of an actual occurrence known to residents in Ione of Mabel, who had missed her white, black spotted Terrier, and going up town and seeing it in a man's arms, demanded it notwithstanding the protest of the man of his ownership, was decidedly so strenuous in her demands the man gave her the dog.*

She took it home and whipped and chained it up. Next

morning she found her dog lying by the one claimed from the stranger.

Lafferty found the clip in the *Ione Valley Echo* while searching for information about his school in old newspapers. "I could have sworn," he wrote, "that I read this same story in one of your books, but I can't find it."

The news item actually contains *two* stories—"Unwitting Thefts" and "Stupid Pet Rescues"—both of which I have addressed in columns. But neither appears in exactly the same form as the 1928 version in any of my previous books. What a lucky coincidence that John Lafferty wrote to me just as I was seeking such stories!

The hitchhiker story is a common variation of an urban legend about the embarrassment of being an unwitting thief. A person, believing himself to have been the victim of a pickpocket, confronts the supposed thief and demands his property back. The startled "thief" complies, giving the person his own property.

These stories usually involve a passenger on a crowded bus or a jogger in a city park. The only hitchhiker variations I'd collected earlier came from the 1930s and 40s.

The second story contained in the *Echo* piece belongs to the category of "Stupid Pet Rescues."

Mabel's experience in Ione sixty-plus years ago seems to have repeated itself, not only in my family, but in the various other stories about the wrong dog or wrong cat being returned quoted above. I don't doubt that some bungled pet rescue stories are true, but I believe that repeated retelling of them have moved these anecdotes toward genuine legend status.

The final bonus from the news item Lafferty sent is the suggested connection between the themes of "Unwitting Thefts" and "Stupid Pet Rescues."

Since I wrote about these two stories months apart, I didn't make this connection, but reading the 1928 story now, I see the logic. Both legends deal with someone who says "Give me my property back!" The punch line, however, shows that it was not that person's property after all.

Not only do the stories themselves depict odd coincidences, but it was an equally odd twist of fate that somebody sent me just the right data at the right time.

Motown Panthers (and Others) Are Hard to Trail

There are legendary big cats in Michigan, and I don't mean the Lions and Tigers of Detroit. During the past several years many southeastern Michiganders claim that they have sighted black panthers—the felines, not the political activists—running wild just thirty or forty miles outside of Motown.

Phantom panthers were reported in Manchester, Michigan, in 1984, in Milford in 1986, and in Imlay City in 1989. In April 1989 a woman, spotting a beast slinking through a nearby field, videotaped it from the deck of her home.

However, investigators from the Michigan Department of Natural Resources repeated the taping while an agent walked a pet cougar through the same field. When the two video shots were superimposed, the "panther" was very small compared to the real cougar. The subject of the woman's video must have been about the size of a house cat, which is probably what the woman saw.

Bill Walker writing in the *Ann Arbor News* on May 14, 1989, summed up the Michigan panther scares in an article headlined "Big Cat Sightings Fiction So Far, DNR Expert Says." And if the DNR experiment didn't cast enough doubt on the reports, there are lots of holes in the stories about beasts roaming southern Michigan.

The Milford panther, for example, was supposed to have been responsible for killing a horse and ripping open its throat. But an animal expert determined that the wound on the horse's neck "was a wound a cat could not make. There were no tooth punctures or claw marks on the animal, just the gash."

He believed that the horse had accidentally slashed its own neck on a barbed wire fence. In the soft earth of a drainage ditch where a panther had supposedly been seen, trackers found only coon and dog prints.

Walker also pointed out that a big cat would have to eat a good-sized animal weekly or so in order to survive. But an escaped pet cougar would lack hunting skills and probably "turn up on back porches looking for handouts."

There were no reports of missing farm stock or of huge pussycats parked on porches in downstate Michigan.

Two Milford police officers thought they spotted a panther through the night-scopes on their rifles, but the scopes proved to have weak batteries that caused spots on the viewing field.

In March 1992 the Motown panthers returned, or at least the stories began anew. The Detroit *Free Press* gave the revived rumors of panther sightings in Oakland, Michigan, lots of coverage on March 5th, 6th, and 7th, but maintained a skeptical, even a mocking, attitude. The headlines said it all: "Cat is on Prowl," "Here Kitty," and "That Mysterious Panther Looks a Bit Cuddly on Film." Indeed, the photo taken by a citizen panther-sighter and published in the *Free Press* was so obviously *not* a panther that it inspired Ronald Watcke of Troy, Michigan, who forwarded me the clippings, to comment, "My short-hair American domestic cat looks more fierce!" The photograph, shot through a zoom lens, was most likely someone's housecat attracted to the raw chicken left out in hopes of luring the elusive panther out of hiding.

If a real black panther does show up in Michigan, it will be a long way from home. It would have to be either a black jaguar from Central or South America, or a black leopard from Africa or Asia, since there are no black panthers native to the United States.

Black panthers are common in American folklore, though. Someone fleetingly sees a shadow, a common wild animal, or a roaming pet, and he or she interprets the sight in terms of familiar folktales and legends.

In Britain, alleged sightings of "The Surrey Puma" and of a big cat dubbed "The Exmoor Beast" have made the news in the past decade. But no one has killed, captured, or photographed a big cat there either.

British journalists often use an ironic style when writing up big cat sightings, which often seem to take place in towns with quaint names like "Worplesdon," "Woking," and "Esher."

A typical article by Nicholas Coleridge appeared on January 14, 1985, in the English newspaper *The Standard*. It described an incident occurring near a village called "Stokenchurch, High Wycombe" in which the big cat "disturbed a canoodling couple in a clump of winter gorse."

I haven't heard any stories of panthers disturbing canoodling Michiganders, but see "The Latest Legends from Italy" in chapter 6 for further European legends about roaming panthers.

"The Hunter's Nightmare"

A Missouri man returning from an unsuccessful hunting trip hit a deer with his car. It seemed like the first good luck of a frustrating weekend, so he decided to keep the deer—illegal though the practice was.

He put the stunned animal into his back seat, but shortly afterwards the deer revived and began thrashing around. Grabbing a tire iron from under the front seat, the man swung at the terrified deer while steering. Unfortunately, he beaned his faithful hunting dog, and the dog bit him.

The man stopped his car and jumped out, pursued by his angry dog. He ran to a telephone booth, slammed the door, and dialed 911. The man screamed to the operator that he was trapped there by his dog, while the deer was kicking out the windows of his car. He begged the police to come and shoot the two animals for him.

Funny story, but is it true?

Elaine Viets, columnist for the *St. Louis Post-Dispatch,* heard the story from a teacher who heard it from a fellow teacher who got it from her husband who had heard it at the brewery where he works. Supposedly the officer on duty made a tape of the emergency call and was duplicating it for his friends.

But local law-enforcement authorities whom Viets called told her that "The Hunter's Nightmare" had not happened in the St. Louis area, but in Poughkeepsie, New York. A St. Louis officer had heard the story told at a conference for 911 coordinators by a policeman from Poughkeepsie.

When Viets called the Poughkeepsie police, she learned that they don't even operate a 911 service there. And when Viets called me, I admitted that I had not heard the story, although it reminded me of urban legends in which stunned animals revive, and mistreated animals gain revenge.

Viets gave up the search for the origin of the incident and wrote a column about it (*Post-Dispatch,* January 3, 1989). She asked her readers, "Is this an urban legend, or did it really happen?"

Within a week Viets heard from twenty-five readers with copies of the tape, three of whom sent her copies. Most respondents had some connection with law enforcement, but they disagreed whether the incident had happened in Missouri, Arkansas, or Colorado.

"They were all wrong," Viets wrote in a follow-up column (January 10, 1989), because by then she had called Poughkeepsie again and spoken to a police officer who said that the emergency call had been received back in 1974 as a regular police report.

The officer claimed that as many as 50,000 copies of the tape were circulating, and that Scotland Yard, the White House, and the FBI academy all had copies.

Impressive explanation, but is it true?

"The Hunter's Nightmare" seems to be an emergent urban legend, possibly based on an actual incident.

The tape recording has extremely poor sound and may have been doctored by someone somewhere along the line during the past fifteen-plus years. The caller's language is very realistic; in fact, it's largely unprintable, as you might expect from a man involved in such a situation.

Although it's a hilarious tape, I doubt if as many as 50,000 copies are floating around, and I don't see what the White House or FBI would want with it.

(In early 1991 readers in Marble Falls, Texas, and Cape Girardeau, Missouri, wrote to me enclosing versions of the stunned-deer story, both supposed to have happened locally. I'm still unable to sort out the real stunned deer, if any, from the deer stunts of urban legend.)

On January 7, 1992, Allen Clouser, a retired officer of the Poughkeepsie, New York, Police Department, wrote to Elaine Viets explaining the truth behind "The Hunter's Nightmare" story. Clouser was the officer who actually took the call in February 1974 from the man claiming to have been attacked by a wounded deer and an angry dog. The man, Clouser believed, was intoxicated, but there was definitely a dog barking excitedly in the background. Several policemen were dispatched to search for and assist the caller, but they were unable to locate him. In a second letter to Viets, on January 31st, granting permission for me to quote his letter, Clouser wrote, "This 'deer' event was merely a routine call for me. It amazes me how it has spread and become a 'legend.' "

"The Flying Cow"

I've never seen a flying cow, except of course in legend. James Horan, a librarian in Huntington, West Virginia, sent me a flying cow story that he found in the June 1–7, 1990, edition of *Moscow News*, an English-language newspaper, and I agree with him that it has the feel of a legend.

According to Yegor Yakovlev, the paper's editor in chief, the story was widely told in Moscow. He commented, "However fantastic it may sound, people swear it is true."

Here's the story:

A capsized boat was spotted near the Pacific coast of the Soviet Union. The only survivor told his rescuers: "A cow fell onto our boat." The poor man was sent to a mental hospital, but continued to stick to his story.

Eventually they decided to find out the facts. . . . An aircraft was ready to fly from one air-base to another when the crew saw a stray cow grazing on the airstrip. "Why not bring her along?" the pilots thought, worrying like everybody else about food. They drove the cow into the plane (via the bomb bay) and took off.

Everything was quiet until they got to cruising altitude. As it grew colder the cow became agitated. "Damn the stupid cow! Let's throw her into the ocean," the pilots decided. And they did—on to the deck of the unfortunate boat.

Yakovlev's purpose in telling the story was to draw an analogy to what had been happening lately in the USSR.

"How can you explain," Yakovlev asked, "a situation in which everyone is trying to resolve their own problems at once, having no idea what the consequences might be for others? Most people have no idea what might suddenly drop on their heads."

His column, "National View," was headlined, "A Mad Cow Story Shows Our Predicament."

My own predicament after reading it was to justify the gut feeling that I'd seen another flying cow story somewhere else; I found it in an urban legend collection from England I've cited several times already, Paul Smith's *The Book of Nasty Legends*. Although this version is not a true parallel, it's pretty close:

Driving along a narrow, winding Scottish road one dark evening, a driver was somewhat surprised when his vision was completely blocked by the body of a flying cow landing on the bonnet [hood] of the car. Being totally unable to explain the phenomenon and also unable to remove the corpse from the bonnet, he pushed the car into a field and walked into the next village to report the incident to the police.

He hesitantly explained his predicament [that word again!] at the police station but, much to his surprise, he was not greeted with incredulity but rather with relief on the part of the police officer.

It turned out that a lorry [truck] driver had just been in to report that he thought he had hit a cow some miles back along the road. Surprisingly, when he searched for the animal its body was nowhere to be found.

The explanation was that the speed and the weight of the truck had sent the cow's body flying a considerable distance back down the road to land on the bonnet of the man's car coming up round the bend.

Smith added a variation he had heard around 1965 in which a driver on a Scottish road struck a cow broadside, catapulting it (so to speak) onto his "bonnet."

"Unfortunately," this story concludes, "the car was an old Austin and he had to smash the flying A symbol off with a rock before the cow could be slid off."

Smith wondered, "What is it about cars, cows, and Scotland?"

And I am wondering—are there other flying cow stories told

in different settings? It seems to me that the story should also exist in the American West where cars and cows occasionally meet on the back roads.

In fact, when I drove out to go fishing on a Colorado mountain stream not long ago, at one point I had to rouse a couple of sleeping cows off the road with my car horn before I could proceed. One cow was even snoozing on a cattle guard built across the road.

Sleeping cows, yes, but *flying* cows? I've never seen one. . . .

"The Missionaries and the Cat"

Mormon missionaries go around two-by-two, wearing dark suits, white shirts, ties, and name tags. They distribute religious tracts and often use a flannel board (a cloth-covered board to which cloth cutouts adhere) to teach prospective converts about their group's beliefs.

A popular missionary legend concerns this low-tech teaching aid. I've heard the story from many of my Mormon neighbors and students here in Salt Lake City where I live, but the flannel board story is also told nearly everywhere that Latter-day Saints missionaries have been assigned around the world.

The LDS folk have no monopoly on flannel boards, but they seem to have perfected their use in leading discussions about their church. The problem with flannel-board teaching, according to the legend, is cats—curious, playful, bothersome cats. Here's how the story goes:

A couple of Mormon missionaries—elder A and elder B—are using a flannel board and cutouts to illustrate a discussion with a prospective convert. The object of their proselytizing is an old lady whose cat is looking on. The cat keeps attacking and carrying off the figures that the two elders stick to their flannel board. So when the old lady briefly leaves the room, elder A reaches down and "kind of flicks the cat on the bridge of its nose with his finger." Not meaning to harm the cat, he evidently flicks his finger much more strongly than he intended. In fact, his blow kills the cat.

The missionary is horrified when he realizes what he has done. But elder B thinks quickly and comes up with a solution. He curls the cat's body around the leg of the chair he is sitting on, and he keeps petting the cat through the rest of the visit. When the missionaries depart, they leave the cat's body leaning up against the chair.

The next time the two elders come to visit, the lady announces sadly, "Oh, I'm so sorry to tell you that my cat that you liked so much has died."

In variations of the story the missionary hits the cat with the corner of the flannel board, only intending to scare it off, but killing it instead. Sometimes, the missionaries hide the cat's body behind a piece of furniture and leave quickly, never returning to resume the discussion.

This legend, in all versions, though it fits the missionary theme perfectly, probably originated in non-Mormon circles. There are at least two other stories about a young man accidentally killing someone's family pet during a visit.

Usually the visitor is a nervous suitor, and in the most popular story—"The Crushed Dog"—he accidentally sits upon and crushes a Chihuahua that is sleeping on a couch in a dimly lighted parlor. Sometimes the young man hides the tiny dog's body inside an umbrella stand and rushes from the house.

I've also heard an English variation on this theme. The suitor is having a terrible time trying to converse with his girlfriend's father, but he finally hits on a topic that seems to interest the man. The suitor then perks up, begins to feel more relaxed, and crosses one leg over the other. Unfortunately, the family pet, a budgerigar, which is allowed to fly freely about the house, is flitting by at just that moment.

The young man's foot, as he brings it up to cross his legs, catches the bird in mid-flight and boots it neatly into the open fireplace where it is immediately burned to a crisp.

No chance to cover the crime this time!

"The Spider in the Cactus"

(Here are my three columns about this legend as they were originally published in the spring of 1989 and 1990, and in the autumn of 1990. I've added a few explanations in brackets, plus an update on the legend as of summer 1991.)

"YUCCA, YUCCA, YUCCA!"

I've got some new angles on the legends called "The Spider in the Hairdo" and "The Spider in the Yucca," both of which tell of bugs in strange places.

Gene Nora Jessen of Boise, Idaho, wrote me in February 1989 about her experience with "The Spider in the Hairdo" legend in the early 1960s when she was a sales demo pilot for the Beech Aircraft Corporation.

"My territory was the forty-eight contiguous states, in which I travelled constantly," she recalled. "At that time we wore beehive hairdos with lots of backcombing or ratting, and we went to the beauty shop weekly rather than doing our own hair.

"I heard the spider in the hairdo story in beauty shops all across the United States over a period of a year. In each shop I was assured that the incident had happened in another shop in that very town.

"Running into that story constantly," said Jessen, "was a revelation to me, as well as an introduction to urban legends."

I recognize the feeling described by my Boise correspondent. I've never worn a beehive hairdo, of course, but wherever I've lived—Michigan, Indiana, Illinois, Idaho, and now Utah—I've always heard the story of the spiders infesting this once-popular hairstyle.

Like all folklorists who have collected the story—and like Gene Jessen's hairdressers—I was generally told that the incident had occurred in the very town I was living in at the time.

Usually it was said that the spiders were discovered when the victim fainted and was taken to a hospital where her hairdo was combed out for the first time in weeks.

Jessen, incidentally, at the time she wrote was president of an international organization of women's pilots, called the Ninety Nines. The group takes its name from the number of charter members who organized the group in 1929. Amelia Earhart was its first president.

If the eensie-weensie spider infests a beehive hairdo in one legend, in the other it comes out of an exotic house plant.

I've related stories told about potted yucca plants, imported into England, that were found to be infested with tarantulas. (See *The Mexican Pet*, pp. 83–84, where the story is quoted from a 1985 English newspaper article about the Marks and Spencer department store being the target of the legend.) And my ace legend correspondent in western Canada tells me that in March 1989 there has been a tarantula-egg and cactus scare in British Columbia.

"The Spider in the Yucca," is also a well-known legend in Scandinavia. In versions told there, the plant's owner discovers the spider or spiders while watering the plant—suddenly the cactus begins to shake or squeak.

The owner calls the store where the yucca was purchased and is advised to keep away from it, or put a plastic bag over the whole plant and pot until store workers can come and remove it safely. (See Bengt af Klintberg, "Legends and Rumours about Spiders and Snakes," *Fabula*, vol. 26, [1985, pp. 274–87].)

In a column last May I discussed this European spidery houseplant story, mentioning that I had not yet encountered it in the United States. But since then I've been sent the following version, told in a recent letter from Geoffrey M. Miller of Kalamazoo, Michigan:

> *A co-worker of my wife's said she purchased a cactus at Frank's Nursery and Crafts. When she took it home, she noticed that it seemed to move on its own.*
>
> *Her husband said it was all in her imagination, but the next*

*day he too decided that it was indeed moving, so they called
the store.*

*The store authorities at first denied that the plant could be
moving, but a while later they called back and said that the
people should get out of their house at once and wait for store
employees to arrive.*

*The workmen came and replaced the cactus plant with
another one, saying that the motion had been caused by a
tarantula having babies inside the plant.*

Before I received this American version, I was skeptical of
Swedish folklorist Bengt af Klintberg's suggestion that "The
Spider in the Yucca" legend reflects women's subconscious sexual anxieties concerning men. But a pregnant tarantula lurking
inside a cactus begins to make that interpretation seem more
plausible.

THE PESTS IN THE PLANT

Dear Professor:

*Last December my sister-in-law told me a "true story"
which her brother, a landscaper, heard from a colleague.*

*I tried to tell her about the guy in Utah that collects these
stories, but she had no doubt that this story is true:*

*"A lady bought a cactus plant from her brother's colleague,
and the night after it was delivered she heard a creaking noise
coming from it. The next morning the cactus was still
creaking, so she called the landscaper.*

*"He told her to get out of the house, taking any pets and
children with her. He rushed over in a van, wearing a
decontamination suit, and went in after the cactus.*

*"As he was walking back to the van with it, the cactus
exploded, releasing thousands of baby scorpions."*

—C.M.

Chapel Hill, North Carolina

Dear C.M.:

I'll guess that the landscaper got his stock from a branch of Frank's Nursery and Crafts, part of the largest plant nursery chain in the United States, and the usual victim of this wild report.

If so, your story is a standard version of the legend I sometimes call "The Critters in the Cactus." If not, the people at Franks—who have been bugged by this fictional story for years—should be relieved that it may be switching targets.

Urban legends about spiders found nesting in cactuses or yuccas imported from Central America surfaced in Scandinavia and Great Britain in the early 1970s. In 1985 a rash of "Spider in the Yucca" yarns zeroed in on a plant supposedly bought from the British retail chain Marks and Spencer.

The plants were said to have hissed, squeaked, shaken, quivered, quaked, and even screamed when they were watered. Specialists from M&S reportedly came and removed the infested plants while wearing protective clothing and using metal extending arms.

I heard my first American version of the story in February 1989 from a reader in Kalamazoo, Michigan, who was told it about a cactus bought at—you guessed it—Frank's Nursery. The plant moved when it was watered, the motion being caused by "a tarantula having babies inside the plant."

No sooner did I mention the Kalamazoo story in a column, than I started hearing it from elsewhere in the Midwest. Several readers in the Chicago suburban area wrote to report stories about cactuses, usually purchased at Frank's, that wiggled when watered and were found to harbor deadly spiders or scorpions, sometimes numbering in the thousands.

Elaine Viets, columnist for the *St. Louis Post-Dispatch,* heard the same story in her area and checked with Frank's District Office. She learned that the legend was circulating in Illinois, Indiana, and Ohio as well as Missouri. (See "A Creepy Addition to Urban Myths," *Post-Dispatch,* June 22, 1989.)

Viets also heard from a reader who was told the story in Buffalo, New York, with the variation that someone had dug up a cactus in the Southwest desert and brought it home.

When the illegally acquired plant started moving, the person put it outside and called firemen; they supposedly turned a flame thrower on the plant, flushing out a nest of tarantulas. At least Frank's didn't get blamed for that mess!

I've also heard the infested-cactus story from Cincinnati; Minneapolis; Milwaukee; Royal Oak, Michigan; and now Chapel Hill.

Frank's, or "a prominent florist," is always mentioned, and the plants either move, "breathe," or make noises when watered or tended. Store officials or firemen are called, and they remove (or burn out) numerous spiders or scorpions—often "newborn" ones. (How can you tell?)

In her letter, the Milwaukee reader who sent the story guessed, "If I heard it twice, I figure you've probably heard it a hundred times."

Not quite, but I have heard about "The Critters in the Cactus" enough times to recognize it as an urban legend that's driving a large nursery chain right up the wall.

EXCUSE ME, BUT THERE'S A SPIDER IN MY PALM

If I ever get to Madison, Wisconsin, I want to eat at the restaurant where Denise E. Klobucar works so we can share some urban legends.

I can just imagine her greeting me something like this: "Good evening, I'm your server, Denise. Our specials tonight are unblackened redfish, Wisconsin Cajun chicken, candied lamb chops, meatloaf Madison, and urban legends explained."

Klobucar recently sent me a four-page letter loaded with legends. She explained, "As a waitress, I get ample opportunity to hear fantastic tales. Believe me, it's a great exercise in self-control to keep my mouth shut when I hear customers tell each other stories like 'The Mexican Pet' or 'Cruise Control.' "

Some patrons she served recently were discussing "The Mexican Pet"; it's the one about the Mexican sewer rat that is adopted and smuggled back home by American tourists who think it's a Chihuahua.

Coincidentally, Denise Klobucar had read my book *The Mexican Pet* and had also heard a version of the story from her roommate, so she recognized the legend immediately when her customers repeated it.

As a discreet but savvy waitress, Denise didn't let on that she knew the story was untrue. She wrote to me instead, saying, "The men at the table told the women the story, the women acted appropriately grossed out, and I kept quiet."

She heard the cruise control legend from members of a wedding party. Concerning this one she wrote, "The story was the same as the one in your book, with the guy driving his camper van who sets the cruise at 60 mph, then steps in back to use the bathroom. He crashes into a tree."

The wedding party had a good laugh, and their waitress bit her tongue and gave nothing away.

This letter suggests to me that waitresses and waiters would make good folklore collectors, if only they could find time to write down the stories they overhear while trying to remember who ordered the house dressing, who wanted the decaf, and who told the one about the spider in the cactus.

Denise Klobucar also heard that story recently, but this time from a coworker. The other waitress told her about a friend of a friend whose new cactus plant leaned over in a peculiar manner whenever it was watered. A horticulturist checked the plant and found hundreds of tiny spiders living inside.

This old legend seems to be enjoying a revival of popularity lately. Maybe it's because of the popularity of the film *Arachnophobia*.

Kate St. John of Pittsburgh recently sent me an account of the same spider-in-cactus story told in her city, also by people while dining out. She wrote:

While we were in a restaurant with friends, they told us that a woman had bought a large cactus from Ikea, a well-known Swedish furniture outlet. After it had been in her home a few days, it began to tremble.

She called the store and also a plant store, but they had no explanation. Finally she called the local botanical garden, and they told her to hang up and leave the house immediately.

They came right over to her house and carted away the cactus, and when the botanists split it open they found it filled with tarantulas.

Besides the patrons, however, the waitress in the Pittsburgh restaurant was also listening to the story. As her customers finished telling it, she blurted out, "Ooh, the spiders! I've heard that too!"

So have I—ever since the early 1970s. And I've heard it from many sources, including European ones. A new book of German urban legends is titled *Die Spinne in der Yucca-Palme* ("The Spider in the Yucca Palm," by Rolf Wilhelm Brednich, Munich: Verlag C. H. Beck, 1990).

If I ever get to Milwaukee, or Munich, I want to eat at a German restaurant and try that version out on the waitress: "Fraulein, bitte, have you heard the one about die Spinne in der Yucca?

UPDATE:

Scholarly notice of "The Spider in the Cactus" was taken by Gary Alan Fine in a note titled "Mercantile Legends and the World Economy: Dangerous Imports from the Third World," in *Western Folklore*, vol. 48, 1989, pp. 153–57. He quotes, among others, Geoffrey Miller's version from my first column, and he suggests that such stories "suggest the inherent dangers when citizens of industrialized nations purchase items from the Third World." He points out that in the versions known to him at that time, in contrast to "The Department Store Snakes" legend, where the emphasis is on the store not the product, in this legend (as well as "The Snake or Spider in the Bananas") the imported raw material is the major concern. Also, Fine notes, the national origin of the plant or bananas is unspecified. But since Fine wrote his analysis, "The Spider in the Cactus" has continued to develop as an urban legend and has, in fact, developed two of the very traits he found missing earlier—a focus on the store selling the plant and information about the plant's origins.

I've continued to receive regular reports of this story being told in literally all parts of the country and right up to the present. From 1990 on, Frank's Nursery was mentioned less often in the legend, as Ikea became the typical target of the story. The fad for Southwestern decor was incorporated into the tradition, not only because this helped explain the popularity of large potted cactuses in homes, but because people were said to be illegally bringing plants home from trips to visit the southwestern deserts. Store-bought cactuses were usually said to have originated in the American Southwest or in Mexico.

The Ikea connection was explored in a column by Brian O'Neill in *The Pittsburgh Press* (May 23, 1990). The manager of a local outlet of that company explained that "Plants sold by Ikea are grown in an enclosed environment; they are not grown wild. They are well-sprayed, and they are repotted before they arrive at the store." (This is essentially the explanation given by Marks and Spencer in 1985.)

A story in the *New York Post* (November 10, 1990) offered this appraisal of the story, given by Pam Diaconis, a corporate spokeswoman for Ikea: "This is one of those folk legends. It apparently started on the West Coast a year ago and recently landed in New York." (This is unlikely, since the story was well known in Europe and the Midwest before being told on the West Coast.)

Diaconis was also quoted in the February 11, 1991, edition

of *Business Week* saying, "Every time we open a new store, [the rumor] hits. We have yet to have anyone call who actually has one. It's always a friend of a friend."

My thick file of letters about "The Spider in the Cactus" suggests how and when such stories are passed on. For example, an Indiana woman's daughter heard it from her teacher; a South Dakota man heard it at a breakfast meeting of his service club; and a southern California agricultural inspector heard it from a person employed as a fruit-fly trapper. A professor at the State University of New York at Stony Brook heard the story told when he was on jury duty, during a delay in the trial when jurors were merely chatting to pass the time; one juror said it happened to a friend of a friend who brought the cactus home from Mexico, while another had heard the Ikea version. Many people wrote me about hearing the story told at school, at work, in beauty shops, or by people engaged in planning or installing home decoration, furniture, landscaping, and the like. However, the typical source statement is rather vague and convoluted; as a Bellevue, Washington, man wrote, "A friend related this story she heard from her mother-in-law. . . . A friend of her in-law's cousins in the Southwest (Phoenix or Tucson) heard it from a relative of the victim."

In January 1991, Mark Chorvinsky, editor of *Strange Magazine*, issued his list of the Top Ten Strange Stories of 1990. Item no. 4 on this widely reprinted list was this:

"The owner of a Saguaro cactus in Arizona called the plant store to complain that the cactus's arms were drooping. The store employee warned, 'Get your kids and get out of the house immediately. We'll be over right away.'

"She did, but before the store employees arrived, the cactus exploded, showering the living room with hundreds of deadly scorpions. Scorpions can reproduce inside the cactus, building up pressure until it explodes."

The really strange thing is that Chorvinsky had not heard the story before, or from enough different places, to recognize its legendary nature. I can't escape variations of this story, and they're still arriving.

The latest, as of this writing: In a letter dated July 18, 1991, Sarah P. Beiting of Kalamazoo wrote to send me a story she had heard from her sister, who lives in New York City. The story was about a friend of a friend who bought a Saguaro cactus from an Ikea store in New Jersey, etc., etc., etc. Ms. Beiting thought the yarn sounded farfetched, and wondered "if you had heard anything about lethal cacti in the past." Evidently the Kalamazoo Frank's-Nursery version of the story had died out, or at least it never reached this correspondent.

"The Snake in the Greens" and
Other Weird Green Things

Three weird green things have shown up on the urban legend grapevine lately. Here they are, as they appeared in news clips sent to me by readers.

"GROCERS FEEL SNAKEBITTEN BY VIPER-IN-GREENS TALE"

This was the headline on a front-page article published June 21, 1990, in the *Vicksburg* (Mississippi) *Evening Post*. The tale told in the news story is actually about a "greens" thing:

"A snake nestling in the greens of a local grocery store bit the hand of a woman reaching into the bin. The victim died either at home, in the hospital, in her car in the store parking lot, or right there in front of the greens."

The news account went on to say that although variations of the rumor were attributed to specific food stores throughout Vicksburg, no local produce department had seen such an accident, nor had police or hospital authorities encountered it.

Tara Jennings, the journalist who wrote the Vicksburg story, called me to ask if I'd heard similar stories. I said it sounded like a take-off on the old "Snake-in-the-Blanket" legend that describes a woman shopping at a discount store who is bitten by a snake concealed in an imported blanket, sweater or coat. I added that snakes or spiders also supposedly infest imported foods.*

Then, to my surprise, within a week I got two letters on this

---

*In the same 1989 *Western Folklore* article mentioned in the previous section, Gary Alan Fine refers to examples of "The Snake in the Greens" from Atlanta, Georgia, in 1983 and from Dayton, Ohio, in 1989. (See Fine, 1989, p. 157, n. 6.)

very theme from Houston. One told of a snake lurking among pineapples from Mexico, and the other described a snake hidden in a shipment of Honduran bananas. In each case, shoppers were supposed to have died shortly after being bitten, but as in the Vicksburg greens rumor, neither case could be authenticated.

In his July 20, 1990, column, "Tracking down slithery rumors," Thom Marshall of the *Houston Chronicle* reported the true Texas counterpart of the story: "Supposedly, two people were bitten by a cobra at the Fiesta supermarket on the Katy Freeway." When some readers were unconvinced that the snake story was false, Marshall rechecked and then wrote in his August 1st column, "No one has come up with any specifics that would change the status of the tale from urban legend to news story. No name of a victim. No date. Important details like that are missing."

I wonder where these southern grocery-store snakes are thought to hide between flurries of the legend. About a year and one-half later, on October 2, 1991, *The Commercial Appeal* of Memphis, Tennessee, reported that slithery rumor again. The headline over a short but bylined story read "Don't Shed Any Tears over Snake in the Onions"; the article, by William Thomas, said that suburban schoolchildren in the area were "telling it for gospel." The odd thing about this report is that, at least according to the newspaper, the children's stories were about "a Mississippi woman" who died after being bitten by a coral snake lurking in a store's onion bin. Maybe some Tennessee child was doing a class project involving reading year-old copies of the *Vicksburg Evening Post,* didn't know what greens were, and substituted onions in the story instead. At any rate, as far as I know *The Commercial Appeal* never explained this anomaly.

We're back to the normal version of the story in a column by Bob Gorman published in early November 1991, in the *Sumter* (South Carolina) *Daily Item*. Headline: "Since When Do Snakes Eat Collard Greens?" Was it a rattlesnake in the Piggly Wiggly grocery store, *two* baby rattlers at the Food Lion store, or a water moccasin somewhere else that bit the poor woman? Could it be true, as the rumors claimed, that the woman died in the front seat of her car in the parking lot and the store's manager paid her husband $90,000 in hush money? Gorman checked out all the best sources, including a class of seventh graders who swore to him that the story was true, and concluded, sensibly, that nothing like this had ever happened, in Sumter or anywhere else.

"THE GREENING OF THE CD"

That headline appeared on an article in "Voice Electromag," a supplement of the June 5, 1990, issue of the New York City weekly newspaper the *Village Voice.* It told a CD (compact disc) story:

"In case you haven't heard . . . someone in California tried coating the thin outer edge of a CD with a green marker pen, and it supposedly improved the sound of the disc."

Bruce Eder, author of the article, reported that "audiophile circles have been abuzz" with the story since February. One company even began producing a special green marker with a notched tip that made coating the disc edge easier.

Eder tested the technique and found it made one of his discs sound "slightly richer," another "very impressive," and gave the rhythm instruments on a third disc "a fuller presence."

Eder concluded, "Professionals are still divided over the effect of green markers, though supporters are gaining the upper hand."

The CD story reminds me of the one about the alleged aphrodisiac power of green M&Ms. I suspect that both these stories are just examples of weird green folklore and that the success stories are products of wishful thinking.

Or, as Patrick Goldstein in an article syndicated by Entertainment News Service put it, beginning another newspaper article on the green-marker/CD story in March 1990, "It sounds crazy. Completely wacko."

Goldstein quoted an industry insider saying "It's half amazing and half-ludicrous," which seems to me to be a pretty good characterization of many urban legends.

"SMEAR ANGERS MAKER"

That headline from the *Brisbane* (Australia) *Courier-Mail* on February 22, 1990, referred to a third bit of hearsay involving the color green:

"Claims that a top-selling hair shampoo turns hair green and causes baldness have caused sales of the brand to drop around the country."

The article went on to explain that a "fake pharmaceutical analysis of the product" had been circulated among Australian hairdressers. It stated that caustic soda and lead-based chemicals supposedly found in the product were responsible for the alleged side effects.

The company denied that any such ingredients or side effects could be traced to its product. Not to mince any words here, the "company" and the "product" referred to were Procter & Gamble and its Pert brand of shampoo.

As if P&G hasn't had enough problems in the past with the false claims that its logo is a satanic symbol, now they have mean green rumors to contend with Down Under.

8

Academic Legends

Back to School Legends

The beginning of a new semester is a good time to report on some academic legends that arrived in my mail lately. Although each of these four stories was told about a particular university, I suspect that they all have counterparts elsewhere.

"THE ZOO SECTION"

One semester a wag in the registrar's office at Yale University supposedly filled one section of Freshman English with students whose surnames were also the names of animals.

The instructor found himself sounding like someone taking inventory at a zoo: "Mr. Bear? Ms. Byrd? Mr. Deere? Mr. Fish? Ms. Finch? Mr. Fox? . . ."

"CARNEGIE MYTHS"

The Tartan, the student newspaper at Carnegie Mellon University in Pittsburgh, debunked several legends commonly heard on campus. One claimed that

"CMU has the second highest workload and the second highest suicide rate of all colleges"; another suggested that "Andrew Carnegie had Baker Hall built with sloped hallways so he could turn it into a factory if the school failed."

The first claim is unverifiable because "workload" in this sense cannot be measured, and suicides at CMU average only about one every three years, a comparatively low figure. The second claim is disputed by a CMU publication on the designs of campus buildings.

My son, a CMU graduate, confirms the truth of another story I've heard: that the computer science students there have wired the Coke machine in their lounge so that they can tell from their office computer terminals whether the machine is filled and whether the Cokes are cold.

"FEATS OF CALTECHIES"

Students of the California Institute of Technology are legendary for their elaborate pranks which are often based on scientific or technical expertise. One favorite Caltech story was sent to me by a Stanford student:

It is reportedly impossible to lock Caltech students out of any room. They say that, as part of the freshman initiation, a student gets back from class one day and finds his room door lock disassembled on his desk.

The student must figure out how to reassemble it. Eventually—from a series of similar pranks—he becomes an expert on locks of all kinds.

Thus, the students gain free access to their teachers' offices, administrative offices, or wherever else on campus they may wish to play pranks.

Is this just a rumor circulated by Stanford students about their Caltech rivals?

"THE BAROMETER PROBLEM"

As a final examination in a physics class, the instructor asks the students to explain how to measure the height of a tall building using a barometer.

Presumably, he intends for them to employ the principle of pressure changes with altitude—say, by measuring the barometric pressure on several floors of the building and comparing the results.

One student, however, submits this solution: "Take the barometer to the top of the building and throw it off. Time its descent with a stopwatch, and compute the height of the building."

The professor finds this answer unacceptable, but gives the student another chance to solve the problem the right way.

The student sits and thinks, until the professor asks if he's giving up.

"No," the student replies, "I'm just trying to decide among several other methods." He outlines them as follows:

1. Lower the barometer with a long rope from the top of the building to the ground; then measure the rope.
2. On a sunny day measure the shadow of the barometer and of the building; then work out the height using proportions.
3. Walk from bottom to top of the building marking off the height on the wall in "barometer units"; then multiply the length of the barometer by the number of units.

Often there are several more similar tactics. The last solution in all versions of the story is always this:

"Take the barometer to the basement of the building to be measured and find the building superintendent or manager. Tell him you will give him the barometer if he tells you the correct height of the building."

Now that's really getting to the bottom of the problem.

"The Obligatory Wait"

One question that seems to puzzle all new college freshmen is "How long are students expected to wait for a tardy professor?" Fortunately, most of the more-experienced students are ready with an answer. Unfortunately, their answers vary wildly, and most of them are wrong.

As Kelly Reese wrote in the May 2, 1990, issue of *Insight,* the California State University at Fresno newspaper, "Collegiate lore has it that students must sit waiting for a late professor anywhere from ten to twenty minutes. Rumors have even held that professors with a doctorate get the full twenty minutes while non-tenured profs get a mere ten."

Even that generally correct summary of this bit of campus folklore has a flaw, since professors could hold a doctorate and not be tenured, or vice versa. Other versions of the belief mention a different waiting period for each academic rank—the shortest time for graduate assistants and the longest for full professors.

Students have told me that classes sometimes sit seriously debating the exact provisions of the campus rule they've heard about that dictates the obligatory wait for a late teacher. Usually, before the class agrees whether to stay or to leave, either the professor arrives or the period ends. Few students attempt to look up the rule, and those who do never find it.

As far as I know, a waiting rule for late professors has never been made an official regulation by a college administration.

Kelly Reese asked Chris Alverado, secretary of the office of student affairs at California State at Fresno, how long the obligatory wait was and got this answer:

"When I was in school, that was something everyone had an

answer for, but they couldn't tell you where they got their information.

"But give me a day and I'll find the answer. I know it's around here somewhere."

Later Alverado admitted that there was no set policy; "It's up to the professor how long they expect students to wait."

Personally, I prefer this "Official Response," as he called it, that I got from a former college registrar who said:

"We don't care, once we have your money. There are no truant officers for colleges, and after you've paid tuition you have the right to sit in class for the entire period, whether the professor shows up or not. You can also leave anytime you wish, provided you don't disturb the rest of the class."

An often-repeated anecdote about George Lyman Kittredge (1860–1941), a famous Harvard philologist, gives another viewpoint. Supposedly, when Kittredge was late to class one day his students became restless. Just as the class started to leave, Professor Kittredge arrived and strode purposefully to the podium as his students scrambled to regain their seats.

When the shuffle of feet and scrape of chairs had died down, Professor Kittredge scowled at the students and said, "In my day at Harvard we would never go back for a late professor!"

Reverend James Haupt, a United Church of Canada minister in Maxwell, Ontario, sent me another waiting-for-the-prof story, based, he said, "on one of those unofficial rules which never seem to appear in print."

He had heard in college that whenever a professor is ten minutes late, his or her class session is automatically cancelled.

"A certain professor," he wrote, "arrived one day a few minutes early to an empty classroom and dropped his hat on the desk. Then he remembered he had left something in his office and went back to retrieve it.

"On the way he ran into a friend and fell into a conversation, losing track of the time. Returning to the classroom just over ten minutes later, he found it empty.

"At the next class session, the professor berated the class, saying that they should have known he was there, since his hat was still on the desk.

"The professor arrived on time for the following session. And he found a hat on every desk, but no students."

Sinking Libraries

Sometimes students tell me that they get a sinking feeling when they study in the University of Utah library. They don't just mean they're worried about finishing a term paper; they mean it literally, the place is sinking!

Campus folklore claims that the architect who designed the library forgot to figure in the weight of the books, so when the librarians filled the shelves, the whole building began slowly sinking into the ground. Sometimes the site is claimed to have been swampy or unstable as well.

I've asked librarians about this story, and they just looked puzzled. I've asked architects, and they raised their eyebrows and shook their heads. But ask the undergraduates, and you'll find that many are convinced it's true. Even if the library isn't sinking, they say, it will never be fully utilized because it can only support a portion of the books that it was planned to hold.

Earlier I had also heard this legend attached to Yale University in New Haven, Connecticut, and Colgate University in Hamilton, New York. More recently the sinking library story has popped up—if that's the right term—elsewhere.

For example, Mark Osbaldeston of Toronto, having read about sinking shopping malls in my book *Curses! Broiled Again!* wrote to report that Robart's Research Library at the University of Toronto is said to be "doomed to remain forever only partially full" because the designer forgot about the books.

Mario Milosevic of White Salmon, Washington, wrote that he first heard the sinking library story told about the campus library at the University of Waterloo in Ontario, Canada, but later he heard the same story applied to Northwestern University (about which, see below).

Then I heard from Frederick D. Glick of Providence, Rhode Island, who said that it was actually the Science and Technology Library at Brown University there that was the victim of its designer's inadequate planning.

Mark Foskey, a student at the University of California at San Diego, says the same story is told about the new library there. Foskey describes the building as having a "futuristic overhanging design with visible exterior concrete supports." But others are convinced that the pillars were added later in order to stabilize the structure.

Another student at UCSD scoffed at the story, telling Mark that the original sinking library is located at Rensselaer Polytechnic Institute in Troy, New York. "It may be a myth here," the student said, "but it really happened at RPI."

Tell that to Tom Rowlands, professor of the history of architecture and art at the University of Illinois at Chicago. He wrote me to report the sinking library story being told by his students about the library at nearby Northwestern University in Evanston, Illinois. Rowland once heard the building's architect, Walter Netsch, being challenged by a student to explain his "mistake" in forgetting the weight of the books. Netsch's immediate denial of the charge, Rowland wrote, was believed by some students to be tacit admission that "something was dreadfully wrong up there in Evanston."

I heard a different legend about a library at Northwestern from Rolf H. Erickson, a librarian there. He wrote:

> *Almost from my first day on campus in 1966, I was told by friend and stranger alike that Frank Lloyd Wright called the Charles Deering Library, "a sow on its back."*
>
> *I was intrigued and sought to get to the source of this story. I always came to dead ends, but discovered that most college campuses have Frank Lloyd Wright stories.*
>
> *St. Olaf College, in Northfield, Minnesota, for example, has the story that Wright admired only one building on the campus—the smokestack.*

Here's my request for students, librarians, or architects. Please send me your sinking-library and Wright-stuff legends.

The Northwestern University Library staff newsletter, *The Lantern's Core,* reprinted my column on sinking libraries in the March 1990 issue and Northwestern alums continue to write me with further details about their version of the sinking library story. One whimsical theory is that the installation of a new lighter-weight carpet throughout the library was done in an effort to halt the sinking.

Another major university with a sinking library legend is Syracuse, where the E. S. Bird Library is the culprit. In an article about the story by David A. Smith published in *The Daily Orange* on September 20, 1990, Associate University Librarian Carol Parke is quoted saying these well-chosen words: "The rumor is a long-standing one that surfaces regularly."

That this legend is sometimes also told about public libraries is indicated in Rebecca Stapleton's article in the October 3, 1990, *Newton* (Massachusetts) *Graphic,* "Library rumors: All wet. Building not about to sink." As the new three-story Newton Library neared completion, rumors spread that the building was sinking into an underground riverbed. When Project Manager Walter Rosenfeld was asked about the story, according to the *Graphic,* he "erupted in peals of laughter" and said that the same rumor had circulated many months earlier.

Ah, but libraries can sink, or at least one library has—it was the Sweetwater County Library in the state of Wyoming. A short report on the disposition of a 1991 case before the Wyoming Supreme Court appeared in *Engineering News Record* for May 13, 1991, under the headline "Cemetery Haunts Sinking Library." In 1977 the county had hired a soils testing firm to evaluate their proposed library site, which had once been a cemetery. The firm approved the site, but, "When the library was completed, serious structural problems began. Eventually, the library began to sink." The court ruled that the suit, filed in 1988, was barred by the ten-year statute of limitations.

Switched Campus Buildings

Dear Professor:

When I was an undergraduate at the University of Virginia in Charlottesville (1982–1987), there was a suspicious story going around, spread in part by the student tour guides, concerning the university chapel.

The chapel is a Gothic looking building built of grey stone and decorated with gargoyles, while the rest of the campus is predominantly colonial red brick with white columns. Legend had it that the chapel was originally designed in red brick as well, but when the building materials were shipped, there was a mix-up with Notre Dame University, which was also building a chapel at the time.

Supposedly, we got their materials, and they got ours. Rather than bothering to exchange the building materials, each school simply used what it had received, leaving each campus with a chapel somewhat out of sync with the rest of the architecture.

I've never been to Notre Dame to check this out, so I would be interested in your findings on the matter.

—Kim Mattingly
Washington, D.C.

Dear Kim:

Presumably the two universities must have switched blueprints for the two chapels as well as the building materials. I assume that Notre Dame University has a chapel, but I have no idea what material it's built of. It would be nice if it turned out to be a red brick colonial design surrounded by grey gothic edifices, but folkloristically speaking, it doesn't matter, since your story is a campus classic.

These switched college-building legends comprise a well-known group that Professor Simon Bronner of Penn State University at Harrisburg calls "architectural folly stories." He gives several examples of such stories in his book *Piled Higher and Deeper: The Folklore of Campus Life* (Little Rock, Arkansas: August House Publishing, 1990). The book's title, incidentally, refers to a list of parody meanings for the three university degrees B.S., M.S., and Ph.D. Figure out "B.S." on your own; the other two mean "More of the Same" and "Piled Higher and Deeper."

At his own university, Bronner found a similar switched building story told about halls built for juniors and seniors in an area called Meade Heights. Students complain that these dormitories are drafty and chilly, and they explain the buildings' inadequacy for a northern climate by claiming that "there's a second Meade Heights in Georgia (or Florida)."

When the two separate housing units were being constructed, the story goes, their plans were accidentally switched. Supposedly, the Meade Heights halls that were built in the South "look like northern fortresses," while those at Penn State are poorly suited for winter weather.

Debra Seltzer of Columbus, Ohio, sent me another mixed-up building story. The library at Oberlin College, she explained, is a huge concrete building with few windows. Seltzer wrote, "One campus rumor was that this is because it was actually designed to be built in Florida." Presumably, in the South, lack of windows would keep the sun from overheating the building, but in the Midwest that design feature merely assured that the building would be dark and cold for much of the year.

The most extreme story of switched campus buildings I've heard came in a letter from M. E. Bolt of Lawrence, Kansas, who wrote:

I was a student at California State University at Hayward in 1972. Supposedly all the buildings there were designed for other universities, and for some reason they were all found unacceptable. But somehow they got built on the Hayward campus instead.

One building—either art or engineering, I've forgotten which—was supposedly designed for a school in the San Fernando Valley where it's very hot. One side of the building is almost all glass, and the windows are sealed.

The original plan called for air conditioning, but since Hayward is pretty cool, air conditioning was dropped from the plans. When the building was put into use, since the windows faced the sunny side of campus and couldn't be opened, the inside became hot as an oven. I heard that there were several cases of student heat exhaustion in that building every year.

Such is supposed to be the result of the folly of those legend-ary college planners who, tradition says, will cut any corners necessary to save a buck.

"The Dormitory Surprise"

I wonder if the freedom and openness characteristic of today's coed college dormitories have rendered obsolete a favorite campus legend told during my own undergraduate days. I call it "The Dormitory Surprise."

Even back when dorms were segregated by gender, there were a few days when visitors of either sex were allowed—such as the periods of moving into and out of the dorm, Parents' Day, Homecoming, etc.

Although I never lived in a dorm, I remember hearing the warning cry "Man on the floor!" once when I helped a girlfriend move some furniture. And I remember often hearing this story:

Forgetting that it was visitor's day, one resident of a men's dorm went down the hall to the shower leaving his two roommates chatting in the room. Coming back, wearing only a towel, the freshly-showered man heard voices coming from the room and assumed it was his roommates still chatting.

He decided to make a dramatic entrance. He whipped the towel off, held his penis in one hand, kicked the door open, and jumped in yelling "Bang, bang, you're all dead!"

The voices he'd heard, however, were those of his mother, father, and hometown girlfriend who had just arrived to visit him.

I heard "The Dormitory Surprise" at Michigan State University in the mid-1950s, but people have written me saying that it "really happened" at Cornell University in 1966, at the University of Illinois in 1967, and at Indiana University sometime in the 1960s. In some versions the naked man wraps the towel around his head like a turban and shouts in some sort of foreign accent. The story might sound like merely a piece of 1960s midwestern and eastern campus lore, but I suspect it is more widely known both over time and space.

"The Dormitory Surprise," like "The Nude Housewife," "The Nude Surprise Party," and other urban legends, dramatizes our fascination with people getting caught with their pants down. It also presents a plausible scenario, given the horseplay and camaraderie that exists in college living units and the possibility for such mistakes to happen in a segregated unit.

But I haven't heard the legend recently, and the only similar tale I've heard about a coed dorm is this one, which is said to have happened at a school in the Northeast:

A male student decides to surprise his girlfriend in their dorm by taking off his clothes and hiding in her closet until she returns. When he hears someone enter the room, he leaps out, thinking it must be the girl. But it's the fire inspectors who are checking for illicit hot pots and coffee makers. The man is expelled from school and banished from campus for life.

Besides the shock value of such stories, there may be a bit of wishful thinking on the part of dorm residents for whom life in a coed living unit is not (usually) nearly as exciting as they had imagined it would be.

After my many years on several college and university campuses—first as a student, then as a professor—I finally saw the inside of a coed dorm at Michigan State University recently when my brother and I stopped to visit my nephew, Stein Brunvand, in his room.

Though our early evening arrival was unannounced, we didn't find ourselves walking down the hall past any orgies, parties, or even hand-holding sessions. Furthermore, everything was about as neat as your average teenagers' domicile might be, neater actually than my own kids' rooms had been at that age.

The behavior of the young people towards the opposite sex seemed to be comparable to that of brother and sisters in my household, maybe even a little more polite. And although I asked them for some campus folk stories, nobody told "The Dormitory Surprise." I wouldn't call this a scientific poll, but it did suggest to me that once the barriers are down between male and female students, the fantasy legends about being caught in the nude are less interesting and may die out.

Of course, I'm prepared to be proven wrong. Have readers heard any dormitory surprise stories lately?

"The Gay Roommate"

The student on the telephone asked his question hesitantly, first assuring me that he had cleared it with his teacher. I was being interviewed in February 1990 via a speakerphone by students in a Mount Pleasant, Iowa, Community High School psychology class when the question arose: Had I heard about a gay college student who sexually attacked his roommate?

Yes, indeed, I had; in fact, "The Gay Roommate" at the time was one of the most common—and most disturbing—urban legends going around.

The Iowa student had heard about a male enrolled at a nearby college who consulted a doctor because of a soreness in his rectal area; the doctor blamed his problem on homosexual activity. But the student insisted he was straight, although he did have a gay roommate. He decided to search their dorm room.

What he supposedly found, hidden among his roommate's possessions, was a bottle of ether and a sponge. The straight student concluded that his gay roommate had been sedating him when he slept in order to have sex with him.

I first heard the story at the October 1989 American Folklore Society annual meeting from University of Illinois folklorist Larry Danielson. In the version he'd heard, the student suffered severe headaches caused by the ether; a physical examination revealed the rectal soreness, which in turn led to solving the mystery. Some students believed the incident happened at Western Illinois University in Macomb and that the straight man had been charged with assault for fighting back strongly enough to break his roommate's arm.

As I heard the story from readers, I found (as one would expect with urban legends) that other details in the story varied. Sometimes, for example, traces of ether or chloroform are dis-

covered in the student's blood sample. In other versions it is
stated or implied that the gay roommate has transmitted AIDS
to his victim. Often the doctor at first prescribes a hemorrhoid
remedy, but this fails to solve the problem. The student returns
a second or third time with the same complaint until the truth is
finally uncovered.

Usually a specific university is named in the legend. For example, an Albion College (Michigan) student wrote that he had
heard that the incident had happened at Michigan State University. At the University of Western Ontario the story was told
about the University of Waterloo. A Harvard student wrote
saying that he heard it happened at Tufts University (Medford,
Massachusetts), and a Maryland college freshman home for
Christmas break in 1989 heard that it happened at the University of Connecticut. Other readers and folklorists reported to
me hearing the story either attributed to specific colleges and
universities in Minnesota, Wisconsin, Nebraska, South Dakota,
and North Dakota, or else told with a generic non-specific setting.

These various local details mean little, since obviously the
story had become widely known, is clearly fictional, and can
easily be adapted to fit different settings. Homophobia—fear of
homosexuals on the part of heterosexuals—is an obvious theme
of the legend. The gay man in the story is stereotyped as being
"evil, opportunistic, desperate, and obsessed with sex," as another folklorist commented when I told him the story.

The straight student, however, bears no responsibility for the
sexual activity and whatever consequences that may result,
such as AIDS, since he is pictured as an unwilling victim who is
drugged, then raped.

Some who have sent me the story expressed outrage at a
heterosexual person being forced into homosexual contact.
But, possibly, the nightmarish attack by the gay roommate also
represents a latent homosexual desire on the part of some men.
Unable to cope with their feelings consciously, they resort to a
fantasy scenario instead. Whether that's plausible or not, I've

discovered that the essential features of "The Gay Roommate" legend are much older and more widely dispersed than the recent popularity of the story in the United States might suggest.

First, here's an Australian version collected in 1978 and published in W. N. Scott's book *The Long & The Short & The Tall* (Sydney: Western Plains Publishers, 1985, p. 80):

"This bloke, he was a terrific winemaker, you know. He was a bit of a homo too, he'd get a lot of young boys out there, drinking this wine, and when they got drunk he'd knock them off. So there's two boys sitting up one morning, talking, and one said to the other 'How do you like old Thingo's wine?'

"He said, 'The wine's lovely, but don't your arse get sore after you drink it. By Jesus, my arse is sore this morning!' "

Scott's note identifies this as "a very old story which I heard at sea in the middle 1940s." He added, in a letter to me, "I heard the story first when I was a gunner in the Navy, about the sailor coming back aboard and telling his mates about the two homosexuals he had met and how generous they had been in buying him drinks."

Scott's version clearly seems to be related to one that the famous Victorian scholar and adventurer Richard F. Burton briefly alluded to in the "Terminal Essay" of his 1886 edition of *The Book of the Thousand Nights and a Night* (privately printed by the Burton Club, p. 201):

"Shaykh Nasr, Governor of Bushire, a man famed for facetious blackguardism, used to invite European youngsters serving in the Bombay Marine and ply them with liquor till they were insensible. Next morning the middies mostly complained that the champagne had caused a curious irritation and soreness in la parte-poste."

Gershon Legman mentions another version of the story in his huge collection of sexual humor called *Rationale of the Dirty Joke* (Second Series, New York: Bell Publishing Company, 1975, p. 156). Here a bellboy is plied with champagne by a homosexual guest; Legman calls this "a well-known joke," but in the United States the military and collegiate versions have taken over.

Eric Walton of Towson, Maryland, wrote me in September 1990 that he had heard the story three times associated with different U.S. Army posts. In one case a commanding officer had even included it as part of a safety briefing, and some soldiers then had T-shirts made up with the slogan "Watch Out for Ether Man." Similarly, at the University of Maryland at College Park, and perhaps elsewhere, the attacker had come to be known as "The Formaldehyde Man."

The latest times I've heard "The Gay Roommate" were in February 1991, as part of a computer bulletin-board posting from Trondheim, Norway, and in May 1991, from a student in Cincinnati who heard that the gay attacker had struck at Bowling Green University using chloroform to knock out his victim. Why had this crime never been reported in the press? Because, according to the Ohio college student who told the story, the victim had been too embarrassed to press charges.

"The Daughter's Letter from College"

At first the letter seems like a pleasant little missive from a daughter who recently entered college: "Dear Mom and Dad," it begins, "I have been remiss in writing, so I will bring you up to date on all my activities."

But before continuing, the daughter's letter cautions, "You are not to read any further unless you are sitting down, OK?"

Then the first bombshell explodes:

"I am getting along pretty well now. The skull fracture and concussion I got jumping out of the window of my dormitory when it caught fire are pretty well healed. I spent two weeks in the hospital, and now I can see almost normally and only get those sick headaches once a day."

The letter goes on to explain that, since her dorm was destroyed, the daughter has moved into an apartment with a gas-station attendant who lives nearby, and they're soon to be married.

"We haven't set the exact date," she writes, "but it will be before my pregnancy begins to show."

Does this bad-news letter sound familiar? If not, it should, since anonymous photocopies of it, with some variations, have been circulating for at least twenty years. During the late 1960s copies of the letter often began with references to the dormitory fire being set during a campus demonstration, but lately this detail seldom appears. (See Alan Dundes and Carl Pagter, *Urban Folklore from the Paperwork Empire*, Austin, Texas: American Folklore Society Memoirs, vol. 62, 1975, pp. 40–41; republished as *Work Hard and You Shall be Rewarded* by Indiana University Press, Bloomington, in 1978.)

"The College Girl's Letter Home," as folklorists call this item, sums up every parent's worst fears about what might happen when a daughter goes off to college. But it is more than likely that no real-life parents have ever received this catalog of disasters, except perhaps as a joke. It's merely a piece of typed and duplicated folklore—often titled "Perspective"—that capitalizes on parents' anxieties and on students' cleverness in knowing exactly what will capture their elders' attentions.

In typical versions of this letter, things get worse before they get better. The next bit of news is usually that the new fiancee "has some minor infection which prevents him from passing our premarital blood tests, and I carelessly caught it from him." There's not much doubt that the infection is a venereal disease, since the letter next says, "This will soon clear up with the penicillin injections I am now taking daily."

I wouldn't be surprised if updated versions of the letter will eventually mention AIDS or even imply a homosexual relationship for the college girl.

Here's another detail about the nice young man that the daughter's letter provides: "He's of a different race and religion than ours, but I'm sure you will love him as much as I do." Some versions of the letter specify further, "I am told that his father is an important gunbearer in the village in Africa from which he comes."

Since I already identified this letter as folklore, and also that it's titled "Perspective," it shouldn't be hard to guess at what the last paragraph reveals. In a typical version:

"There was no dormitory fire; I did not have a concussion or a skull fracture; I was not in the hospital; I am not pregnant; I am not engaged. I do not have syphillis, and there is no boyfriend in my life. However, I am getting a D in History and an F in science, and I wanted you to see these grades in the proper perspective." (A text of the same letter is quoted by Harlan Cleveland in the Foreword to his *The Knowledge Executive: Leadership in an Information Society,* New York: E. P. Dutton, Truman Talley Books, 1985. Cleveland mentions that during a particularly trying day as a university president "a kind and perceptive friend" handed him a copy of the college girl's letter home so he would see his problems in perspective.)

Other versions of the letter provide slightly different details, but all of them follow the same general formula, reporting a fire, injuries, pregnancy, illness, and a boyfriend who is not likely to win the hearts of most white middle-class Moms and Dads, though clearly the parents are regarded by the student as being liberals.

Sometimes there is also an ironic reference to one of a parent's dearest wishes: "You always wanted a grandchild, so you will be glad to know that you will be grandparents next month."

The two low grades reported are always D and F, but occasionally they are received in other subjects, such as French, Chemistry, or Sociology.

It's too bad the student who wrote the letter wasn't taking a folklore class. Then she could have collected some variant versions of "Perspective," analyzed their meanings and functions, and probably have received at least a B in the course.

Lending a Hand at Med School

Medical students are notorious pranksters, at least according to campus legends. Their favorite escapade, so the stories claim, is one that folklorists call "The Cadaver Arm," and I warn you, it's a shocker.

Ann Cary of Seattle wrote recently reminding me of this grisly yarn, which she has never seen printed. Years ago a doctor in Bellingham, Washington, had told her the same story was attributed to students at every medical school in America.

His version seems to have sprouted at a time when the presence of women in medical school was a notable exception. According to the doctor, after a new female medical student enrolled, the males in her class, hoping to scare her into dropping out, placed a pickled arm cut from a cadaver into her bed.

Upon finding it, the woman went insane, and was discovered gnawing on the pickled arm. (Remember—I warned you about this legend!)

Years later, Cary heard the same story told in Portland, Oregon, by a coworker who said she knew someone whose daughter's best friend was related to a nurse at the insane asylum where the victim of the prank was said to be confined. Supposedly, the unfortunate girl was still clutching and occasionally chewing upon the same pickled arm.

Back in 1945, Ernest Baughman writing in *Hoosier Folklore Bulletin* (vol. 4, no. 2, pp. 30–31) summarized thirteen variations of "The Cadaver Arm," and the story is still widely repeated in medical schools with many of the same details. (Baughman assigned the legend motif number N384.0.1.1. in his *Type and Motif Index of the Folktales of England and North America,* Indiana University Folklore Series, no. 20, 1966.) Some accounts may describe pranks that someone actually played, but most versions are probably just repetitions of the old legend.

Usually the cadaver arm is said to have been put into the woman's bed, but sometimes it's hung from a light cord or a shade pull, or else placed into a dresser drawer or hung in her closet. Besides madness and limb-gnawing, the motif of the victim's hair instantly turning white may occur. Occasionally the victim is found rocking the arm like a baby and singing a lullaby.

Also in 1945 Bennett Cerf printed a version of "The Cadaver Arm" in his *Saturday Review* column "Trade Winds" (vol. 28, no. 17, March 24, 1945). He reported the arm had supposedly been painted with luminous paint, and that the prank had been played at the University of Pennsylvania.

Besides the frightened-student version, other versions tell of a cadaver arm or hand that was left behind with toll-takers, or hung from a strap on a New York City bus, or extended to a politician shaking hands on the campaign trail.

This handshake version has the oldest pedigree I've found so far. In 1928 the Spanish novelist Pío Baroja included it in his novel *The Tree of Knowledge* (original title *El arbol de la ciencig;* see translation by Aubrey F. G. Bell published by Howard Fertig, New York, 1974). In chapter 6, which is about the lives of medical students in Madrid, Baroja wrote:

"A second-year student . . . took a dead man's arm, wrapped it in his cloak and went up to greet his friend.

" 'How do you do?' he said, putting out the hand of the corpse from beneath his cloak."

According to Baroja's tale, the friend was horrified, but nothing is mentioned about his going mad, gnawing on the hand, or having his hair turn white. But Baroja does add this revealing comment:

"Many other stories of the kind, true or not, were told with real glee. These medical students had a tendency to a class spirit consisting of a disdain for death, a certain enthusiasm for surgical brutality, and a great contempt for sensibility."

In the modern context, I believe medical students tell such stories—and it's possible that they actually play a few tricks with cadavers—to demonstrate bravado in the face of having to regard the human body as a complex mechanism to be viewed dispassionately in the dissecting lab.

An excellent discussion of the whole subject with copious references and examples is Frederic W. Hafferty's article "Cadaver Stories and the Emotional Socialization of Medical Students," in *Journal of Health and Social Behavior,* vol. 29, 1988, pp. 344–56.

Lessons in Compassion

One of my students told me a story belonging to the ever popular "final exam" category of campus legends. It seemed that the details of the story couldn't possibly fit any school other than the University of Utah, where I teach, but it turned out to be told elsewhere.

Here is my student's version of the story:

"An instructor at the Institute of Religion was teaching a course on the life of Christ over in the new East Institute building.

"On the last day of class, when students arrived for the final exam, they found a note on the chalkboard from their instructor saying that their final would be given in the old West Institute building across campus.

[The note was referring to one of the buildings, located off-campus at opposite ends of our university, where instructors from the Latter-day Saints Church—the Mormons—teach noncredit religion classes to LDS students who desire them.]

"The note on the board sent all the students rushing off to the West Institute, in order not to arrive late. On the way, in the middle of the campus, they all passed a pathetic old beggar who petitioned them for help as they hurried by.

" 'Nobody stopped for the beggar, however,' the student said.

"When the students reached the other classroom on the west side of campus, their instructor was waiting. He asked the class if anyone had helped the beggar, and learning they had not, he informed them all that they had failed the final exam.

"The beggar, the instructor explained, was really an actor he had planted in their path. By ignoring him, the students had shown that they had studied the facts of Jesus' life, without acquiring any of his compassion."

In a variant version, one student does stop to help the beggar, and only he (or she) receives an "A" for the course. In the only other variation my student had heard, the incident was supposed to have taken place at the Mormon-owned Brigham Young University in Provo.

According to my student, the "Lesson in Compassion" story is sometimes told as an instructive example at LDS meetings, but he has never met anyone who was either a member of that institute class, knows someone from the class, or who can name the instructor involved.

"The Lesson in Compassion" has three typical features of a campus legend: It's unverifiable, it contains its own moral, and it's told with slight variations. I'd be very surprised not to hear from someone beyond the borders of the Beehive State who could tell me a different local version of the same story.

UPDATE:

OK, so now I'm "very surprised," as I wrote in the above column, because the only two readers who commented on the "Lesson in Compassion" story were *both* from Utah. Still, as expected, it turned out to be more than just a local story.

Marjorie Draper Conder of Midvale, Utah, wrote that she encountered the story, not in a religion class, but in a social psychology class right here at the University of Utah. She supplied me with a reference to the article in which is reported the original research that surely underlies this legend: John M. Darley and C. Daniel Batson, " 'From Jerusalem to Jericho': A Study of Situational and Dispositional Variables in Helping Behavior," *Journal of Personality and Social Psychology*, vol. 27, no. 1, 1973, pp. 100–108.

Darley and Batson's experiments, which are also summarized in several textbooks, involved sending the experimental subjects—who were seminary students—from one building to another with little time to spare between assignments. Some of the subjects had been directed, as part of a supposed test of their abilities in religious education, to prepare a talk on a biblical topic. All of the subjects passed by an actor who posed as someone in distress, slumped in a doorway. The experimenters' conclusion: "A person in a hurry is likely to keep going . . . even if he is hurrying to speak on the parable of the Good Samaritan." While pondering the parable of the Good Samaritan proved not to increase the subjects' willingness to help another person, being in a hurry definitely decreased their willingness.

The simplified campus-folklore version of the story—which clearly derives from accounts of this actual experiment—substitutes study of the life of Jesus rather than a specific parable, and it introduces the final-exam theme to the story.

M. Dell Madsen of Salt Lake City gave me another angle on the story. He did his good turn for the day when he wrote to tell me how he encountered a variation of the compassion test during a training session for adult Boy Scout leaders that he attended in Missouri in the early 1970s:

We did a series of outdoor training exercises, and as we completed each one we were admonished to be punctual in arriving at the location for the next event.

The route between two training locations led past a large oak tree, and as we approached the tree we saw the member of the staff who was serving as chaplain searching the grass beneath the tree with a worried look on his face.

He said that he had lost a medal that he prized highly, and by his looks and actions he clearly indicated that he would appreciate some help in finding it. But, as I recall, none of the trainees stopped to help him.

At the opening of the next event a few minutes later, the trainer told us that the "lost medal" incident was a test to see how we would respond to the opportunity to help another person whose need for help conflicted with our established priorities.

Thus, what the Biblical parable teaches in story form, the Boy Scout training exercise taught in a practical way. With the campus legend of "The Lesson in Compassion" we are back to the narrative as a teaching device, although it's possible that some actual professor has used the trick.

Dissertation Blues

A doctoral dissertation that represents "an original contribution to knowledge" is the final hurdle a candidate must clear to be awarded a Ph.D.

The traditional term for someone who has finished Ph.D. course work and exams, but not yet written a dissertation, is "ABD" ("All But Dissertation"). An ABD degree and a quarter (25¢) will get you a cup of coffee, they say.

Would a candidate cheat in order to gain the degree? Possibly; so, not surprisingly, plagiarism and deceit are common themes of the urban legends about dissertations. A history professor from the Midwest, for instance, wrote to tell me that he had several times heard this story:

Supposedly, a graduate student working in a European archive who translated the unpublished Ph.D. dissertation of a foreign student who had died, then submitted this as his own work. When the work was published in English, the dead European student's adviser recognized it. He exposed the plagiarist, who was stripped of his doctorate.

Another legend depicts a candidate who successfully tricks a faculty advisor into awarding him academia's highest degree. The candidate completes the dissertation and submits it to the adviser. Eventually the adviser returns the manuscript to the student. Attached to the title page is a long list of minor corrections to be made before the work will be accepted by the supervisory committee.

Between the pages the student finds a carbon copy of the same list. Hoping the adviser failed to retain a copy of the required changes, the student keeps the dissertation for a suitable interval, then returns it unaltered with a note: "All of your corrections have been incorporated." The dissertation is quickly approved, and the degree is granted.

Several dissertation legends reflect every Ph.D. candidate's worst nightmare—finally finishing the dissertation, then losing the only copy of the manuscript before it can be submitted for approval. Graduate students, the legends claim (no names, just the generic "students"), have allegedly lost their dissertations in home fires, floods, robberies, and in automobile accidents or thefts. Some professors advise students to keep an extra copy of the dissertation wrapped up in their freezer, where, presumably, it would survive almost any disaster.

All of the legends seem to make an emphatic point: Without a little common sense, academic knowledge isn't worth the paper it's printed on.

Here's a typically southern Californian version of the lost-dissertation legend. Supposedly a doctoral candidate finished typing his dissertation, which ran to hundreds of pages, and placed the manuscript in a cardboard box on the back seat of his open convertible. As the candidate drove to the university to photocopy and turn in his work, the top of the box blew off and his opus flew page-by-page out onto the freeway.

The latest versions of the lost-dissertation legend claims that an entire work was destroyed when the computer crashed. This is a possibility, but a remote one, since the first thing any student learns when using computers is always to back up your data—make duplicate copies of your writing, that is.

In the summer of 1987 the Associated Press carried a story describing a Swedish author who was trying to reassemble his 250-page book manuscript which had accidentally been slashed into 50,000 tiny strips. The story said that the book, the product of thirteen years of research, was destroyed when a secretary mistook a shredder for a photocopy machine.

I thought the news story sounded fishy, right down to the name of the author, "Ulf af Trolle." So I wrote to Bengt af Klintberg, my folklorist friend in Stockholm.

Bengt assured me that the story was trustworthy, mentioning that Ulf af Trolle is a well-known consultant to companies with economic problems. Ulf's nickname in this regard (roughly translated) is "Doc of the Business World."

So, if the story is true, it's a pity that "Doc" af Trolle got an honorary degree attached to him by his clients before he proved that he could complete his book without succumbing to the curse of a dissertation legend. I haven't heard yet—several years after the disaster—whether he has finished piecing together his shredded manuscript.

But I *have* learned, from a short item in *The Chronicle of Higher Education* (May 22, 1991, p. A13) that Alleen Pace Nilsen, Assistant Vice President for Personnel at Arizona State University, collects true lost data stories, beginning with her own, concerning the time her briefcase containing three hundred completed questionnaires was stolen. One of her examples tells of:

"A graduate student, now a genetics professor, who was working on a six-month-long experiment that involved breeding 300 mice in total darkness. The student was in her laboratory during the final stage of her experiment when two maintenance workers lifted an air-conditioning unit out of the wall, exposing the entire room to light. (The surprised student soon began cleaning out cages to get ready to breed 300 new mice.)"

Three hundred seems to be almost a ritual number in such stories. Maybe there's a dissertation topic there.

A TYPE-INDEX OF URBAN LEGENDS

(*My books are cited, by page references, in the order published:* VH = *The Vanishing Hitchhiker*, CD = The *Choking Doberman*, MP = *The Mexican Pet*, Curses = *Curses! Broiled Again,* and BT = *The Baby Train*. A few currently circulating legends are indexed that are not found in any of my books.)

1. Legends about Automobiles

Ghost Stories:

"The Vanishing Hitchhiker" Ghostly or heavenly hitchhiker vanishes from moving car, sometimes after giving warning or prophecy. Portrait identification and sweater-on-grave motifs may occur.—VH, 24–40; CD, 210–12; MP, 49–51; BT, 251.

"The Corpse in the Car" Hitchhiker's prophecy supposedly validated by accurate prediction of a corpse in car later.—VH, 30.

"The Ghost in Search of Help for a Dying Man" Doctor summoned by person later proven to be a ghost.—VH, 34–35.

"The Haunted Street" Thump heard while driving on a Detroit street explained as sound of a fatal accident that occurred there.

Travel Mishaps:

"The Runaway Grandmother" Car with grandmother's corpse on top is stolen, never recovered.—VH, 112–22; CD, 219; Curses, 14–15; BT, 237, 240.

"The Nude in the RV" Person steps out of RV, nude or partly clothed, is left behind on highway. (Compare **"The Cut-Out Pullman"** Man stranded in wrong pullman car without clothes.—VH, 136–38.)—VH, 132–36.

"The Wife Left Behind" Wife forgotten at highway stop.—Curses, 126; BT, 231–32.

"The Baby on the Roof" Baby forgotten on roof of car.—CD, 55–57.

"The Kangaroo Thief" (**"The Gucci Kangaroo"**) and **"The Deer Departed"** Stunned animal, thought dead, walks off with coat, rifle, etc.—MP, 24–25; BT, 233–36.

"The Nut and the Tire Nuts" Asylum inmate explains how motorist can replace lost tire nuts.—MP, 63–64.

"The Day Trip" Vacationer in England returns wrong drunken day-tripper to his home.—BT, 229–30.

"The Mystery Trip" Vacationers in England take mystery trip to their own home city.—BT, 230.

"The Ice-Cream Car" Flavor of ice cream ordered affects performance of person's car.—Curses, 121–22.

"Celebrity Has Car Breakdown" Grateful celebrity (Perry Como, etc.) gives expensive present to helper.—Curses, 114–16.

Rolls-Royce Legends—RRs never break down, or factory never admits it.

Accident Stories:

"The Elephant That Sat on the VW" Mistakes small red car for stool in circus act.—CD, 58–61.

"The Gerbil—(or Snake)—Caused Accident" Animal escapes from box, driver stops; slapstick attempts at aid by others.—MP, 60–61.

"The Unlucky Driver Examination" Following examiner's instructions leads to accident.—BT, 214–15.

"Old vs. Young" Young driver steals parking place, old one crashes into car for revenge.—MP, 67.

"The Smashed VW Bug" Crushed VW and passengers found between two crashed trucks.—Curses, 89–91.

"The Body on the Car" Accident victim found stuck to front of car.—Curses, 92–95; BT, 23.

"The Wrong Rest Stop" Picknickers in runaway-truck escape lane.—BT, 232.

"The Lost Wreck" Car wreck hidden for years in thick brush or woods.—Curses, 99–100.

"The Pig on the Road" (**"Road Hog"**) Warning about pig thought to be insult and ignored; car strikes actual pig.—MP, 62; Curses, 127–28.

"Fear of Frying" Anti-seat-belt stories.—Curses, 96–98.

Automobile Horror Stories:

"The Boyfriend's Death" Boyfriend killed, girl loses mind, after being stranded without gas.—VH, 5–10; BT, 240.

"The Killer in the Backseat" Would-be killer lurks in back, detected by motorist or gas-station attendant.—VH, 52–53; CD, 214; MP, 58–59.

"The Hairy-Armed Hitchhiker" Man dressed as woman has hatchet in handbag, but crime is foiled.—CD, 52–55; MP, 157–59; BT, 240.

"The Slasher under the Car" Ankle-slashing men hide beneath cars.—BT, 134–38.

Amputation Stories:

"The Hook" Hookman leaves hook-hand dangling from door handle. VH, 48–52; BT, 14, 27–29.

"The Severed Fingers" (Car story) Fingers of threatening pedestrians torn off by car.—CD, 34–37; MP, 65–66.

"The Decapitated Pet or Person" Head stuck out of window (or head of cyclist) is cut off.—MP, 56–57.

Toll Booth Pranks. Severed hand extended to toll collector.—Curses, 299–301; BT, 316.

Cheap Car Fantasies:

"The Economical Carburetor" Experimental car model accidentally sold, then recalled.—VH, 175–78; MP, 161–63.

"The Death Car" Car permeated by smell of death offered at low price.—VH, 20–22; CD, 212–13; MP, 12–13, BT, 133.

"The $50 Porsche" Husband's expensive car sold cheaply by abandoned wife.—VH, 22–24.

"The Bargain Sportscar" Mother sells dead son's car cheaply, unaware of its value.—Curses, 123–25.

Mint Condition Vintage Vehicles. New Model T's, A's, Jeeps, etc. or Harley Davidson motorcycles found in freight car, garage, barn, etc.—VH, 178.

Dalliance or Nudity Involving Automobiles: (See **"The Nude in the RV"** above.)

"The Solid-Concrete Cadillac" Husband fills own new car with cement, thinking it belongs to wife's lover.—VH, 125–32; CD, 220.

"The Unzipped Mechanic" (or plumber) Man under sink (or car) unzipped by wife, thinking he's her husband.—VH, 147–48. (Compare **"The Unzipped Fly"** in Section 5)

"The Wife's RV Revenge" Wife traps husband and his lover in RV, gives them a wild ride.—CD, 66–67.

"The Stuck Couple" Penis captivus in a sportscar.—CD, 142–45.

Technical Incompetence: (Compare some **"Travel Mishaps"** above)

"Push-Starting the Car" Driver hits stalled car at speed required to turn over engine.—CD, 65.

"Cruise Control" Cruise confused with auto pilot.—CD, 63–66.

"*R* Is for for Race" Misunderstanding of automatic transmission settings; *D* for Drag, *L* for Leap, etc.—Curses, 117.

Automobile Sabotage or Crime:

"The Rattle in the Cadillac" Note from auto worker in sabotaged new car mocks owner—CD, 62–63.

"The Dishonest Note" Driver who hit parked car pretends to leave his name and address.—Curses, 118–120.

"Truckers and Bikers" Trucker(s) revenge on motorcyclists.—VH, 179; BT, 213–14.

Bikers vs. Smokers. Angry smoker leaves restaurant and vandalizes wrong motorcycle; attacked by biker.—BT, 212–13.

Other Biker Legends. Good deeds, better than their image, etc.—BT, 210–12.

"The Arrest" Driver escaping DUI citation takes the wrong car, a police cruiser.—Curses, 101–103.

"The Stolen Specimen" Urine specimen in booze bottle left in car or bike basket, is stolen.—CD, 127–30; MP, 89–90.

"The Double Theft" Thieves return car with tickets as thanks; burglarize home while owners are attending show, concert, game, etc.—CD, 193–94.

"Take My Tickets, Please!" Tickets for poorly-performing team left conspicuously in unlocked car, hoping for theft of same; owner returns to find more tickets left by others.

"The Two Hitchhikers" Clean-cut hitchhiker attempts theft;

scruffy hitcher, a thief on vacation, protects the driver.—Curses, 108–110.

"The Unstealable Car" Heavily locked and protected car is moved by thieves who leave a mocking note.—Curses, 104–107.

Car Theft during Earthquake. Car thief is found in flattened car—BT, 146–48.

"The Stolen Speed Trap" Thought to be lost microwave oven.—Curses, 111.

"Stripping the Car" Man changing tire on busy highway joined by car stripper who offers to split the loot.—Curses, 111–12.

"The Unfortunate Gas Thief" Attempts to siphon gas from toilet holding tank on RV.—VH, 181–82.

"Stopping the Detroit Car in Canada" RCMP stop car for minor infraction; passengers take stance to be frisked.—Curses, 112–13.

2. Legends about Animals

Animal Disasters:

"The Microwaved Pet" (See also **"The Hippy Babysitter"** in Section 3) Explodes in oven.—VH, 62–65; CD, 215–16; BT, 241.

"The Dead Cat in the Package" Stolen or switched package contains dead cat.—VH, 103–12; CD, 216–19; MP, 31–34; BT, 20–22, 245–46.

"Dog's Corpse Is Stolen" Dead dog in suitcase stolen at subway turnstile.—MP, 32–33.

"The Wildcat in the Suitcase" Prank: Suitcase left where motorists see and steal it.

The Dead Pet Replaced:

Air-Freighted Dead Pet. Baggage handlers replace dead pet with live one; owner was shipping body home for burial.—Curses, 156–58.

"The Hare Dryer" Dead rabbit cleaned and replaced in hutch; it had died, been dug up by dog.—Curses, 151–61.

"The Poisoned Pussycat at the Party" Guests have stomachs pumped, but cat was killed by a car not food it stole.—VH, 111–12.

"The Bump in the Rug" Carpet layer crushes pet canary, hamster, gerbil, etc.—CD, 93–94.

"The Pet Nabber" Cat or small dog carried off by large bird.—Curses, 129–31.

"The Flying Kitten" Attempt to rescue cat from tree launches it over fence.—Curses, 162.

"The Flying Cow" Lands on passing car or boat.—BT, 273–75.

"The Missionaries and the Cat" Mormon lad drives cat from flannel board, accidentally kills it.—BT, 276–77.

"The Ice-Fishing Dog" Dives into hole after fish, comes up at another hole.

"The Bungled Rescue of the Cat" Volunteer fire crew backs truck over cat rescued from tree.—Curses, 163–65.

"Stupid Pet Rescues" Wrong pet returned to supposed owner.—BT, 262–66.

Exploding Animals. Bird eat rice, bees gassed in vacuum cleaner bag.—CD, 107; MP, 35; BT, 254–55, 260–61. (See also **"The Loaded Dog"**)

Hunting Legends:

    "Shooting the Bull" Prank backfires; hunter shoots valuable farm animal.—Curses, 138–41.

    "The Naive Hunter" Mistakes mule, horse, etc. for deer—Curses, 139.

    "The Hunter's Nightmare" Stunned deer, presumed dead, wreaks havoc in car.—BT, 270–72.

"The Animal's Revenge" or **"The Loaded Dog"** Dog wired with explosive crawls under car, truck, or camper.—CD, 67–68; MP, 36–40; BT, 235. Variant, **"The Plant's Revenge"** Saguaro cactus crushes man who shot at it.—Curses, 44–46.

Dog Disasters:

    "The Dog's Dinner" Cooked and served to owners, tourists in Hong Kong.—CD, 94–96; BT, 240.

    "The Dog in the Highrise" Follows tossed ball out window to death.—CD, 96–97.

    "The Leashed Dog" Dog tied to garage door or car, forgotten and dragged.—Curses, 149–50.

    "The Crushed Dog" Guest sits on small dog, hides body.—Curses, 135–37; BT, 277.

    "Fifi Spills the Paint" Painter blames spill on dog.—Curses, 132–34. Variant: **"Kitty Takes the Rap"** Person blames food theft on cat or dog.—BT, 25–27.

Animal Infestations or Contaminations: (See also **"Medical Horrors"** in Section 3)

"The Spider in the Hairdo" Infested beehive hairdo.—VH, 76–81; BT, 16.

"The Spider in the Cactus" Infested succulent brought home.—MP, 83–84; BT, 240–41, 278–87.

"The Snake in the Discount Store" Lurking in coat, sweater, etc.; bites shopper.—VH, 160–71.

Contaminated Comforters. Maggots wriggling inside move it off the bed.—BT, 237–38.

The Snake (Spider, etc.) in Bananas (Greens, etc.) Bites Shopper.—BT, 288–90.

"Alligators in the Sewers" Flushed baby pets grow up.—VH, 90–98.

"Big Cats (Panthers, etc.) Running Wild." Beasts out of their range.—BT, 247–48, 267–69.

Bosom-Serpent Legends. Snake enters body.—CD, 107–112.

　"The Snake in the Strawberry Patch" Creeps into baby's mouth.—Curses, 82–84.

　"Octopus Eggs Impregnate Swimmer" Enter woman.—CD, 110–111.

　"Sperm in the Swimming Pool" Woman becomes pregnant.—CD, 110.

　"Tapeworms in Diet Pills" Secret of diet's success.—CD, 111–12.

"Ants or Termites under a Cast [or in sinuses]" Infested flesh produces terrible itch.—VH, 80.

"The Fatal Boot" Rattlesnake fangs kill several generations.—Curses, 76–78.

"A Bug in the Ear" Earwigs eat through the brain.—CD, 109; Curses, 40–43.

"The Mexican Pet" Stray Chihuahua adopted, actually a rat.—MP, 21–23; BT, 15–16, 248.

"The Giant Catfish" Size of small car; frighten divers.—MP, 26–27.

Watersnake Stories:

　"The Can of Snakes" Baby snakes used for fish bait.—MP, 28.

　"The Hapless Waterskier" Falls into nest of snakes.—MP, 29.

"The Incautious Swimmer" Dives into snake nest.—MP, 30.

"Snakes in the Tunnel of Love" Bite patrons of ride.—Curses, 37–39.

Food and Restaurant Stories:—CD, 118–120. (See also **"Hold the Mayo"** in Section 5)

"The Rat in the Rye Bread" Baked into the bread.—CD, 120–21.

"The Kentucky-Fried Rat" Batter-fried rodent served as chicken.—VH, 81–84.

"Spider Eggs in Bubble Yum" Infested chewing gum.—VH, 89–90.

"Worms in Burgers" Worms substituted for hamburger.—VH, 90.

Foreign Matter in Foreign Food:

Ethnic Restaurant Stories. Finger, cat meat, etc. in chop suey, etc.—VH, 84; CD, 121–22.

"The Eaten Pets" Asian immigrants eat cats and dogs.—CD, 96, 122–27; MP, 99–103; BT, 255–58.

"Urine in Corona Beer" Mexican import contaminated.

"The Mouse in the Coke" Contaminated soft drink or beer. Variant: **"The Finger in the Pickle Jar,"** etc.—VH, 84–89; CD, 119.

"Not my Dog" Follows guest into home, but belongs to neither guest nor host.—Curses, 146–48.

Lawn Order. Dogs repelled by water-filled bottle.—Curses, 142–45.

Trusty Watchdogs:

"The Choking Doberman" Fingers of intruder stuck in throat.—CD, 3–49; MP, 41–47; BT, 237.

"The Licked Hand" Murderer licks hand in dark, assumed to be dog.—CD, 73–77; Curses, 203–205.

3. Horror Legends

Babysitter Stories:

"The Babysitter and the Man Upstairs" Threatens her on telephone; traced to upstairs extension.—VH, 53–57; CD, 214–15.

"The Clever Babysitter" Uses stove gas to quiet baby.—CD, 77–78; MP, 69–70.

"The Hippy Babysitter" (See also "The Microwaved Pet" in Section 2) Cooks baby.—VH, 65–69.

"Baby Trapped in Highchair" Starved to death when parents return.—CD, 57; BT, 73.

Medical Horrors: (See also **"The Ghost in Search of Help for a Dying Man,"** in Section 1)

Malpractice Stories:

"Flopped X-Rays" Lead to incorrect treatment.—CD, 98.

"Wrong Organs or Limbs Removed"—CD, 98.

"The Escalating Medical Problem" Treatment of minor ailment causes major problems.

"Dental Death" Dentist disposes of "corpse" that revives. Curses, 68–69.

"The Second Death" "Corpse" in hearse revives, but killed in collision with ambulance.—Curses, 66–68.

"The Frozen Brain" Finnish boy fails to wear his hat.—BT, 241.

"The Runaway Patient" Elderly patient forgotten on hospital elevator.

"CPR Annie" Practice dummy modeled on accident victim.—CD, 98.

"The Proctological Examination" Scope causes explosion in colon.—CD, 98–99.

"The Relative's Cadaver" Recognized by med student.—CD, 99–102.

"The Corpse in the Cask" Preservative alcohol is drunk.—CD, 114–18.

"The Accidental Cannibals" Cremains mistaken for food or seasoning.—VH, 117; CD, 114–15; BT, 75–79.

"The Spider Bite" Swells and bursts, releasing spiders.—CD, 108; MP, 76–77.

"The Fatal Golf Tee" Chewed tee has insecticide on it.—Curses, 65–66.

"The Hair Ball" From chewing on pigtail ends.—MP, 77–78.

"The Colo-rectal Mouse" or **"Gerbilling"** Rodent in rectum.—MP, 78–79.

"The Poinsettia Myth" Plant thought to be poisonous.—MP, 91–92.

Other Horrors:

Satanic Panic. Rumors of cults, kidnappings, and sacrifices.

"The Graveyard Wager" Clothes caught in dark (Type 1676B).—Curses, 79–81.

"The Dream Warning" Dream about elevator operator or phantom coachman comes true.

"The Well to Hell" Geologists drill through ceiling of Hell in Siberia.—BT, 105–108.

"The Devil in the Dancehall" Recognized by his deformed or animal feet.—VH, 180–81.

"The Jersey Devil," "Mothman," "Greenman," and other local monsters. BT, 95–100.

"The Poison Dress" Absorbs embalming fluid, kills next wearer.—CD, 112–14.

Shampoo Turns Hair Green.—BT, 291.

"The Message under the Stamp" Smuggled note from war prisoner.—Curses, 73–75.

"The Last Kiss" Worker caught in couplers or other machinery, killed by rescue attempt, has last farewell to wife.—Curses, 70–72.

"The Mother's Threat Carried Out" (See also **"Accidental Multiple Deaths"** in Section 4.) Child carries out mother's threat, kills sibling.—MP, 72–73; BT, 68–71.

"The Climax of Horrors" Telling the worst news last (Type 2040).—BT, 92–94.

"I Believe in Mary Worth" Ritual summons mirror witch.—MP, 80–82.

"Flights of Fancy" Boy plays Superman or Popeye, tries to fly.—BT, 65–67.

"Razor Blades in Waterslide" Injury from sabotaged ride.—Curses, 37.

Tourist Horror Stories. Kidnappings, killings, etc.—CD, 92; Curses, 85–87.

"The Body in the Bed" Found in smelly Las Vegas hotel room.—BT, 131–33.

Ethnic Stereotype Stories. Unsanitary conditions, crowding, unsavory food, general "uncivilized" behavior.—MP, 104–105; BT, 226–28.

4. Accident Legends

Gruesome Accidents: (See also **"The Last Kiss"** in Section 3)

"Atomic Golfballs" Explode when cut open; poison centers.—CD, 154; BT, 203–4.

"The Exploding Butane Lighter" Ignited by a spark, blows chest open.—CD, 155–57; MP, 164–65.

"The Fused Cornea and Contact Lenses" Welding accident fuses eye and lens.—CD, 157–60; MP, 165–66.

"Curses! Broiled Again!" Woman cooked in tanning salon.—Curses, 29–36.

"The Lawnmower Accident" Amputated fingers from lifting mower.—CD, 160–62; MP, 164.

"The Sawed-off Finger" Worker demonstrates and repeats accident.—BT, 178–80.

"The Death of Little Mikey" Pop Rocks and soda explode in stomach.—VH, 89; CD, 103–106.

"Michael Jackson's Dancing Partner" Dies while break-dancing.—MP, 183.

"The Scuba Diver in the Tree" Scooped up from lake by fire-fighting plane.—Curses, 47–48.

"The Stuck Diver" Hand caught in crevice by large crab or clam.—BT, 72.

"The Stuck Santa" Father, playing Santa, stuck in chimney.—BT, 74.

"Shrink-to-Fit Jeans" Squeezed to death while worn in bathtub.—CD, 154.

Accidental Multiple Deaths. Rush to rescue one kills other(s).—BT, 68–71.

Air Crash Legends. Miraculous survivals, near misses, etc.

"The Exploding Airplane" Bullet decompresses cabin.—BT, 83–85.

Hilarious Accidents:

"The Exploding Toilet" Wife sprays, husband hurt.—VH, 181; MP, 13–16; BT, 237.

"The Exploding Bra" Air pressure expands inflatable bra.—BT, 80–82.

"Stuck on the Toilet" Painted or varnished seat.

"The Barrel of Bricks" Mishap with rope and pulley; comical letter requests sick leave.—Curses, 180–88.

"The Man on the Roof" Secured by rope tied to car; pulled off.—VH, 181.

"The Laughing Paramedics" Typical ending motif of hilarious accident legends: "They laughed so hard they dropped him."

"The Heel in the Grate" Shoe comes off, grate comes up, bride falls in.—Curses, 167–72.

"The Ski Accident" Woman relieves herself and slips; man injured while watching her.—VH, 181; MP, 117–20.

"The Golf Bag" Thrown in pond, but contains car keys.—BT, 203.

"The Failed Suicide" Multiple methods of death cancel each other.—BT, 86–87.

"The Unlucky Contacts" Swallowed when water in glass is drunk.—MP, 85–86.

"The Wrong Teeth" Two pair of false teeth lost because of prank.—MP, 87–88.

"The Caned Telegraph Boy" Mistaken identity, wrong boy beaten.—BT, 169–71.

"Bungling Brides" Fails to question mother's cooking tip.—Curses, 191–92.

5. Sex and Scandal Legends

Aphrodisiac Stories:
"Green M&Ms" Said to "make you horny."—MP, 111–13.
"The Girl on the Gearshift Lever" Impales herself in sexual frenzy.—CD, 133–34.

Contraception Stories:
"The Baby Headache" Birth-control replaced with baby aspirin.—CD, 132.
Plastic wrap used as contraceptive by naive young person.—CD, 131–32.

Sex Education Stories:—CD, 132. (See also **"Sex in the Classroom"** in Section 10)
Themes include **"Students Practice Sex,"** **"The Teacher Demonstrates"** and **"Sex Crimes Follow Classes"**

Sex Scandals:
Caught in the Nude:
"The Nude Bachelor" Stranded in apartment's hallway when he goes for newspaper.—VH, 138.
"The Nude Housewife" Caught naked and wearing football helmet by meter reader or plumber.—VH, 139–40; Curses, 15.
"Waiting for the Iceman" Woman surprised in nude says the wrong thing.—Curses, 193–94.
"The Blind Man" Man delivering window blinds meets naked housewife.—Curses, 213–15.

"The Nude Surprise Party" Surprisers surprised by nude man or couple.—VH, 140–46; CD, 221–22.

> Variant: **"The Fart in the Dark"** Blindfolded person thinks he or she's alone.—VH, 148–49.

"Come and Get It" Wife pulls penis of wrong man in shower.—VH, 146–47.

"The Dormitory Surprise" Man returns to room naked, surprises girlfriend and parents.—MP, 201; BT, 305–307.

"Sex in the Camper" Tent trailer collapses.—Curses, 211.

"Superhero Hijinks" Costumed husband knocked unconscious; naked wife tied to bed.—BT, 38–42.

"The Cat (or Dog) and the Nude Man" Animal startles naked man who has accident.—CD, 220–21.

> Variant: **"A Snake Story"** Snake in house triggers cat or dog accident. MP, 114–16.

"The Unzipped Fly" Zipped to tablecloth.—VH, 138–39. (See also **"The Unzipped Mechanic"** in Section 1)

"Something in the Disco Pants" Cucumber or sausage cuts off circulation; man faints.—VH, 81.

"Sex with the Wrong Partner" Couple in Halloween costumes or on camping trip swap partners.—Curses, 209–12.

"The Hairdresser's Error" Cleaning glasses under sheet, mistaken for masturbating.—BT, 44–46.

"A License to Practice" Tourist's vice arrest; prostitution permit sold.—CD, 141.

"The Witness's Note" Rape victim's written testimony mistaken by juror for solicitation.—CD, 141.

"State Police Don't Have Balls" Speeder offers to buy tickets to policemen's ball.—CD, 139.

"The Blind Date" #1 Man buys condoms from date's father.—MP, 126.

"The Blind Date" #2 Woman has date with ER doctor who removed stuck tampax.—CD, 138.

"Buying Tampax/Thumbtacks" Terms confused on store PA system. CD, 138.

"Dentist Seduces Patient" Headline: "Dentist Fills Wrong Cavity."—CD, 133.

"Drugged and Seduced" Campus date rape story.—CD, 133.

"The Gay Roommate" Anesthesizes and sodomizes straight roommate.—BT, 308–11.

"The Unexpected Inheritance" Man gives partner's name in affair with innkeeper. ("The Kilkenny Widow").—CD, 133; MP, 127–28.

"The Turkey Neck" Stuck in open fly of sleeping drunk; nibbled by cat.—MP, 129–31.

"The Butcher's Prank" Sausage stuck in open fly cut off.—BT, 47–49.

"The Bothered Bride" Calls off wedding, announcing groom's misbehavior to guests.—MP, 134–35.

"The Bad Bachelorette" Sleeps with black stripper, bears black baby.—BT, 50–52.

Caught in the Act:

"The Evidence" Toilet clogged with condoms, but husband doesn't use condoms.—MP, 132.

"Walking the Dog" Dog leads wife to home of husband's lover.—MP, 132–33.

"Filmed in the Act" Honeymoon hotel films guests for porn films.—CD, 139–40.

"The Sexy Videotape" Amateur sex tape circulates in community.—BT, 61–64.

Other Sex Stories:

"The Baby Train" Early train wakes couples; birth rate zooms.—BT, 33–37.

"The Bullet through the Balls" Woman impregnated by sperm on bullet.—CD, 134–38.

"The Promiscuous Cheerleader" Semen in stomach of cheerleader or rock star.

Masturbating into Food. Contamination of fast food by disgruntled employee.—CD, 121.

"The Sheriff's Daughter" Cops bribed by sex with a girl inside a tent; at his turn, the sheriff recognizes his own daughter as the donor.—CD, 145–46.

"The Avon Flasher" Salesman exposes himself to housewife.—MP, 121.

"Green Stamps" Gynecologist wisecracks about stamps stuck to woman,—CD, 139; MP, 122–25.

"Superglue Revenge" Wife fastens husband's penis to his leg.—CD, 146–49.

"AIDS Mary" and **"AIDS Harry"** Victim welcomed to world of AIDS.—Curses, 195–202, 203–205; BT, 237, 240.

6. Crime Legends (See also FBI legends under Government Legends, Section 8)

Theft Stories:

> **"All That Glitters Is Not Gold"** Thief gets fake gold necklace, "victim" grabs his real gold one.—BT, 125.
>
> **"The Robber Who Was Hurt"** Recognized by injured fingers.—CD, 37–41; BT, 121–24.
>
> **"The Helpful Mafia Neighbor"** Arranges return of stolen property.—MP, 147.
>
> **"The Misguided Good Deed"** Wrong passenger's glove tossed from subway car.—BT, 125.
>
> **"The Lottery Ticket"** (See also **"Pass It On"** under Drug Crimes) Winning ticket stolen when passed around in a bar.—MP, 142; Curses, 19–21.
>
> **"The Videotaped Theft"** Wedding guest revealed as pickpocket.—CD, 140.
>
> **"Indecent Exposure"** Photo taken by thieves shows toothbrushes stuck in rectum.—BT, 54–60.
>
> **"Stolen Sod"** Unlikely theft of heavy load of sod.—BT, 126.
>
> **Stolen Casino Cash.** Dropped into boot top; thief cannot walk.—BT, 129.

Unwitting Thefts:

> **"The Jogger's Billfold"** Innocent man mistaken by jogger for pickpocket, gives up own billfold.—CD, 188–91; BT, 265–66.
>
> **"The Five-Pound Note"** (or **"The Accidental Stickup"**) Innocent person mistaken for thief.—CD, 190–91.

Thefts of Food:

> **"The Grocery Scam"** Man's "mother" said he'd pay for food.—Curses, 247–52.
>
> **"The Packet of Biscuits"** Wrong cookies or candy eaten by strangers in snack bar.—CD, 191–93; MP, 137–40.
>
> **"The Guilty Dieter"** Caught stealing sugared donut from plate in café.—MP, 141.
>
> **"The Shoplifter and the Frozen Chicken"** Hidden under hat, thief faints from cold. (Variant: blood drips from meat under hat.)—MP, 143–44; Curses, 178–79.
>
> **"The Pregnant Shoplifter"** Accused of stealing basketball.—MP, 144; Curses, 177–79.

Atrocities and Kidnappings:—VH, 182–83; BT, 247, 250–51.

"The Mutilated Boy" and **"The Attempted Abduction"**
Boy castrated by gang as part of initiation; girl disguised, but recognized by mother.—CD, 78–92; MP, 48–56; Curses, 16, 206–208.

"The Kidney Heist" Kidney stolen for transplant.—BT, 149–54, 247.

"The Cut-off Finger" Finger amputated to steal rings.—BT, 121.

"The Phantom Clowns" Clowns in vans kidnap children.—BT, 101–104.

"Halloween Sadists" Razor blades in apples, etc.—Curses, 51–54.

Drug Crimes:

"Mickey Mouse Acid" Fliers warn parents of drug-laced tattoos.—CD, 162–69.

"Blue Star Acid" Pattern on tattoos.—Curses, 55–64; BT, 249.

"Bart Simpson Acid" Image on tattoos.

"Pass It On" During danger-of-drugs lecture, samples are stolen; more are replaced.—CD, 163; MP, 142.

Drug Horror Stories. Staring at the sun, gouging out eyes, etc.—BT, 109–112.

"A Drug-Smuggling Legend" Drugs inside dead baby.—MP, 145–46.

Cocaine-Contaminated Money. Teller tests positive from handling it.—BT, 130.

7. Business and Professional Legends (See also some animal infestation and contamination legends in Section 2)

Companies and Businesses:

"Red Velvet Cake" Rip-off recipe from Waldorf-Astoria.—VH, 154–60; Curses 221–24.

"The Mrs. Field's Cookie Recipe" Further rip-off recipe stories.—Curses, 219–26.

Trademarks, etc.

"The Procter & Gamble Trademark" Alleged satanic symbolism.—CD, 169–86.

666 and Mark of the Beast. (See also science/technology section below)

"The Jewish Secret Tax" Kosher markings on food labels represent a tax on non-Jews.—MP, 106–107.

Rumors about Marlboro Cigarettes. Filters contain addictive substance, label markings reveal KKK ownership, etc..—CD, 154.

"The Cabbage Patch Tragedy" Doll returned for repair; death certificate issued.—MP, 74–75.

McDonald's Rumors. Wormburgers, spoons for cocaine use, etc.—VH, 90; CD, 173.

"Don't Mess with Texas" Second meaning of littering slogan.—MP, 93–98.

"The Secret Ingredient" Collagens in cosmetics come from aborted fetuses.—MP, 93–98.

"Redemption Rumors" Pull Tab saved for charity.—MP, 169–74.

"Postcards for Little Buddy" Sick child wants Guinness record.—Curses, 227–32.

SCA Legends. Costumed member of Society for Creative Anachronisms acts the part.—BT, 207–209.

"The Ghost Airliner" Haunted by late captain.—VH, 178–80.

"The Locked Out Pilot" Use fire ax to re-enter cockpit.—Curses, 48–50.

Telephones:

"Burt Reynolds' Telephone Credit Card Number" Star offers free calls to fans to use judgment award from telephone company.—CD, 203–208.

"Michael Jackson's Telephone Number" Included in UPC on record cover—MP, 181–82.

"Dial 911 for Help" Person cannot find eleven on phone dial.—CD, 208–209; BT, 42–43.

"The Lover's Telephone Revenge" Calls Tokoyo time service, leaves phone off hook.—Curses, 216–17.

Other Technology:

"Sinking Malls and Leaning Towers" Inept architect; building sags.—Curses, 253–55.

"Sinking Libraries" Architect forgot weight of books.—BT, 299–301.

"Switched Campus Buildings" Building material switched, so structures are on wrong campus.—BT, 302–304.

"Built in a Day" Tour guide pretends not to recognize imposing building; "It wasn't there yesterday."—BT, 195–98

Backwards Buildings and Statues. Architect commits suicide because of error; statue has back to church.—Curses, 255–58

"The Psychic Videotape" Ghost seen in "Three Men and a Baby" tape.—BT, 88–91.

Greenroom Legends. Stories about origin of the name.—BT, 185–87.

Computer Folklore:

> **Naive User Stories.** White Out on screen, etc.
>
> **Viruses, "The Mystery Glitch,"** etc. Creative hacking.—CD, 201–202.
>
> **USENET Lore.** Slang and chit-chat on computer net.—BT, 191–93.
>
> **"The Modem Tax"** Rumor of tax persists after request denied. BT, 188–90.
>
> **"The Technology Contest"** Wispy wire drilled by foreign competitor.—BT, 174–77.
>
> **Enhancing CD sound.** Green marker does the trick.—BT, 290–91.
>
> **"Trouble with Technology":** Lore of Miscellaneous Modern Gadgets.—Curses, 189–92.
>
> **"The Tube on the Tube"** Fluorescent tube mistaken for subway handrail.
>
> **"The Helpful Citizen"** Curtain rod mistaken for blind person's white cane.

Professions and Trades: (See also Medical Horrors and Academic Legends in Sections 3 and 10)

Written Traditions:

> **"Hilarious Reports"** Illiterate welfare letters, funny insurance reports, etc.—Curses, 236–39.
>
> **"Those Good Old Days"** Tough rules for teachers.—Curses, 240–42.
>
> **"Grandma's Washday"** Hard hand work described, but "Count your blessings."—Curses, 243–46.
>
> **Legal Horror Stories ("Atrocity Stories")** Unbelievable judgments.—CD, 160–61; MP, 167–68.
>
> **"The Will"** Fortune goes to one person who attended funeral, a stranger.—Curses, 267–68.
>
> **"The Homemade Lie Detector"** Guilty person tricked into revealing self; the only one not to touch something.—Curses, 269–73.

"The Colander Copier Caper" Police fake a lie detector until suspect confesses.—BT, 139–45.

"The Bedbug Letter" Polite apology from RR company is a form letter.—BT, 158–62.

"Bookeeper in a Brothel" Illiterate man becomes successful businessman by accident.—BT, 155–56.

"Find the Hat" Business traveler hides lost hat in expense account.—Curses, 259–60.

"The Roughneck's Revenge" Oil driller throws tool back into hole when fired. BT, 163–65.

"The Wife on the Flight" Free flights for spouses used by others.—BT, 166–68.

"Fixing the Flue" Bricklayer glasses in fireplace until paid.—Curses, 260.

"The Holy Place" Catholics genuflect at spot in church where they once merely had to duck an obstruction.

Buried Saint Sells Property. St. Joseph buried in the yard.—BT, 181–84.

"Start the Music" Orchestra and solist wait for the other to begin piece.

Translation errors with comic results.—Curses, 24.

"Waiting for the Verb" German translator explains long pause.

8. Legends about Governments

Inefficiency:

    "The Wordy Memo" Takes many words to set price of cabbage or other commodity.—CD, 195–96.

    Overstuffed Government Warehouses. Contain too much and the wrong things.—CD, 196.

Conspiracy:

    "The Landed Martians" Government cover up.—CD, 198.

    "The Communist Rules for Revolution" The master plan. CD, 184; MP, 108–109.

Science versus Religion:

    "The Missing Day in Time" NASA computers verify biblical miracle.—CD, 198–99.

    "Madalyn Murray O'Hair's Petition" Demands a ban on religious broadcasting.—CD, 184.

Military and Wartime Legends: (See also **"The Message under the Stamp"** in Section 3)

Legends from Wartime Poland. Fooling the Germans, etc—BT, 242–44.

"The Veterans' Insurance Dividend" Only paid if you apply.—Curses, 261–64.

War Profiteer Legends. He wishes war to continue.—MP, 71

"Inner Golf" Prisoner of war improves golf game by mental practice.—BT, 204–205.

Pearl Harbor Rumors and Legends. Japanese pilot fails in try to bomb Mormon temple, converts to the faith after the war.

"Grenadians Speak English" But army seeks Spanish speakers.

"The Veggie Missile" Potato painted green imitates hand grenade. BT, 127.

Miscellaneous Government:

FBI Stories: New identity, "Watch the Borders," etc.—BT, 128–29.

"Funny Money" and Postage Stamp Stories: Hidden meanings in designs. (See also **"The Kennedy Note"** in Section 9)

"The Bug under the Rug" Screw removed in hotel floor; chandelier falls in room below.—CD, 94.

Culture Clash Legends: Tea bag misused, etc.—BT, 223–25.

Food Stamp, Homeless, Senior Citizen, and Welfare Stories—CD, 126–27.

9. Celebrity Rumors and Legends (See also various celebrity stories in Sections 1, 4, 5, and 7.)

Celebrities:

"The Elevator Incident" Black man mistaken for mugger; white passengers sit on floor.—CD, 18–28; Curses, 21–23; BT, 15.

Generation Gap Legends: Who was first man on moon?—BT, 217. (See also "The Youngest Fan" below under musicians.)

"The Gay Jesus Film" Christ portrayed as gay swinger.—MP, 175–77.

"The Kennedy Note" $1 bill has coded references to assassination.—MP, 179.

How Bronko Nagurski Was Discovered. Strong man points with plow.—BT, 156–57.

"Bozo the Clown's Blooper" Children's TV show character curses, or is cursed by kids, on the air or "Uncle Don's Blooper" Radio character (i.e., Don Carney) supposedly cursed on air, was fired. (Attributed to various people.).—MP, 184–85.

Musicians:
> **Buddy Holly Legends.** Circumstances of his discovery, death, guitars, etc.—CD, 204.
>
> **Grateful Dead Legends.** Origin of group's name, traditions about their tours, songs, etc.
>
> **"Paul Is Dead"** Rumors of McCartney's demise. CD, 203.
>
> **"The Dolly Parton Diet"** Features "T.J.'s Miracle Soup" (Variant: "The Stress Diet," a parody)—MP, 186–90.
>
> **"Who Bought the Car?"** Pop star pays cash—BT, 233 [variant].
>
> **"Backward Masking"** Satanic messages on records.
>
> **"What Is Jazz?"** Musician says, "Don't mess with it."—BT, 220–22.
>
> **"The Youngest Fan"** Paul McCartney was in a band before Wings.—BT, 217–19.

Talk Show Hosts: Groucho's off-color remarks, Johnny Carson's Comments, Dave's Behind, etc.—CD, 204–205; Curses, 233–35.

Mistaken Identities. Lead to comical results.—BT, 169–73.

"The Ice Cream Cone Caper" Celebrity sighting causes woman to put cone in purse.—Curses, 173–76.

Tour Guide Stories. Rescuing Richard Nixon, Point Out a Mormon, etc. (See also **"Built in a Day"** in Section 7.)—BT, 199–202.

10. Academic Legends (See also **"Sinking Libraries"** and **"Switched Campus Buildings"** in Section 7)

Faculty and Research:
> **"The Small World Legend"** Small number of links between individuals.—Curses, 314–17.
>
> **"Sex in the Classroom"** Instructor puts down female student with double entende.
>
> **"The Acrobatic Professor"** Enters through the transom with pop quiz.—MP, 192–95.
>
> **"The Trained Professor"** Behavior modified by class.—Curses, 311–13.

"The Resubmitted Term Paper" Gets higher or lower grade than before.—Curses, 286–87.
Dissertation Legends: Lost data, plagiarism, etc.—BT, 322–24.

Students: (See also **"The Dormitory Surprise," "Drugged and Seduced,"** and **"The Gay Roommate"** in Section 5)
"The Roommate's Death" Scratches at door, but roommate inside afraid to open it.—VH, 57–62; MP, 202–204.
Campus Rumor Scares: Predictions of murders at certain time and place.—BT, 116–119.
"The Suicide Rule" Surviving roommates given 4.0 grades by administration.—Curses, 295–98.
"The Obligatory Wait" Specific periods depending on rank of late professor.—BT, 296–98.
"The Zoo Section" Entire class of people with animal names.—BT, 293.
"The DC Schoolchild's Question" Asks "Why haven't white people accomplished anything in history?"—BT, 125–26.
Carnegie-Mellon Myths, Cal Techies, etc. Legends of colleges' pasts.—BT, 293–94.
Medical Student Pranks (See also **Toll Booth Pranks** in Section 1) **Fun with cadavers.**—CD, 99; Curses, 299–301; BT, 315–17.
"Roaming Gnomes" Postcards from stolen garden ornaments.—Curses, 305–310.
Other Student Pranks: Leading the general public into foolish behavior.—Curses, 302–304.
"The Fatal Fraternity Initiation" Hazing is fatal.
"The Tell Tale Report" Absent students' cover-up backfires. (Often told on Mormon missionaries.)—Curses, 292–94.
"The Daughter's Letter from College" List of disasters untrue, but low grades real.—BT, 312–14.

Blue Book and Other Examination Legends:
"The Unsolvable Math Problem" Solved by student unaware the problem is not a test or homework.—Curses, 278–83.
"The Barometer Problem" Ingenious "wrong" solutions to determining height of building using a barometer.—BT, 294–95.
"The Lesson in Compassion" Actor confronts students rushing to exam; no Good Samaritans among them.—BT, 318–21.
"The Open-Book Exam" Student carries in a graduate student.—Curses, 284–85.

"The Stolen Exam" Professor identifies thief by modifying exams not stolen.—Curses, 285–86.

"The Announced Quiz" Classified ad announces it.—Curses, 284.

"The Tricky Answer" Student changes the subject on essay exam (often a biblical topic).—Curses, 289–91.

"Define 'Courage' " Blank page is definition.

"The One-Word Exam Question" Question is "Why," answer, "Because," "Why Not?" etc.—Curses, 286.

"Don't Jump!" Student opening window during exam thought to be committing suicide.

"Writing High" Student on drugs writes whole answer on one line.—MP, 199–200.

"The Second Blue Book" Various strategies to cheat on essay exams by using two blue books.—MP, 196–98.

"Do You Know Who I Am?" Late essay stuck into middle of pile of blue books.—MP, 198–99; Curses, 275–76.

"The Bird Foot Exam" After identifying birds by their feet, student shows professor his foot as identification.—Curses, 275–77.

INDEX